Uncle John's

FIFTH
BATHROOM
READER

The Bathroom Readers'
Institute

Bathroom Reader's Press
Berkeley

Produced and Packaged by Javnarama
Design by Javnarama
Cover Art by William Cone
Cover Art Direction by Michael Brunsfeld
B.R.I. Technician Pictured on the Back Cover: Larry Kelp

THIS BOOK IS AVAILABLE IN "BULK" RATES

For information, write to
The Bathroom Reader's Press
1400 Shattuck Avenue, #25
Berkeley, CA 94709
or call 510-841-5866

THANK YOU

The Bathroom Readers' Institute thanks all the people whose advice and assistance made this book possible, including:

John Javna
John Dollison
Jack Mingo
Penelope Houston
Mike Litchfield
National Insecurity Council
Berkeley Pop Culture Project
Joanne Miller
Fritz Springmeyer
Lyn Speakman
Lenna Lebovich
Emma Lauriston
Sharilyn Hovind
Carol Schreiber
Ray Broekel

Melissa Schwartz
Eric Lefcowitz
Charles Panati
Michael Silverstein
Larry Kelp
Jesse
Bob Shannon
Steve Tally
Ross Owens
Mike Brunsfeld
William Cone
Kelly Rogers
Thomas Crapper
Hi to Emily and Molly Bennett
...and all the bathroom readers

WE'RE ON A ROLL!

Wow! We're up to our fifth volume of Uncle John's Bathroom Reader.
*In fact, our books have become so popular that we've started our own
publishing company: The Bathroom Reader's Press. Imagine that! A
publishing company devoted entirely to quality bathroom reading!
To celebrate, we're reprinting the introduction to* Uncle John's
First Bathroom Reader. *Every year we've tried to top it,
but so far we haven't been able to. So here it is again.*

There are two kinds of people in the world—people who read
in the bathroom, and people who don't.

People who do share a few of the subtler joys and frustra-
tions of life—e.g., the joy of discovering a really interesting article
in the latest issue of a favorite magazine as you head to the head, or
the frustration of trying to find something suitable to read...at the
last minute. This isn't something we talk about, but it's understood.

People who don't read in the bathroom haven't got a clue about
why people who do, do. This book isn't for them.

Uncle John's Bathroom Reader, the first book especially for people
who love to read in the bathroom, was conceived in 1987. A group
of socially active citizens in Berkeley, California, realized that the
publishing industry had plenty of books for every room of the house
(bedside readers, cookbooks, coffee-table books, etc.) except the
bathroom—where up to 60% of Americans read. It was clearly time
for bathroom readers to come out of the water closet and say it
loud: "I read in there and I'm proud!"

Consequently, they formed The Bathroom Readers' Institute to
fight for the rights of bathroom readers everywhere.

The *Reader* has been specially designed with the needs of bathroom readers in mind: it's full of brief but interesting articles that
can be read in a few seconds, or a few minutes. It covers a variety of
subjects (so a reader never has to settle for the "same old thing").
And it's arranged so a reader can just flip it open to any page; no
planning, no searching. We hope you enjoy it. As we say at The
Bathroom Readers' Institute:

"Go with the flow."

CONTENTS

NOTE
Because the B.R.I. understands your reading needs, we've
divided the contents by length as well as subject.
Short—a quick read
Medium—1 to 3 pages
Long—for those extended visits, when something
a little more involved is required.

CAT FACTS

Ready? Comfortable? Settled in? Okay...Let's start our Fifth Bathroom Reader *off with some info about America's purr-fectly popular pets.*

THE INSIDE POOP

Nearly all domestic cats bury their feces—but in the wild, only timid cats do. Aggressive cats in the wild actually leave their droppings on tiny "advertising hills" that they create. This leads researchers to believe that domestic cats see themselves as submissive members of their human families and environments.

FAMILY FLAVOR

Does your cat lick its fur clean after it rubs against you? That's its way of "tasting" you—becoming familiar with the taste and scent of the people in its life.

CAT & MOUSE

Why do cats play "cat and mouse" with their victims? Experts believe it's because they're not hungry. Wild cats, who eat nothing but the food they catch, rarely, if ever, play cat and mouse.

PURR-FECT

Do cats purr because they are happy? Probably not, researchers say; even dying cats and cats in pain purr. The researchers think a cat's purr is a sign it is receptive to "social interaction."

THE BETTER TO SEE YOU WITH

Unlike human eyes, a cat's eyes have pupils that are shaped like vertical slits. These vertical slits work together with the horizontal slits of the cat's eyelid to give it greater control over how much light it allows into its eyes.

WHISKED AWAY

Because a cat's whiskers are sensitive to the slight air currents that form around solid objects (such as furniture and trees), they help it to "see" in the dark. They're especially helpful when the cat hunts at night.

Elvis Presley's favorite amusement park ride was the bumper cars.

WHERE-ING CLOTHES

*Ever wonder how fabric designs and clothing styles got their names? Well, at
least a few are named after locations. Here are a half dozen examples.*

CALICO. In the early 1700s, a fabric from India became so
popular with the British public that they stopped buying
English cloth and English weavers began losing their jobs.
The weavers rioted. (In fact, they started attacking people wearing
the cloth.) The result: Parliament banned imports of the fabric,
and English weavers began making it themselves. They named it after the place it was originally made, the Indian town of Calicut.
Eventually, *Calicut* cloth evolved into *calico* cloth.

PAISLEY. These amoeba-like patterns were originally found on
shawls imported into England from India in the 1800s. Scottish
weavers in the town of Paisley began producing their own versions
of the design.

BIKINI. Daring two-piece swimsuits were introduced at end-of-
the-world parties inspired by America's 1946 A-bomb tests on the
Bikini Atoll in the Pacific.

BERMUDA SHORTS. Bermuda, an island in the Atlantic, was a
popular warm-weather tourist resort in the 1940s. But female vacationers had to use caution when they relaxed—a law on the island
prohibited them from walking around with bare legs. The fashion
solution: knee-length shorts, worn with knee-socks.

CAPRI PANTS. Fashion designer Emilio Pucci met a beautiful
woman while vacationing on the Isle of Capri in the 1950s. The
encounter inspired a line of beach fashions that featured these skin-
tight pants.

JODHPURS. These riding pants were created by English horse-
men living in Jodhpur, India.

Batter Up: An estimated 41 million Americans play softball in their free time.

FAMOUS FOR 15 MINUTES

We've included this feature—based on Andy Warhol's comment that "In the future, everyone will be famous for 15 minutes"—in several previous Bathroom Readers. Here it is again, with new stars.

THE STAR: Oliver Sipple, an ex-marine living in San Francisco.

THE HEADLINE: "Man Saves President Ford's Life by Deflecting Assassin's Gun"

WHAT HAPPENED: President Gerald R. Ford was visiting San Francisco on September 22, 1975. As he crossed the street, a woman in the crowd, Sara Jane Moore, pulled out a gun and tried to shoot him. Fortunately, a bystander spotted Moore and managed to tackle her just as the gun went off. The bullet missed the President by only a few feet.

Oliver Sipple, the bystander, was an instant hero—which was about the last thing he wanted. Reporters investigating his private life discovered that he was openly gay—a fact he'd hidden from his family in Detroit. Sipple pleaded with journalists not to write about his private life, but they ignored him. The next day, the *Los Angeles Times* ran a front-page story headlined "Hero in Ford Shooting Active Among S.F. Gays."

THE AFTERMATH: The incident ruined his life. When Sipple's mother learned of his sexual orientation, she stopped speaking to him. And when she died in 1979, Sipple's father would not let him attend the funeral. Sipple became an alcoholic. In 1979 he was found dead of "natural causes" in his apartment. He was 37.

THE STAR: Hiroo Onoda, a Japanese army lieutenant during World War II.

THE HEADLINE: "Japanese Soldier Finally Surrenders...29 Years After the War"

WHAT HAPPENED: In February 1945 the Allied forces overran

Lubang Island in the Philippines. Most of the occupying Japanese soldiers were captured, but a few escaped into the hills. There they waited to be "liberated," unaware that Japan had surrendered. They survived by living off the forest and raiding native villages for food. Villagers called them "the mountain devils."

The U.S. and Japanese governments knew there were holdouts on the island, and for more than 25 years they tried to reach them by dropping leaflets, organizing search parties, and bringing relatives to coax them out of hiding. But nothing worked.

By 1974 there was only one soldier left: 53-year-old Hiroo Onoda. One day, he spotted a young Japanese man drinking from a stream in the hills. The stranger turned out to be Norio Suzuki, a university dropout who'd come to the island specifically to find Onoda. Suzuki explained that the war had been over for 27 years and asked Onoda to return with him to Japan. But Onoda refused—unless his commanding officer came to the island and delivered the order personally. Suzuki returned to Japan, found the commanding officer, and brought him back to Lubang Island, where Onoda finally surrendered.

THE AFTERMATH: Onoda was regarded as a curiosity in the world press, but in Japan he was a national hero. More than 4,000 people greeted him at the airport when he returned to Japan. He sold his memoirs for enough money to buy a 2,870-acre farm in Brazil, stocked with 1,700 head of cattle.

THE STAR: Roy Riegels, captain of the football team at the University at California, Berkeley during the 1929 season.

THE HEADLINE: "Blooper of the Century: Cal Captain Runs Wrong Way, Gives Away Rose Bowl Game"

WHAT HAPPENED: It was the 1929 Rose Bowl game: U.C. Berkeley was playing Georgia Tech, and the score was 0-0 in the 2nd quarter. Berkeley had the ball deep in Georgia Tech territory, but in four attempts, they failed to score. Now Tech took over the ball...but on first down, the Georgia quarterback fumbled. In the confusion, Roy Riegels recovered the ball and started running for a touchdown. The only problem was, he was running *the wrong way*.

Benny Lom, Cal's center, realized what was happening and chased Riegels, shouting and screaming. But Riegels outran him, carrying the ball 69-1/2 yards down the field. Lom finally tackled him—6 *inches* from the California goal line.

Heavy Fact: Pound for pound, earthworms make up half of all animal life.

THE AFTERMATH: On the next play, Tech nailed Cal for a safety, making the score Georgia 2, California 0. They added a touchdown in the third quarter, but failed to make the extra point. Now the score was Georgia 8, California 0. In the fourth quarter, California scored a touchdown and made the extra point—but that was it. Final score: Georgia Tech 8, California 7. Riegels's blunder had cost Cal the game. The next day, Riegels was the most celebrated sports figure in the country. In fact, he's still known as "Wrong Way" Riegels.

THE STAR: William Figueroa, a 12-year-old student.

THE HEADLINE: "New Jersey Student Makes Vice President Look Like a Foole."

WHAT HAPPENED: In June 1992, Vice President Dan Quayle visited a Trenton, New Jersey, elementary school where a spelling bee was being held. Quayle took over. Reading from a cue card, Quayle asked Figueroa, a sixth-grader, to spell the word "potato." The boy spelled the word correctly, but Quayle insisted that he change it, because "potato" was spelled with an 'e' at the end. "I knew he was wrong," Figueroa later told reporters, "but since he's the vice president, I went and put the 'e' on and he said, 'That's right, now go and sit down.' Afterward, I went to a dictionary and there was potato like I spelled it. I showed the reporters and the book and they were all laughing about what a fool he was."

THE AFTERMATH: Figueroa became an instant celebrity. "Late Night with David Letterman" had him on as a guest, and he was asked to lead the pledge of allegiance at the 1992 Democratic National Convention. Afterwards, an AM radio station paid him $50 a day to provide political commentary on the Republican National Convention. He was also hired as spokesperson for a company that makes a computer spelling program.

• • • •

TV QUIZ: THE ADDAMS FAMILY

1. What language drove Gomez crazy?
2. What did Gomez called Morticia?
3. How did Uncle Fester produce electric light?
4. What kind of creature was Wednesday's pet, Homer?
5. How was Itt, the 4-foot ball of hair, related to Gomez?

Answers: 1.French; 2. Tish; 3. He put a bulb in his mouth; 4. A black widow spider; 5. Cousin.

FAMOUS PHRASES

We've supplied the origins of familiar phrases in every edition of the Bathroom Reader so far...here are a few more.

NOT UP TO SCRATCH

Meaning: Inadequate, subpar

Background: In the early days of boxing, there was no bell to signal the beginning of a round. Instead, the referee would scratch a line on the ground between the fighters and the round began when both men stepped over it. When a boxer couldn't (or wouldn't) cross the line to keep a match going, people said he was not "up to the scratch."

CAUGHT RED-HANDED

Meaning: Caught in the act

Background: For hundreds of years, stealing and butchering another person's livestock was a common crime. But it was hard to prove unless the thief was caught with the dead animal...and blood on his hands.

CAN'T HOLD A CANDLE TO (YOU)

Meaning: Not as good as (you)

Background: Comes from England. Before there were streetlights, when wealthy British nobles went walking at night they brought along servants to carry candles. This simple task was one of the least-demanding responsibilities a servant could have; people who weren't able to handle it were considered worthless. Eventually, the term "can't hold a candle" came to mean inferiority.

GIVE SOMEONE THE BIRD

Meaning: Make a nasty gesture at someone (usually with the middle finger uplifted)

Background: Originally referred to the hissing sound audiences made when they didn't like a performance. Hissing is the sound that a goose makes when it's threatened or angry.

CHEERS

A few facts about the show that critics agree was the best sitcom of the '80s.

ORIGIN. Producers Glen and Les Charles and producer/director James Burrows were part of the team that created the successful 1970s sitcom, "Taxi." When they left that show, they decided to work together on a comedy set in a hotel... so they'd be able to bring in new characters whenever they wanted. However, when they sketched out plots, they found that most of the action would take place in the hotel bar. So they dumped the hotel and kept the bar.

The show debuted on September 30, 1982. But despite critical acclaim, it was a flop. The first episode was rated 60th out of 63 programs, and it didn't do much better for the rest of the season. To everyone's surprise, NBC decided to renew the sitcom anyway (because it had faith in its creators). Result: By the following season it was in the top 20, and a year later it was in the top 10.

INSIDE FACTS

• Ted Danson got his start on TV in the 1970s soap opera, "Somerset." The turning point in his career was a guest appearance he did on "Taxi," playing an obnoxious beautician who gave Elaine Nardo a dreadful new-wave hairdo. He was so impressive that the producers took him aside and convinced him to audition for the lead role in a new series they were developing—"Cheers."

• The "Cheers" creators intentionally picked the name Norm for George Wendt's character because he's supposed to be the guy who represents the "norm."

• The exterior of the "Cheers" bar belongs to a real Boston bar called the Bull and Finch. It's on Beacon Street, right across from the Boston Common, but don't go there expecting to find Sam Malone's bar. The dimly lit, crowded interior is nothing like "Cheers."

• Shelley Long was pregnant during most of the third season. It was covered up by strategically placed trays and by having her stand behind the bar a lot. "I'm sure," Long recalls, "there were times when the audience said, 'My God, she's pregnant.'"

About 1 in 4 Americans who eat breakfast away from home eat it at McDonald's.

BUY AMERICAN?

It may not be as easy as you think. This cautionary info is taken from a sparkling little volume called Buy American—Buy This Book, *by Eric Lefcowitz (Ten Speed Press).*

THE TOWN CALLED USA

Before World War II, products stamped MADE IN USA were not necessarily made in the United States or its territories. Many items were made in the town of Usa, Japan (current pop: 27,994). Usa is known to tourists as the home of a beautiful Shinto shrine....However, prior to World War II it was notorious for manufacturing articles stamped MADE IN USA, which, according to the *Encyclopedia Americana*, was used "as a means of circumventing American boycotts of Japanese goods."

AMERICAN QUILTS

In 1992, the Smithsonian Institution outraged American quilt makers by licensing the reproduction of four antique quilts in its collection to a firm in China. The American quilt industry protested that the Smithsonian had undercut their business and cheapened the quality of traditional quilting. The Chinese replicas, which could be mass-produced at a fraction of the cost due to cheap labor, were available for $200-$400 at the Smithsonian gift shop as well as through the Land's End and Speigel catalogs. Only a removable hang tag identified the quilts as imports. Ironically, one of the quilt patterns was "America's Great Seal."

AMERICAN FLAGS

According to industry experts, approximately 15% of all American flags are imported from abroad. This phenomenon is not new: prior to World War II, the American Legion of Cambria County, Pennsylvania, complained that it was "unable to find any small American flags that were not made in either Germany or Japan." In recent times, Taiwan has become the primary source of imported flags, although these imports are often difficult to detect because their labels can be torn off. The easiest way to spot an imported flag, experts say, is to examine its quality—printed rather than

---

Talking Trash: 80% of U.S. men say they're the ones who take out the garbage.

stitched—and its colors, which will rarely match the official Old Glory red, Old Glory white, and Old Glory blue.

FLORIDA ORANGE JUICE

Just because your glass of orange juice has Florida's Seal of Approval does not mean that it comes from the United States. In 1991, 320 million gallons' worth of frozen citrus concentrate were shipped to the United States from Brazil and then reconstituted, packaged, and sold to American consumers. Under the guidelines of the Florida Department of Citrus, any orange juice, regardless of origin, can receive the Florida Seal of Approval provided it meets state standards. Only the "100% Florida" label guarantees an American-grown glass of orange juice.

• • • •

...AND NOW FOR SOMETHING COMPLETELY DIFFERENT

Supermarket Sweepstakes

According to the latest 1992 research, here are the Top 10 bestselling items in your supermarket:

1. Pepsi Cola (2 liters)

2. Coca Cola (2 liters)

3. Campbell's Chicken Noodle Soup

4. Campbell's Cream of Mushroom Soup

5. StarKist Chunk Tuna in Spring Water

6. Campbell's Tomato Soup

7. Kraft Macaroni and Cheese

8. Scott Bathroom Tissue

9. Diet Coke (2 liters)

10. Coca Cola (six-pack of cans)

HOORAY FOR HOLLYWOOD

Hollywood is so closely identified with the glamorous film industry,
it's hard to imagine that it started out as a prim Victorian town...but it did.

HISTORY. In 1886 Kansas prohibitionists Harvey and Daeida Wilcox "bought a 120-acre citrus farm in sleepy Cahuenga Valley, a suburb of Los Angeles, for $150/acre." They built an elaborate Victorian house in the middle of a fig orchard, then began subdividing the property. Liquor wasn't allowed, and only "well-educated, worldly, decent" people were offered the property.

In 1903, the subdivision was big enough to become the city of Hollywood. But it didn't last long. In 1910, the citizens voted to make Hollywood an official district of L.A. The reason: They wanted access to L.A.'s water system. Since then, one historian laments, "Hollywood has been reduced to a mere 'northwest sector of the city of Los Angeles.'"

NAME. While her California house was being built in 1886, Daeida Wilcox went East to visit her family. On the train, she met a woman who described a lovely Illinois summer estate, called Hollywood, that was sprinkled with holly trees.

Mrs. Wilcox was taken with the idea. She repeatedly tried to grow holly on her citrus farm before deciding that the climate wasn't suitable. Perhaps to console herself, she named their ranch Hollywood anyway. In 1887 she registered the name with the Los Angeles recorder.

MAIN INDUSTRY. In the early 1900s the film industry was centered in both New York City and Fort Lee, New Jersey. But soon movie companies were headed west:

• **The First West Coast Studio.** In 1907 Colonel William Selig was producing crude silent movies in Chicago, "whenever the sun was shining—which was not frequently enough to make [his business] a profound success." He happened to read a promotional pamphlet sent east by the Los Angeles Chamber of Commerce that mentioned the city was "bathed in sunshine some 350 days of the year." This impressed Selig, and he sent two men—Francis Boggs and Thomas Parsons—to see if it was true.

To give the area a true test, Boggs and Parsons set up a temporary studio in L.A. and began making pictures, recruiting actors off the streets of the city. When they'd completed several pictures, they left to test another location—Colorado—where they compared the climate and photographic possibilities to those on the coast. The West Coast won. Not only was there almost unlimited sunshine, but the varied scenery—mountains, rivers, deserts, and ocean—was unbeatable. Boggs and Parsons shared their discovery with other filmmakers in the east, and in early 1909, Selig went to Los Angeles to build the first L.A. studio.

The First Hollywood Studio. Ironically, it was the Wilcoxes' puritanism that brought moviemakers to Hollywood. When the couple subdivided their estate, one plot of land wound up in the hands of a tavern owner...who opened a bar there. The outraged Victorians passed a law prohibiting booze, bankrupting the bar. So when the Nestor Moving Picture Company arrived from New Jersey in 1911, they were able to buy the abandoned tavern cheap and convert it into the first Hollywood studio. Within a week, Nestor's had produced Hollywood's first film, *Her Indian Hero*, a western featuring real indians. Within three months, they were sharing Hollywood with fourteen other film companies—despite the "Actors Not Welcome" signs posted all over town.

HOLLYWOOD FACTS
• Early filmmakers who moved West weren't just looking for a place in the sun; they were looking for a place to hide. So many were violating Thomas Edison's motion picture patents that a legal battle known as the Patents War erupted. Southern California was the perfect refuge—as far from the federal government as possible and close enough to the Mexican border for a quick getaway.

• The famous "HOLLYWOOD" sign in the hills above the film capital originally said "HOLLYWOODLAND." It was built in 1923 to promote a real estate development. The last four letters fell down during WW II.

White is the most common color for houses in the United States.

THE LAST LAUGH: EPITAPHS

In the second Bathroom Reader, we included some unusual epitaphs sent to us by B.R.I. members. Here's a bunch we've gotten since then.

Seen in Medway, MA:
In Memory of Peter Daniels,
1688-1746:
Beneath this stone, a lump of
  clay,
Lies Uncle Peter Daniels,
Who too early in the month of
  May
Took off his winter flannels.

Seen in Ribbesford, England:
Anna Wallace
The children of Israel wanted
  bread,
And the Lord he sent them
  manna.
Old clerk Wallace wanted a
  wife,
And the Devil sent him Anna.

Seen in Westminster Abbey:
John Gay
Life is a joke, and all things
  show it;
I thought so once and now I
  know it.

Seen in Death Valley, CA:
May Preston
Here lies the body of fat May
  Preston
Who's now moved to heaven
To relieve the congestion.

Seen in Falkirk, England:
Jimmy Wyatt
At rest beneath this slab of
  stone
Lies Stingy Jimmy Wyatt;
He died one morning just at
  ten
And saved a dinner by it.

Seen in Thanet, England:
Against his will, here lies
  George Hill
Who from a cliff, fell down
  quite stiff.
When it happened is not
  known,
Therefore not mentioned on
  this stone.

Seen in Shutesbury, MA:
To the Four Husbands
Of Miss Ivy Saunders
Here lies my husbands, One,
  Two, Three,
Dumb as men could ever be.
As for my fourth, well, praise
  be God,
He bides for a little above the
  sod.
Alex, Ben and Sandy were the
  first three's names,
And to make things tidy I'll
  add his—James.

HAPPY BIRTHDAY!

It may come as a surprise to learn that celebrating birthdays is a relatively new tradition for anyone but kings and queens. Here are a few inside facts.

BIRTHDAY CELEBRATIONS. The first people known to celebrate birthdays were the ancient Egyptians—starting around 3000 B.C. But only the queen and male members of the royal family were honored. No one even bothered recording anyone else's birthdates.

• The ancient Greeks expanded the concept a little: they celebrated the birthdays of all adult males...and kept on celebrating, even after a man had died. Women's and children's birthdays were considered too unimportant to observe.

• The Greeks also introduced the birthday cake (which they got from the Persians) and birthday candles (which may have been used to honor Artemis, goddess of the moon, because they symbolized moonlight).

• It wasn't until the Middle Ages that German peasants became the first to celebrate the birthdays of everyone in the family. Children's birthday celebrations were especially important. Called *kinderfestes*, they were the forerunner to our toddler birthday parties.

THE BIRTHDAY SONG. Mildred and Patty Smith Hill, two sisters from Louisville, Kentucky, published a song called "Good Morning to All" in a kindergarten songbook in 1893. They wrote it as a "welcoming" song, to be sung to young students at the beginning of each school day.

In 1924 a songbook editor changed the lyrics to "Happy Birthday to You"...and published it without the Hill sisters' permission. The new lyrics made it a popular tune, but the Hill family took no action...until the song appeared in a Broadway play in 1933. Then Jessica Hill (a third sister) sued for copyright infringement. She won, but most singers stopped using the song rather than pay the royalty fee. In one play called *Happy Birthday*, for example, actress Helen Hayes *spoke* the words to avoid paying it.

Today whenever "Happy Birthday" is sung commercially, a royalty still must be paid to the Hills.

REAL-LIFE SONGS

What's the inspiration for a popular song? Often, an event in the life of the songwriter. Behind the Hits, by Bob Shannon, offers good examples of the kinds of experiences that become hits.

THE DOCK OF THE BAY—OTIS REDDING. One warm morning in late 1967, Redding relaxed on a houseboat he'd rented in Sausalito, across the bay from the city of San Francisco. He was "just wastin' time"—and he could afford to. A few days earlier, he'd electrified the audience with his midnight show-closing performance at the Monterey Pop Festival. Then, he had headed north to the legendary Fillmore Auditorium in San Francisco and knocked out the audience there. He was definitely on his way to rock stardom. Satisfied, Redding kicked back in the sunshine, played a few chords on his guitar, and dreamed up a little tune: "Sittin' in the mornin' sun..."

When Redding got back to Memphis, he went into the studio and recorded his song. At the end he wasn't sure what to sing or say—so he just whistled, capturing the casual mood he'd been in on that houseboat in Sausalito.

For the Record: Three days later, Redding died in a plane crash near Madison, Wisconsin. "The Dock of the Bay" became the first posthumous #1 record in history—and Redding's only #1 pop hit.

ROXANNE—THE POLICE. On October 20, 1977, the Police—a starving "art rock" band—were scheduled to be the opening act for a punk band in a Paris club. So they loaded up their car with equipment and drove to France. But when they arrived at the club, they found that there was no gig. They weren't opening for anybody, and no one had come to watch them. They played to an empty house anyway, and left disconsolate, because they could scarcely afford to have made a trip to Paris for nothing.

Things got worse: As they drove around the city right after the gig, their car broke down; it had to be towed back to London.

Sting decided that as long as he had to walk, he might as well take a stroll through Paris's famous red-light district. "It was the first time I'd seen prostitutes on the streets," Sting recalls. "I imagined being in love with one of those girls. I mean, they do have fellas. How would I feel?" He translated the experience into a song called "Roxanne." Two years later it became the first big new wave hit and established the Police.

For the Record: Where did he get the name? "It's a beautiful name, with such a rich history....Roxanne was Alexander the Great's wife, and Cyrano de Bergerac's girlfriend."

UP, UP AND AWAY—THE FIFTH DIMENSION. Here's songwriter Jimmy Webb's version of writing the song: "A friend of mine named William F. Williams, who was at radio station KMEN in San Bernardino, was using this hot air balloon for promotions in the San Bernardino area. He and I were just kind of hanging out, and he took me up a couple of times. The first time, he and I started thinking about doing a film about hot air balloons...just because they were so colorful and so big and so different....He said, 'I've got a great idea for a title—*Up, Up and Away*.' And I said, 'Oh, that's good, I like that.' I was still going to San Bernardino Valley College, so that afternoon I sneaked into a practice room and I wrote 'Up, Up and Away.' The next time I saw him, I said, 'Well, I've got the music for the film.' As it turned out, there never was a film made. But the Fifth Dimension recorded it a few years later, and it worked out nicely for everybody."

SOMEONE SAVED MY LIFE TONIGHT—ELTON JOHN. "She was six-foot tall and going out with a midget in Sheffield," Elton John told *Rolling Stone* about a woman he'd met in 1968. "He used to beat her up! I felt so sorry for her...I fell desperately in love." When they moved in together, "It was just like six months in hell....I tried to commit suicide. It was a very Woody Allen-type suicide. I turned on the gas and left all the windows open." Still, Elton planned to marry her. The night before the ceremony, his friend and manager, John Baldry, came over and convinced him to call it off. Some time later, Elton and Bernie Taupin wrote "Someone Saved My Life Tonight" about Baldry's eleventh-hour wedding intervention.

For the Record: Elton didn't like the record. "I thought it was the worst vocal of all time." But it hit #4 on the charts and was nominated for a Grammy.

THAT WAS NO LADY...

When Dolly Madison passed away, a critic noted that "the first lady of the nation" had died. Since then, we've referred to all presidents' wives as "First Ladies."

Following doctor's orders, Eleanor Roosevelt ate 3 chocolate-covered garlic balls every day of her adult life. Her physician assured her it would improve her memory.

Lady Bird Johnson was such a fan of TV's "Gunsmoke" that she sometimes left official functions early to watch the show.

President William McKinley's wife, Ida, suffered from seizures. (She was believed to be an epileptic.) She and her husband took the problem in stride: whenever she suffered a seizure during a state dinner, President McKinley would drape a handkerchief over her face. When the fit had passed, Ida would remove the handkerchief herself and continue as if nothing had happened.

President Harry S Truman met his future wife, Bess, when both were only 5 years old. One thing he liked about her: she was the only girl in Independence, Missouri, who could whistle through her teeth.

Martha Washington was such a poor speller (she spelled the word "cat" with two t's) that George often had to write her letters for her.

Dolly Madison was addicted to snuff.

Edith Wilson (Woodrow Wilson's wife) was a direct descendant of Pocahontas.

Elizabeth Monroe, wife of James Monroe, liked to have the White House staff address her as "Your Majesty."

Zachary Taylor's wife hated public life so much that she rarely attended White House functions. Many people never even realized the president had a wife until he died in office in 1850...and she attended the funeral.

Louisa Adams (John Quincy Adams's wife) had a unique hobby: she spun silk from silkworms living in the mulberry trees on the White House lawn.

Bad Year: Nobody won the Nobel Peace Prize in 1972.

A TOY IS BORN

*You've bought them. You've played with them. You've wondered where
they came from and who created them. Now the B.R.I. offers
this bit of useless information to satisfy your curiosity.*

W IFFLE BALLS
In 1953 David Mullaney noticed that his son and a friend
were playing stickball in the small backyard of their Fair-
field, Connecticut, home....But they were using one of Mullaney's
plastic golf balls instead of a rubber ball. It seemed like a good idea;
that way the ball couldn't be hit or thrown too far.

Mullaney cut holes in some of his plastic golf balls with a razor
blade and discovered that, with the right configuration, players using a lightweight plastic ball could even throw curves and sliders.
In 1955 he began manufacturing his new creation, marketing it as a
Wiffle Ball—a name he adapted from the baseball term "to whiff,"
or strike out.

SUPERBALLS
In the early '60s a chemist named Norman Stingley was experimenting with high-resiliency synthetics when he discovered a com-
pound he dubbed *Zectron*. He was intrigued; when the material was
fashioned into a ball, he found it retained almost 100% of its
bounce...which meant it had six times the bounce of regular rubber
balls....And a Zectron ball kept bouncing—about 10 times longer
than a tennis ball.

Stingley presented the discovery to his employer, the Bettis Rubber Company, but the firm had no use for it. So, in 1965, Stingley
took his Zectron ball to Wham-O, the toy company that had created Hula Hoops and Frisbees. It was a profitable trip. Wham-O
snapped up Stingley's invention, sold it as a "Superball" and sold 7
million of them in the next six months.

Scientific Curiosity
Stingley wasn't the only "scientist" interested in superballs. During
the Superball craze, aficionados in Australia made a giant Superball
and dropped it from a skyscraper to see if it would bounce all the

way back up.

Unfortunately, the experiment went awry: when the ball hit the ground, it split in half and one part went crashing down the street, bouncing off cars and buildings until it crashed through the front window of a store.

PIGGY BANKS

"For almost 300 years," writes Charles Panati in *Extraordinary Origins of Everyday Things*, "the predominant child's bank has been a pig with a slot in its back." Yet, he points out, pigs have no symbolic connection to saving money. So why did people pick a pig?

According to Panati, "The answer is: by coincidence. During the Middle Ages, mined metal was scarce, expensive, and thus rarely used in the manufacture of household utensils. More abundant and economical throughout Western Europe was a type of dense, orange clay known as pygg. It was used in making dishes, cups, pots, and jars, and the earthenware items were referred to as pygg.

"Frugal people then as now saved cash in the kitchen pots and jars. A 'pygg jar' was not yet shaped like a pig. But the name persisted as the clay was forgotten. By the 18th century in England, pygg jar had become pig jar, or pig bank. Potters, not usually etymologists, simply cast the bank in the shape of its common, everyday name."

TROLL DOLLS

In the early '50s a Danish woodcarver named Thomas Dam made a wooden doll as a birthday gift for his teenage daughter.

The doll, Dam's interpretation of "the mythical Scandinavian elves visible only to children and childlike grown-ups," was so popular with local kids that a Danish toy store owner insisted he make more of them. Eventually, to keep up with European demand, Dam began mass-producing them out of plastic.

In the early 1960s they were exported to the United States as Dammit Dolls...and quickly became a teenage fad, adapted to everything from key chains to sentimental "message" dolls. But since Dam had no legal protection for the design, dozens of manufacturers jumped on the troll-wagon with knockoffs called Wish Niks, Dam Things, Norfins, etc.

The original Dammit Dolls are now collectors' items.

Some toothpastes contain antifreeze.

OL' BLOOD 'N' GUTS

*General George Patton was famous for his one-liners
as he was for his military victories in World War II.*

"In war, just as in loving, you've got to keep on shoving."

"To be a successful soldier you must know history....What you must know is how man reacts. Weapons change but man who uses them changes not at all. To win battles you do not beat weapons—you beat the soul of the enemy man."

"Wars may be fought with weapons, but they are won by men. It is the spirit of the men who follow and of the man who leads that gains the victory."

"The most vital quality a soldier can possess is self-confidence, utter, complete, and bumptious."

"Never tell people *how* to do things. Tell them *what* to do and they will surprise you with their ingenuity."

"A pint of sweat will save a gallon of blood."

"Untutored courage is useless in the face of educated bullets."

"Take calculated risks. That is quite different from being rash."

"A piece of spaghetti or a military unit can only be led from the front end."

"Use steamroller strategy; that is, make up your mind on the course and direction of action, and stick to it. But in tactics, do not steamroller. Attack weakness. Hold them by the nose and kick them in the pants."

"There's one thing you men can say when it's all over and you're home once more. You can thank God that twenty years from now when you're sitting by the fireside with your grandson on your knee, and he asks you what you did in the war, you won't have to shift him to the other knee, cough and say, 'I shoveled crap in Louisiana.'"

Tax Break: 75% of Americans get a refund from the IRS.

THE MYTH-ADVENTURES OF CHRISTOPHER COLUMBUS

Who was Christopher Columbus and what did he really do? Much of what we were taught in school is untrue, according to The Myth-Adventures of Christopher Columbus, *by Jack Mingo. Here are some examples.*

THE MYTH: Columbus was born in Genoa, Italy.

BACKGROUND: The only documentary proof is a will written in 1498, purportedly by Columbus, that begins with "I, being born in Genoa...."

THE TRUTH: According to his son Fernando, Columbus never revealed where he was born; he preferred to call himself "a man of the sea." And historians doubt whether the 1498 will is genuine. Meanwhile, dozens of places claim to be Columbus's birthplace, including:

• **Corsica.** The town of Calvi claims both his birth and his remains; Columbus has a tombstone there.

• **France.** In 1687 French lawyer Jean Colomb claimed Chris was his ancestor.

• **England.** A book published in 1682 in London states that Columbus was "born in England, but lived in Genoa."

• **Spain, Armenia, Poland, and even Norway.** Norwegians say his real name was Christopher Bonde.

THE MYTH: Christopher Columbus was named...Christopher Columbus.

BACKGROUND: This name first appeared in 1553, long after his death, in a book by Petrus Martyr.

THE TRUTH: He was never called Columbus in his lifetime. In fact, when Columbus was alive he was known by at least 5 other names:

• **Cristoforo Colombo.** Most historians believe he was born Cristoforo Colombo (although one Genoese source referred to him as Christofferus de Columbo).

• **Christovam Colom.** When he settled in Portugal and became a

---

successful merchant-seaman, he was known as Christobal (or Christovam) Colom (or Colombo).

• **Cristobal Colon.** He adopted this name after he moved to Spain (also, occasionally, Christoual or Colamo). This was his name during his voyages and what he's still called in Spanish countries.

• **Christophorus Colonus.** This is the name preferred by his son Fernando, who wrote a biography of his dad. Other Latin forms of the name: Christoforus Colom, Cristoferi Colom.

• **Xpoual de Colon.** This is what he was called in his agreement with the King and Queen of Spain before his first voyage across the Atlantic. After 1493, he signed his name Xpo FERENS, using only his first name, in the fashion of royalty. Later he began to sign his name like this:

.s.
.S. A .S.
X M Y
: Xpo FERENS/

Nobody in the past 500 years has been able to explain what this signature means.

THE MYTH: Columbus's boats were officially named the *Nina,* the *Pinta,* and the *Santa Maria.*

BACKGROUND: Blame historians for spreading the story. For example, in *Three Ships at Dawn,* Augustus Heavy wrote: "*Pinta,* meaning 'Lovely Lady,' was called that because she floated so gracefully; *Nina,* meaning 'Baby,' was named that because it was so small; and the devoutly religious sailors called the last ship the *Santa Maria* in honor of Saint Mary."

THE TRUTH: In Columbus's time, if a ship had any kind of name at all, it was unofficial—usually something that the crew came up with. This was true of Columbus's ships as well:

• The *Pinta* might have been called that in honor of the Pinto family in Palos, where the ships were readied for the voyage. But a more likely explanation: "Pinta" also meant "Painted Lady"—a prostitute.

• The *Nina,* smallest of the three ships, had previously been known as the Santa Clara. "Nina" means "Little Girl"—sailor slang for a woman who's easy with sexual favors.

• And the *Santa Maria?* Many of the crew knew it under its long-

Sigmund Freud had a morbid fear of ferns.

time name of "La Gallega" (the Lady from Galicia), so-called because it was built in that region of Spain. But it had picked up a newer nickname, "Marigalante"—"Dirty Mary." The devout Columbus objected to the name. He demanded that the crew call the boat *Santa Maria* in honor of Jesus' mother.

THE MYTH: Queen Isabella of Spain believed so firmly in Columbus's project that she pawned her jewels to finance it.

BACKGROUND: Two of Columbus's biographers—his son Fernando and Bartolome dé Las Casas—told this tale decades after his death.

THE TRUTH: Isabella didn't pawn a single pearl. The queen had a special fondness for Columbus: they were both in their mid-30s, fervently religious, enthusiastic about reforming the world, and may both have had fair complexions and red hair. Queen Isabella would listen to Columbus for hours as he laid out his maps of the world and described his plans for carrying Christianity across the ocean. Despite that, he couldn't get her to finance his plans, because the crown's funds were tied up in a holy war against the Islamic Moors in southern Spain.

Though Isabella had a great many virtues, religious tolerance wasn't one of them. She made war on the Moslems and ordered all Jews expelled from Spain. Christians found to be "insincere" were burned alive at the stake while choir boys sang to protect Isabella's ears from their screams.

With the fall of Granada, the last Islam stronghold, in January, 1492, the queen was full of goodwill and generosity. Columbus saw his chance to plead his case again and received a more benevolent hearing this time. Isabella was now soundly behind his vision of taking Christianity across the waters to save thousands more souls.

But she didn't need to pawn her jewels. As monarch of Castile, she had plenty of her own resources. She used funds from her government coffers, fattened by confiscating property from Jews, Moslems, and "infidels." She even figured out a way to cut expenses. Shippers in the harbor town of Palos, Spain, had been caught smuggling African goods without paying royal duties. As a punishment, the town was ordered to supply ships and provisions for Columbus's journey.

The screwdriver was first used to help knights put on their armor.

THE DEATH OF JIM MORRISON

Did Jim Morrison really leave the land of the living in 1971...
or did he just slip out of the limelight? From It's a
Conspiracy! *by the National Insecurity Council.*

T he Deceased: Jim Morrison, the lead singer of the Doors, one of the most popular rock bands of the 1960s.

How He Died: In the summer of 1971, Morrison and his girlfriend, Pamela Courson, went to Paris on vacation. On July 5, Courson allegedly found him dead in the bathtub. Two days later, he was buried in a quiet service attended by five close friends. The official cause of death was listed as a heart attack. He was 27.

SUSPICIOUS FACTS

• Nobody but Courson ever saw Morrison's dead body; neither Morrison's friends nor his family were given the opportunity to view it. After Morrison died, Courson asked Bill Siddons, the Doors' road manager, to come to Paris. He said that when he arrived on July 6, he "was met at the flat by Pamela, a sealed coffin, and a signed death certificate." He never saw Morrison's body.

• When asked the name of the doctor who signed the death certificate, Siddons said he didn't know, and Courson said she didn't remember. Moreover, according to *No One Here Gets Out Alive*, a 1980 biography of Morrison, "There was no police report, no doctor present. No autopsy had been conducted."

• When Courson filed the death certificate at the U.S. Embassy on July 7, the day of the funeral, she claimed there were no living relatives—which meant that since there was no one to be notified, Morrison could be buried quickly. In fact, Jim's family lived in Arlington, Virginia.

• Morrison's friends kept the story of his death a secret for almost a week. Siddons told his story to the media six days after Morrison died, two days after the funeral. Beyond noting that Morrison had died of "natural causes," Siddons had no more to add.

It's Auto-matic: 40% of American couples first discuss marriage in a car.

POSSIBLE CONCLUSIONS

• **Morrison is really dead.** His friends say they hushed up his death to protect his privacy. A statement prepared for the public said, "The initial news of his death and funeral was kept quiet...to avoid all the notoriety and circus-like atmosphere that surrounded the deaths of such other rock personalities as Janis Joplin and Jimmy Hendrix."

• **Morrison is hiding out.** At the time of his death, Morrison's life was a mess. He had been convicted on two counts of profanity and indecent exposure in Miami and faced a jail sentence if his appeal failed; he faced a possible 10-year sentence after being busted by the FBI for being drunk and disorderly on an airplane; and more than *twenty* paternity suits were pending against him.

Morrison was sick of his life as a rock star and had been saying so for years. He said he wanted to start over anonymously, so he could just write. With Courson's help, he could easily have faked his own death to give himself a fresh start.

√ For years, Courson had urged Morrison to quit the band and develop himself as a poet.

√ She, or someone else, started a rumor that Morrison may have visited a Paris hangout earlier in the evening and obtained some heroin. That, mixed with alcohol, is what supposedly killed him. Yet for all the drugs he ingested, no friends ever mentioned heroin, and Morrison was afraid of needles.

√ The absence of an autopsy and police report is very suspicious, and the lie about his parents and the quick "burial" forestalled any further inquiries. A doctor could have been bribed to fake a death certificate.

√ Finally, Morrison had repeatedly talked about Paris. According to one close friend of the singer, "he thought it was a place where he could be himself and not have people hounding him and making a circus out of his life, making him something he wasn't."

RECOMMENDED READING

All of the quotes in this chapter are from *No One Here Gets Out Alive,* by Jerry Hopkins and Danny Sugerman (Warner Books, 1980).

Texas Rangers pitcher Nolan Ryan earned $1.8 million signing autographs in 1991.

PARKING METER TRIVIA

Fortunately for us, no one's figured out how to put parking meters in bath-rooms...but it seems like they're everywhere else. Here's a little parking meter history, from The Little Book of Boston Parking Horrors, *by Michael Silverstein and Linda Elwood (Silverwood Publications, 1986).*

THE ORIGIN OF PARKING METERS
- In the early '30s Carl Magee, an Oklahoma City journalist, decided he was sick of looking for a parking space every time he drove to town.

- He was sure there was a way to build a machine that kept track of how long a car was parked in a space, but didn't know how to do it. So in 1933 he sponsored a contest at the Engineering Department of Oklahoma State University, offering to pay a cash prize to the student who designed the best working model. A number of students entered the contest, but none came up with a workable design.

- Finally, two engineering professors at the university submitted their design. Magee liked it so much that he formed a company to sell their "parking meters."

TAKING IT TO THE STREET
- The first parking meter, the "Park-O-Meter" #1, was installed at the intersection of 1st St. and Robinson in July 1935. Cost: 5¢ an hour.

- When the first batch of 150 meters was installed, curious motorists came from miles around to witness the unveiling and try one out.

- One local farmer tied his horse to the meter (he told reporters it was cheaper than keeping the horse in a stable); another family pumped a day's worth of nickels into the meter, set up a card table, and spent the day playing bridge with their neighbors.

- The first person to get a ticket was Reverend H. C. North, a local clergyman. He was also the first person to talk his way out of a fine: he told the judge he'd gone to get change when the meter expired.

- R. H. Avant, another local, was the first person to actually *pay* a fine for a meter violation. He handed over $11, an enormous amount of money in 1935. (Not all early fines were that steep; one woman only had to pay $3—and her fine was suspended until she sold enough chickens to come up with the money).

Superman's dog is named Krypto.

THE TV SPEECH THAT MADE A PRESIDENT

No one would have believed Ronald Reagan could be elected president—or even governor of California—until he gave a pro-Goldwater TV speech in 1964 called "A Time for Choosing." Then he was on his way.

BACKGROUND. In 1954, Ronald Reagan was having such a hard time getting acting jobs that he had to work as a Las Vegas emcee. Then came General Electric.

G.E. was looking for someone to host its new half-hour television show—"a man," says one historian, "who could act, sell General Electric products, help build the company's corporate image, and visit General Electric plants to improve company morale." Reagan's agent at MCA got wind of it; he thought the assignment was tailor-made for Ronnie...and G.E. agreed.

Reagan started at $125,000 a year...then got a quick boost to $150,000—because G.E. loved him. "He was a superb TV salesman," one biographer says. "There was a joke in Hollywood about someone who watched him deliver an institutional advertisement for GE's nuclear submarine and remarked, 'I really didn't need a submarine, but I've got one now.' "

G.E. Spokesman

Between TV appearances on "G.E. Theater" from 1954 to 1962, Reagan traveled the country representing the company. He visited 125 G.E. plants, spoke to thousands of Rotary Clubs and other service organizations, and met with 250,000 workers. At each stop, he gave a standard address that became known as "the speech." It was a conservative diatribe extolling free enterprise and warning against the evils of big government.

Republican

In 1962 G.E. canceled "G.E. Theater," and Reagan became host of "Death Valley Days." He also became more active in Republican politics, speaking on behalf of Richard Nixon (who ran for California governor in 1962), and right-wing causes like Dr. Fred Schwartz's Christian anti-Communist campaign. He even produced

Ronald Reagan Record Kits "to warn listeners of...the spreading virus of socialized medicine."

Goldwater Supporter

When Barry Goldwater was nominated for president in 1964, Reagan became co-chairman of Californians for Goldwater.

"In late October," writes Larry Learner in his book *Make-Believe*, "Goldwater was unable to speak at the big $1000-a-plate dinner at the Ambassador Hotel in Los Angeles." Reagan was asked to pinch-hit.

"Asking Ronnie to talk about the 'cause,' " says Learner, "was like getting Billy Graham to discuss sin. He had been preparing his speech for more than a decade as he toured the country for General Electric. He had tried out each bit and piece scores of times. He had tested the response to each of his anecdotes, each of his stories of outrage, each of his shocking facts a score of times."

Naturally, the speech went over well. In fact, it raised so much money around the state that California Republicans decided to televise it nationally. They called it "A Time for Choosing."

THE SPEECH

"On October 27, 1964," writes Lou Cannon in *Ronald Reagan*, "a washed-up 53-year-old movie actor...made a speech on national television on behalf of a Republican presidential candidate who had no chance to be elected....Most of his address was standard, anti-government boilerplate larded with denunciations of communism and a celebration of individual freedom. His statistics were sweeping and in some cases dubious. His best lines were cribbed from Franklin Roosevelt." He only mentioned Goldwater five times in the entire half-hour speech. Yet it was a magic moment in TV political history. Here are a few excerpts:

• "You and I are told increasingly that we have to choose between a left or a right, but I would like to suggest that there is no such thing as a left or a right....There is only an up or a down: up to man's age-old dream—the ultimate in individual freedom consistent with law and order—or down to the ant heap of totalitarianism."

• "We have so many people who can't see a fat man standing beside a thin one without coming to the conclusion that the fat man got that way by taking advantage of the thin one! So they are going to solve all the problems of human misery through government and government planning."

● "We cannot buy our security, our freedom from the threat of the bomb, by committing an immorality so great as saying to a billion human beings now in slavery behind the Iron Curtain, 'Give up your dreams of freedom because to save our own skin, we are willing to make a deal with your slave-masters.'"

● "You and I have a rendezvous with destiny. We will preserve for our children this, the last best hope of man on Earth, or we will sentence them to take the last step into a thousand years of darkness. We will keep in mind and remember that Barry Goldwater has faith in us. He has faith that you and I have the ability and the dignity and the right to make our own decisions and determine our own destiny. Thank you."

THE REACTION
Before the speech, powerful California conservatives considered Reagan "little more than an after-dinner entertainer and cheerleader." Afterward, he was regarded as the new star of the Right.

"Everyone thought I'd done well," recalls Reagan, "but still you don't know always about these things. Then the phone rang about midnight. It was a call from Washington, D.C., where it was 3 a.m. One of Goldwater's staff called to tell me that the switchboard was still lit up from the calls pledging money to his campaign. I then slept peacefully. The speech raised $8 million [at that time, more than any speech in history] and soon changed my life."

Washington columnist David Broder called it "the most successful political debut since William Jennings Bryan electrified the 1896 Democratic convention." A group in Michigan immediately formed a Reagan for President committee. And legend has it that after watching the speech, President Johnson himself turned to aide Bill Moyers and drawled, "Y'know, the Republicans have the wrong damn boy runnin' for president." The direct result of the speech: California Republicans insisted that Reagan run for governor of California. He did, and won two times. His next elected office was the presidency.

DEFINITIONS

In previous Bathroom Readers we've included some uncommon words, and their meanings, to help build weak vocabularies. Here's another batch.

Ambivert: A person who's half introvert and half extrovert.

Backclipping: Shortening a longer word into a smaller one, like *chrysanthemum* to *mum.*

Boomer: A male kangaroo.

Callipygian: Having shapely buttocks.

Chad: The little circles of paper your hole-punch makes.

Furfurrate: What dandruff does when it falls from your scalp.

Genuglyphics: Painting or decorating a person's knees to make them more erotic.

Hypocorism: Baby talk.

Infix: A word placed inside another word to change its meaning, as in fan-f-----tastic.

Izzard: The name of the letter "z."

Kith: Your friends.

Lecanoscopy: The act of hypnotizing yourself by staring into a sink filled with water.

Liveware: People who work with computer software and hardware.

Nidus: A place where bacteria multiplies

Otorhinolaryngologist: An ear, nose, and throat doctor.

Otoplasty: A surgical procedure to fix ears that stick out.

Pandiculate: To yawn.

Paradog: A military dog that's been trained to parachute out of airplanes.

Paranymph: The bridesmaid or best man at a wedding.

Pica: A desire to eat non-foods (like dirt).

Pilomotor reaction: What your hair does when it stands on end.

Pip: What an unhatched chick does to break through its eggshell.

Pullet: A female chicken one year old or younger.

Puwo: An animal that's half poodle and half wolf.

Taresthesia: The tingling sensation you get when your foot falls asleep.

Tautonym: A word consisting of two identical parts, like *tutu.*

Ucalegon: A neighbor whose house is burning down.

Zoonoses: Diseases humans can get from animals.

INSIDE "JEOPARDY!"

"If I had a TV in my bathroom," writes B.R.I. member J. Haines, "I'd be a regular "Jeopardy!" watcher. Unfortunately, I don't. How about a few pages on the program, so I can still think about 'Jeopardy!' in the john?" Okay, J.—here's some info from The Jeopardy! Book, by Alex Trebek.

ORIGIN. In 1963 Merv Griffin and his wife, Juliann, were on a flight to New York when they began discussing game shows. Griffin describes the conversation:

"After the quiz show scandals of the late fifties, the networks were leery of shows where contestants answered questions for money....I mentioned how much I liked the old quiz shows, but reminded her that the scandals had created credibility problems for producers.

" 'So,' Juliann joked, 'Why not just give them the answers to start with?' She was kidding, but the thought struck me between the eyes. She said to me, '79 Wistful Vista.' And I replied, 'What's *Fibber McGee and Molly*'s address?' " "Jeopardy" 's format was born.

THE SHOW GOES ON

As soon as the plane landed in New York, Griffin began working on the show. "I decided to create separate categories of answers, such as History, Literature, Motion Pictures. Put the categories in columns and assign dollar values to each square. That was it. One big board with ten categories and ten answers in each category. We called the game 'What's the Question?' and had a game board built to show to NBC."

The Name. "During the development process, I showed our efforts to network executive Ed Vane, who commented, 'I like what I see, but the game needs more Jeopardies,' " or portions of the game where the players risk losing it all. "I didn't hear another word he said after that. All I could think of was the name: goodbye 'What's the Question?,' hello 'Jeopardy!' "

Showtime. At first, NBC executives disliked the show. During the final sales presentation to the network, NBC head Mort Werner played the game with Merv Griffin acting as host. Halfway through the game Werner threw up his hands and shouted, "I didn't get one question right; it's too hard." But before he could reject the show out of hand, one of his assistants leaned over and whispered, "Buy it." Werner bought it. (His young assistant, a man named Grant Tinker, eventually became head of NBC himself).

THE HOSTS

• **Art Fleming.** The first "Jeopardy!" host was an announcer Merv Griffin had seen on a TWA commercial. Fleming hosted the program for more than 12 years, ultimately appearing on 2,858 shows between 1964 and 1979.

• **Alex Trebek.** Trebek took over when the show was revived in 1984. Earlier that year Chuck Wollery, host of "Wheel of Fortune" (another Merv Griffin game show) became ill. The producer needed a replacement host to tape the program. So he called Alex Trebek, who was emceeing a game show called "Battlestars." Trebek agreed to fill in, and did so well that he was hired to host the new "Jeopardy!"

ANSWERS & QUESTIONS

• How do they come up with their questions?

√ A research staff of 12 writers drafts the questions and provides at least two sources verifying the information.

√ Then the show's editorial associate producer edits the questions and assigns dollar amounts.

√ The questions are then sent back to a different researcher, who verifies them again.

√ From there the questions are given to the show's producer, who can ask for even further verification.

√ Then on game day Alex Trebek reviews the questions himself.

• In the show's 20 seasons, nearly 300,000 questions—61 per episode—have been through this review process.

CONTESTANTS

Where do they get the contestants?

√ Every year 250,000 people apply for an audition, either through the station that broadcasts the show in their area, or by contacting the show itself.

√ Only 15,000 are chosen for the initial screening exam, and only 1,500 qualify to become contestants.

√ Only 500 actually make it on the air.

IN THE BLINK
OF AN EYE

In the time it takes to read this 4-page piece, you'll blink at least 30 times.
Or at least that's what Jay Ingram says in his fascinating book,
The Science of Everyday Life.

B ACKGROUND
"We blink an average of fifteen thousand times a day, each
one lasting roughly three-tenths of a second. That's about an
hour and fifteen minutes each day we spend with our eyes partly or
completely closed. But it's only in the last few years that scientists
have really begun to understand what's going on when we blink.
There are some situations where you expect to blink: when dust or
smoke gets in your eyes, when you're startled by a sudden noise or
the sudden appearance of something close to your eye. But those
account for only a small proportion of the total number of blinks
during the day. The others have nothing to do with cleaning or
protecting your eyes—they are actually signals of what's going on
in your brain."

PHYSICAL DETAILS
• "A blink in detail is a remarkable event. As light as the eyelid
is—it's the thinnest piece of skin in your body—it doesn't get up to
maximum speed immediately."
• "Slow-motion replays show that the eyelid begins to drop, builds
up speed to a maximum, then begins to slow again before your eye
is actually closed. All of that takes about one-tenth of a second."
• "The eyelid stays closed for about one-twentieth of a second,
then it starts accelerating back upward again, leaving a film of tears
behind. The odd thing is that even though your eye is partly or
completely closed for three-tenths of a second or more, you aren't
aware of missing anything."

WHY BLINK?
• "Most of us blink about fifteen times a minute, yet apparently
only one or two of those are necessary to keep the surface of the

eye lubricated. In some forms of Parkinson's disease, patients only blink once or twice a minute, yet have no problem with dryness of the eyes."

• "In fact, scientists Eric Ponder and W. P. Kennedy of Edinburgh University showed in the 1920s that it made no difference to the frequency of blinking whether subjects were in the extremely humid conditions of the botany department's hothouse or in the extreme dryness of a Turkish bath."

• "Ponder and Kennedy also tried to determine if there was a sex difference in blinking. They found that on streetcars men blinked every two and a half seconds, while women blinked every six seconds. But curiously, the results reversed in a library: while the women again blinked roughly every six seconds, the men had reduced their rate dramatically to one blink every eleven seconds."

• "As it turns out, the sex differences they measured have never shown up again in controlled situations, but they hit on something important when they showed that different kinds of mental activity are accompanied by different rates of blinking."

CONCENTRATION IS THE KEY

• "Research since then has boiled that relationship down to one simple rule: the harder you are concentrating, the less you blink. This has been demonstrated in all kinds of circumstances:

√ "Pilots in flight simulators cut their blinking in half when they move from the co-pilot's seat to take control of the aircraft. If the simulated flight is low level and high speed, both co-pilot and pilot blink even less."

√ "Car drivers blink less in city traffic than on highways, and don't blink at all as they're passing trucks at high speed. Even in situations where there's no apparent hazard, concentration reduces the number of blinks."

√ "Doing mental arithmetic or remembering series of numbers reduces blinking."

√ "If you are conversing you blink at the normal rate, about fifteen per minute, but that drops to six a minute if you're reading."

LEARNING BY READING

• A closer look at reading begins to reveal what blinking really means. Studies more than forty years ago showed that readers blink most often when they reach a punctuation mark or the end of the page. In other words, when there's a pause in the flow of information coming into the brain, there's a blink. A blink is a visible signal that the brain is taking a breath.

• It's not just with visual activities like reading. Subjects who are being quizzed by researchers blink very little during a question and in the short period immediately following, presumably because they're thinking about the answer. As soon as they start to answer, they blink, sometimes repeatedly.

• In another experiment people were required to distinguish between a long musical tone and a short one. They usually blinked sometime after the end of the short tone, but often right in the middle of the long tone. The explanation is simple: when the short tone ends, there is a brief delay before the brain realizes it's over. It then recognizes that fact with a blink. But as soon as the long tone stretches beyond a certain length, the brain knows it must be a long tone, and blinks even before it's over.

• So a blink appears only after the brain has processed a certain amount of information, and the greater the amount of information, the longer the delay before a blink. If it takes twice as long to memorize six numbers as two...the blink will appear that much later.

BRAIN FOOD

• Why should blinking reflect what's going on in our brains? Apparently it's not necessary. Those same patients who blink only a couple of times a minute think perfectly well. Blinking isn't a cause of the thinking process, it's a result.

• Some psychologists think that blinking just represents a spillover of brain activity. The flurry of nerve impulses produced during reading or thinking somehow escapes into the nerves controlling the eyelid muscles, and those muscles twitch.

• "It's also true that people who are asked to recite the alphabet to themselves or to count upward from one hundred silently blink much less often than if they're asked to do the same things aloud. Somehow the act of speaking (without changing the thoughts involved) increases the rate of blinking."

• "This supports the idea that there's some kind of spillover, and in

Water Babies: Baby sea lions have to be taught how to swim.

fact the area in the brain that directs movement of eyelid muscles is...adjacent to the area controlling the tongue and face."

THE ANXIETY FACTOR

• Most people believe that anxiety increases the rate of blinking—former U.S. president Richard Nixon blinked twice as much as normal when answering hostile questions about Watergate as he did when answering non-threatening ones, and during the 1988 television debates between Michael Dukakis and George Bush, both debaters blinked more when questions were directed their way.

• But these findings are confounded by the fact that thinking and talking both increase the rate of blinking anyway. Ponder and Kennedy...did note that witnesses in court blink more rapidly—sometimes twice as fast as normal—when they are being cross-examined. But more recent studies showed that subjects who were measurably anxious (because they had been threatened with electric shocks), did not increase their blinking rate. And even if anxiety plays some role in increasing blinking, no one has any idea why this should be so.

BLINKING WARS

• The other common belief about blinking is that it reveals a certain timidity in the face of a threat. Two enemies stand toe to toe, the first to blink is the loser, and the winner proclaims, "He blinked." The phrase is used to describe confrontations between individuals or superpowers, and... its origin is clear. An exhaustive survey of blinking in animals revealed that, on average, carnivores blink less often than herbivores. Or, if you want to put it another way, the predator blinks less than the prey.

• One explanation offered in the 1940s was that the prey needs to survey the landscape continuously for danger, is therefore changing focus and direction of gaze constantly, and blinks with each shift of attention. The carnivore, on the other hand, must fix its gaze on its prey—without a blink.

• Unfortunately, the victors in the human versions of these situations, while crowing that the opponent blinked, forget that an unblinking face may front an unthinking brain.

Galileo went blind studying the sun through telescopes.

10 CANDY BARS YOU'LL NEVER EAT

These tasty tidbits about candy bars that are gone for good come from Dr. Ray Broekel, chocolate and candy bar historian and publisher of Candy Bar Gazebo, a newsletter on old and new candy bars.

THE AIR MAIL BAR. Introduced in 1930 to honor the first airmail flight in the U.S.—in 1918, from Washington, D.C. to New York City. Ironically, the first flight never made it to New York. After takeoff, the pilot noticed someone had forgotten to fill the fuel tank. Then he got lost over Maryland and had to land in a cow pasture. The Air Mail candy bar had a similar fate.

FAT EMMA. In the early1920s the Pendergast Candy Company in Minneapolis introduced a candy bar with a nougat center. They planned to call it the *Emma* bar. But when it wound up twice as thick as expected (they accidentally put too much egg white in the mixture), they changed the name to Fat Emma. Later, Frank Mars copied the idea to create the Milky Way bar.

THE SAL-LE-DANDE BAR. The first candy bar named after a stripper—Sally Rand, whose "fan dance" at the 1933-34 Chicago World's Fair in shocked and titillated the nation. In the '60s another stripper bar was available briefly: the Gypsy bar, named after Gypsy Rose Lee.

THE RED GRANGE BAR. Endorsed by Red Grange, the most popular football player of his day. After starring at the University of Illinois, he joined the Chicago Bears in 1925 and helped keep the National Football League in business. Unfortunately, he couldn't do the same for his candy bar.

THE VEGETABLE SANDWICH BAR. One of the weirdest "health" bars ever made, this 1920s vegetable concoction contained cabbage, celery, peppers, and tomatoes. Its makers claimed it aided digestion and "will not constipate."

THE ZEP CANDY BAR. "Sky-High Quality." One of several candy bars that capitalized on the popularity of "lighter-than-air" dirigibles in the 1930s. This one featured a sketch of a Graf Zeppelin on the wrapper. It was taken off the market after the Hindenburg exploded in 1937.

THE CHICKEN DINNER BAR. One of the bestselling bars you've never heard of. It was introduced in the 1920s and remained on the market for about 50 years. The original wrapper featured a picture of a roasted chicken on a dinner plate—a bizarre way of suggesting it was a nourishing meal and encouraging consumers to associate it with prosperity ("a chicken in every pot"). The manufacturer, Sperry Candy Co., even dispatched a fleet of Model A trucks disguised as giant sheet-metal chickens to deliver the candy to stores. Several years after the bar's debut, Sperry dropped the chicken from the wrapper. But it kept the name.

THE BIG-HEARTED "AL" BAR. George Williamson, owner of the Williamson Candy Company, was a good Democrat and a good friend of New York Governor Al Smith, Democratic nominee for president in 1928. Smith lost in a landslide to Herbert Hoover, and his candy bar soon followed.

THE SEVEN UP CANDY BAR. Got its name from having seven connected pieces, each with a different center. The bar came out in the 1930s, before the 7-Up Bottling Company began producing its soft drink—so the Trudeau Candy Company owned the trademark rights to the name. Eventually the 7-Up Bottling Company bought the bar and retired it, so they had exclusive use of the name no matter how it was spelled—*Seven Up* or *7-Up*.

THE "IT" BAR. The #1 female sex symbol of the silent movie era was Clara Bow—known as the "It Girl." (She had that special quality her movie studio called "It.") In 1927, the McDonald Candy Company of Salt Lake City tried cashing in on her popularity with a candy bar featuring her face on the wrapper. It did well for a few years, then disappeared along with Bow. (She wasn't able to make the switch to talkies, because although she was lovely to look at, her Brooklyn accent made her impossible to listen to.)

Also Gone: The Betsy Ross bar, the Lindy (for Charles Lindbergh), Amos 'n' Andy, Poor Prune, Vita Sert, and Doctor's Orders.

During the Middle Ages you could be accused of witchcraft if your pets disobeyed you.

THAT'S A LOAD OF GARBAGE

You think it's a pain to take out the garbage at home?
Just be glad you haven't got these problems.

Garbage: 400,000 pounds of "pizza sludge" (flour, tomato paste, cheese, pepperoni, etc.)
Location: Wellston, Ohio

Source: A Jeno's, Inc., frozen pizza plant.

Problem: Jeno's produced so much waste in their pizza factory that the local sewage system couldn't accommodate it. They couldn't bury it either, because environmental experts said "it would 'move' in the ground" once they put it there. They had to truck it out.

Garbage: 27 years' worth of radioactive dog poop.

Location: Unknown

Source: Department of Energy experiments. For almost three decades, the DOE studied the effects of radiation by feeding 3,700 beagles radiation-laden food. Each ate the food for a year and a half, and was then left to live out its life.

Problem: No one anticipated that while the experiment was going on, the dog-doo would be dangerous and would have to be treated as hazardous waste. They saved it for decades...and finally took it to a hazardous waste facility.

Garbage: 1,000 pounds of raspberry gelatin and 16 gallons of whipped cream.

Location: Inside a car in Provo, Utah

Source: Evan Hansen, a student at Brigham Young University. He won a radio contest for "most outrageous stunt" by cutting the roof off a station wagon and filling the car with the dessert.

Problem: Hansen couldn't find any way to get rid of the Jell-O. He finally drove to a shopping center parking lot, opened his car doors, and dumped it down a storm drain. He was fined $500 for violating Utah's Water Pollution Control Act.

An estimated 61% of American adults read the newspaper every day.

WHAT, ME WORRY?

Is there a bathroom reader anywhere in the U.S. who's never toted a copy of Mad *magazine into the john at least once in his or her life?*

BACKGROUND
In 1947 Max Gaines, owner of Educational Comics (which published Biblical, scientific, and historical comic books), was killed in a boating accident. He left the business to his 25-year-old son, William, a university student who wanted to be a chemistry teacher.

The younger Gaines renamed the company Entertaining Comics (EC) and phased out its stodgy line of educational comics in favor of more profitable war, true crime, suspense, and horror comics like *Tales from the Crypt, Vault of Horrors,* and *House of Fear.*

THE BIRTH OF *MAD*
Gaines paid his writers and artists by the page. Most of his employees preferred this—but not Harvey Kurtzman. Kurtzman was a freelancer who worked on *Frontline Combat,* a true-to-life battle comic that portrayed the negative aspects of war. He enjoyed writing this comic, but it took so long to research and write that he couldn't make a living doing it. So he went to Gaines and asked for a raise. Gaines refused, but suggested an alternative—in addition to his current work, Kurtzman could produce a satirical comic, which would be easier and more profitable to write. Kurtzman liked the idea and immediately started creating it.

The first issue of *Tales Calculated to Drive You Mad: Humor in a Jugular Vein* debuted in August 1952. It was a flop...and so were the next two issues. But Gaines didn't know it; it took so long to get sales reports that the fourth issue—which featured a *Superman* spoof called *Superduperman*—was already being published before Gaines realized he was losing money. By then, *Mad* had started to sell well.

RED SCARE
Gaines didn't expect *Mad* to be as successful as his other comics, but it turned out to be the only one of his titles to survive the wave of

anti-comic hysteria that swept the country during the McCarthy era.

In 1953 Frederic Wertham, a noted psychiatrist and self-proclaimed "mental hygienist," published *The Seduction of the Innocents*, a scathing attack on the comic book industry. Few comics were left untouched—Wertham denounced Batman and Robin as homosexuals, branded Wonder Woman a lesbian, and claimed that words such as "arghh," "blam," "thunk," and "kapow" were producing a generation of illiterates. The charges were outlandish, but the public believed it; churches across the country even held comic book burnings.

To defend themselves, big comic book publishers established the Comics Code Authority (CCA) to set standards of "decency" for the comic industry and issue a seal of approval to comics that passed scrutiny. (Among the so-called reforms: only "classic" monsters such as vampires and werewolves could be shown; authority figures such as policemen, judges, and government officials could not be shown in a way that encouraged "disrespect for authority," and the words "crime," "horror," and "weird" were banned from comic book titles.) Magazine distributors would no longer sell comics that didn't adhere to CCA guidelines.

Gaines refused to submit his work to the CCA, but he couldn't withstand public pressure. By 1954 only four EC titles were left. Amazingly, *Mad* was one of them.

MAD LIVES

Gaines knew *Mad* wouldn't survive long unless he did something drastic to save it. So rather than *fight* the CCA, he avoided it: he dropped *Mad*'s comic book format and turned it into a full-fledged, "slick" magazine. Thus, it was no longer subject to CCA censorship.

The first *Mad* "magazine" was published in the summer of 1955. "We really didn't know how *Mad*, the slick edition, was going to come out," one early *Mad* staffer later recalled, "but the people who printed it were laughing and getting a big kick out of it, so we said 'This has got to be good.' "

The first issue sold so many copies that it had to be sent back for a second printing. By 1960 sales hit 1 million copies, and *Mad* was being read by an estimated 58% of American college students and 43% of high school students.

The average bird's eyes take up 50% of the space in its skull.

In 1967 Warner Communications, which owned DC Comics, bought *Mad*, but it couldn't affect sales or editorial content: as part of the deal, Warners had to leave Gaines alone. In 1973 sales hit an all-time high of 2.4 million copies; since then they've leveled off at 1 million in the United States. There are also 12 foreign editions. Gaines died in 1992, but *Mad* continues to thrive.

WHAT, ME WORRY?

Alfred E. Neuman has been *Mad* magazine's mascot for years. But his face and even his "What me worry?" slogan predate the magazine by 50 years. They were adapted from advertising postcards issued by a turn-of-the-century dentist from Topeka, Kansas, who called himself "Painless Romaine."

Mad artists were able to rationalize their plagiarism, according to Harvey Kurtzman, after they discovered that Romaine himself had lifted the drawing from an illustration in a medical textbook showing a boy who had gotten too much iodine in his system.

Kurtzman first dubbed the boy "Melvin Koznowski." But he was eventually renamed Alfred E. Neuman, after a nerdy fictional character on the "Henry Morgan Radio Show." Strangely enough, *that* character had been named after a real-life Alfred Newman, who was the composer and arranger for more than 250 movies, including *The Hunchback of Notre Dame* and *The Grapes of Wrath*.

MAD FACTS

• In 1965 *Mad* magazine was turned into an off-Broadway play called *The Mad Show*. Notices were sent out to New York theatre critics in the form of ransom notes tied to bricks. The show gave performances at 3:00 p.m. and midnight, and sold painted rocks, Ex-Lax, Liquid Drano, and hair cream in the lobby. The play got great reviews from the press and ran longer than two years, with bookings in Los Angeles, Chicago, Boston, and other major cities. It was reportedly a major influence on the creators of "Laugh In."

• *Mad* magazine's luck has not been as good in Hollywood. *The Mad Movie*, Gaines's first try for the silver screen, was dumped before production began, and *Up the Academy*, Mad's second attempt, was so bad that Gaines paid $50,000 to have all references to the magazine edited out of the film. An animated TV series in the early 1970s was pulled before it aired.

Bird droppings are the chief export of Nauru, an island nation in the western Pacific.

PRETTY FLAMINGOS

They're America's beloved symbol of bad taste—as designs for lawn ornaments, lamps, cups, and so on. B.R.I. member Jack Mingo tells us how these strange-looking birds became as American as apple pie.

THE FLAMINGO BOOM

During the 1920s, Florida was the hottest vacation spot in the U.S. Tens of thousands of real estate speculators and tourists swarmed to the semitropical state to spend their stock market "profits"...and many brought home souvenirs bearing pictures of a bizarre pink bird that lived there—the flamingo.

In the North, these items—proof that their owners were rich enough to travel to exotic places—became status symbols. Everyone wanted them. So manufacturers started incorporating flamingos into a variety of new product designs.

They were so popular that by the 1950s, the image of a flamingo was as much a part of middle-class America as Wonder Bread or poodles.

THE LAWN FLAMINGO

In 1952, the Union Plastics Company of Massachusetts introduced the first flamingo lawn ornament. It was "flat and unappealing."

• To boost sales, the company decided to offer a more lifelike, three-dimensional flamingo. But the second generation of lawn flamingos "was made of construction foam and fell apart rather quickly," recalls a company executive. "Dogs loved to chew it up."

• Finally, in 1956, Union Plastics hired a 21-year-old art student named Don Featherstone to sculpt a new lawn flamingo. "I got a bunch of nature books and started studying them," says Featherstone. "Finally, I sculpted one, and I must say it was a beautiful looking thing."

• The first atomic-pink molded plastic lawn flamingo went on sale in 1957. It was an immediate success; in the next decade, Americans bought millions of them. But by the 1970s, lawn flamingos were, "gathering dust on the hardware store shelves along with other out-of-date lawn ornaments such as the scorned sleeping

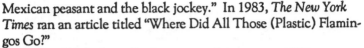

Mexican peasant and the black jockey." In 1983, *The New York Times* ran an article titled "Where Did All Those (Plastic) Flamingos Go?"

• Then suddenly, lawn flamingos were flying again. 1985 was a record year, with 450,000 sold in the U.S. Why the resurgence? Critics suggested a combination of nostalgia and the popularity of the television show "Miami Vice." "They are a must for the newest hot social events—'Miami Vice' parties," reported a California newspaper in 1986.

• Featherstone never got any royalties for his creation. But he did become a vice president of Union Plastics...and in 1987, he was honored when Union started embossing its flamingos with his signature. "I'm getting my name pressed into the rump of every flamingo that goes out the door," he announced proudly.

FLAMINGO: THE BIRD

History. Flamingos, looking pretty much as they do today, were roaming the earth 47 million years before humans came along.

• They were well known in Egypt during the pyramid-and-Sphinx period. A flamingo played a prominent role in Aristophanes' 414 B.C. play *The Birds*.

• The American flamingo is extinct in the wild—captive flocks (most with wings clipped so they don't fly away) at zoos and bird sanctuaries are the only ones left.

Body. Flamingos' knees don't really bend backward. But their legs are so long that the joint you see where it seems the knee ought to be is really the flamingo's ankle, and it bends the same way yours does. The knee is hidden, high up inside the body.

• The flamingo is the only bird that eats with its head upside down—even while it is standing up.

Color. While flamingos are known to sometimes eat small fish, shrimp, and snails, they are primarily vegetarians. They consume vast quantities of algae, and this is what makes them pink. Without the "food coloring," flamingos are actually white.

• Flamingos in captivity are, as a result of algae deprivation, quite a bit paler than their wild cousins. Zoos attempt to keep their flamingo flocks in the pink by feeding them carotene to compensate for the algae they'd get in their natural habitats.

There are more plastic flamingos in America than real ones.

GIVE 'EM HELL, HARRY

Here are a few words from President Harry Truman.

"I never did give anybody hell. I just told the truth, and they thought it was hell."

"The C students run the world."

"The only things worth learning are the things you learn after you know it all."

"You know what makes leadership? It is the ability to get men to do what they don't want to do, and like it."

"You want a friend in this life, get a dog."

"The best way to give advice to your children is to find out what they want and advise them to do it."

"Men don't change. The only thing new in the world is the history you don't know."

"It's a recession when your neighbor loses his job; it's a depression when you lose yours."

"If you can't convince them, confuse them."

"A politician is a man who understands government—and it takes a politician to run a government. A statesman is a politician who's been dead ten or fifteen years."

"Whenever you have an efficient government, you have a dictatorship."

"Whenever a fellow tells me he's bipartisan, I know he's going to vote against me."

"Polls are like sleeping pills designed to lull voters into sleeping on election day. You might call them 'sleeping polls.' "

"I think there is an immense shortage of Christian charity among so-called Christians."

"I look with commiseration over the great body of my fellow citizens who, reading newspapers, live and die in the belief they have known something of what has been passing in the world around them."

"Secrecy and a free, democratic government don't mix."

On average, twins are born 24 days earlier than single babies.

SECRETS OF DISNEYLAND

Well, they're not really secrets—more like gossip. But most people don't know much about the history and operations of the original mega-theme park. And it's pretty interesting stuff.

INSPIRATION

A couple of Walt Disney's top animators were real train buffs. They got Uncle Walt interested in the hobby and he set up a miniature steam railroad that circled his house and gardens (note: *Bathroom Reader #2*, p. 62), big enough to ride. After several train-theme parties, Walt got the idea that if his friends got such a kick from this one ride, maybe a whole amusement park would lure vacationers visiting Hollywood to star-gaze.

HOW WALT GOT THE MONEY

Walt proposed the idea to his brother Roy, the Disney stockholders, and their bankers...but they rejected it. In fact, they thought he was nuts. (In those days, amusement parks were sleazy places full of carnival side-shows, rip-off games, and cheap mechanical rides.)

So Disney was on his own. He went on a relentless search for financing. He sold his Palm Springs home and cashed in his $100,000 life insurance policy to finance his research. He lined up corporate sponsors, who were willing to pay for exhibits and restaurants in exchange for name recognition.

But the turning point came when he made a deal with ABC-TV. At the time ABC, a relatively new network, was a distant third in the ratings. It was desperate for the high-quality, high name-recognition programming Disney could provide. But Disney had already turned down offers from other networks. Why should he join forces with a loser like ABC? The answer: financing for his amusement park. In exchange for doing the show, Disney received a substantial sum of money and ABC agreed to call the show "Disneyland," virtually making the weekly show a one-hour commercial for the park. But perhaps more important, later, in an "unrelated" deal,

ABC purchased a 34% interest in Disneyland, Inc., the company set up to build the park.

When Roy saw the package Walt had put together, he changed his mind and hopped on the Disneyland bandwagon. In 1954, ground was broken in an Anaheim orange grove.

OPENING DAY

In the wake of its enormous success, people have forgotten that Disneyland's opening day was a disaster. Nearly 33,000 people—twice as many as the number invited—packed the park with the help of forged tickets and surreptitiously placed ladders. Not all the rides were operational, and the restaurants ran out of food after a few hours. In some parts of the park, concrete and asphalt hadn't hardened properly, and women walked out of their high-heel shoes.

Also, there had been a plumber's strike during construction, and there weren't enough drinking fountains. The press thought it was a ploy to get visitors to purchase soft drinks. What they didn't know was that, in order to be ready for opening day, Walt had to choose between installing toilets or drinking fountains.

Thanks to nationwide TV coverage emceed by Ronald Reagan, the entire country learned of the mess. The next day's newspaper headlines read, "Walt's Dream A Nightmare"—and Disney seemed to agree: for the rest of his life he referred to opening day as "Black Sunday."

LAND OF ILLUSIONS

When Uncle Walt bought the property for Disneyland in Anaheim in the early 1950s, he couldn't afford to buy all the land he wanted. So, in order to fit everything in, he used movie makers' tricks to make everything look bigger.

One trick was to use things that are familiar, but make them smaller than normal. Unless you look carefully and measure with your eyes, you'll assume, for instance, that the Disneyland train is normal size. It isn't. It is built to 5/8 scale. Many of the Disney buildings use the same trick, but that's just the beginning.

If you look carefully at some of the Disney buildings, especially those on Main Street, you'll notice there's something a little odd about them. They are not only smaller than normal, but their second and third stories are smaller still. This is known in art and in movie making as "forced perspective." By tapering the upper stories, the designers fool your eye into believing that they are bigger and taller than they really are.

This is done especially skillfully on Sleeping Beauty's Castle, even to the point that the bricks get smaller and smaller with each level.

In making Disney World this was less of a problem, because by that time the company could afford to buy an area bigger than most cities. It used many of the same tricks, but on an even bigger scale.

DISNEYLAND DEATHS

According to an article in *Egg* magazine, at least 53 people have died at Disneyland. According to *Egg*:

• The first Disney death was apparently a suicide: In 1964, after an argument with his girlfriend, a passenger on the Matterhorn stood up on the ride and was catapulted onto the tracks when his car came to a sudden stop. He never regained consciousness, and died four days later.

• The Matterhorn killed again in 1984, when a 48-year-old woman fell out of the ride and was struck by the following car. (For the rest of the day the Matterhorn was closed due to "technical difficulties.")

• Two people have been killed in accidents in Tomorrowland's "PeopleMover" ride, two others drowned in the river surrounding Tom Sawyer's Island. Another person was run down by the Monorail when he tried to sneak into the park without paying; and a park employee was crushed by a moving wall in the "America Sings" attraction.

• The park's first homicide occurred in 1981, when a man was stabbed after touching another man's girlfriend. (Disneyland was found negligent in the death and fined $600,000 after a park nurse neglected to call paramedics—and instead had the victim driven to the hospital in a park van.)

• Not all of the accidents happen inside the park: in 1968, 44 people were killed in two separate helicopter accidents traveling between Disneyland and Los Angeles International Airport; and in 1987 a teenage male was killed during a gunfight in the parking lot.

WHAT'S IN A NAME?

You know these corporate and product names, but not where they come from. Well, the B.R.I. will fix that. Here's a little trivia you can use to entertain store clerks next time you're shopping.

Kodak. No meaning. George Eastman, founder of the company, wanted a name that began and ended in the letter K. "The letter K has been a favorite with me," he explained. "It seems a strong, incisive sort of letter."

Chanel No. 5 Perfume. Coco Chanel considered 5 her lucky number. She introduced the perfume on the fifth day of the fifth month of 1921.

Lucky Strikes. Dr. R. A. Patterson, a Virginia doctor, used the name to sell tobacco to miners during the California Gold Rush in 1856.

Ex-Lax. Short for *Excellent Laxative.*

Reebok. An African gazelle, "whose spirit, speed, and grace the [company] wanted to capture in their shoes."

Avon Products. Named for Stratford-on-Avon, William Shakespeare's birthplace.

Random House. America's biggest publisher started out in the 1920s, offering cheap editions of classic books. But founder Bennett Cerf decided to expand the line by publishing luxury editions of books selected "at random."

Kent Cigarettes. Herbert A. Kent, a Lorillard Tobacco Company executive, was so popular at the office that the company named a cigarette after him in 1952.

Toyota. Sakichi Toyoda made the first Japanese power loom. His son Kiichiro expanded into the automobile business.

Xerox. The Haloid Company originally called its copiers "electrophotography" machines. In the 1940s, they hired a Greek scholar at Ohio State University to think up a new name. He came up with "Xerography" for the process (after the Greek words for dry and writing) and called the copier itself a *Xerox* machine.

TANG TWUSTERS

Ready for a workout? Here are 20 difficult tongue twisters. Try to say each of them five times fast...and don't pay any attention to the people banging on the bathroom door, asking what's going on in there.

If you must cross a coarse cross cow across a crowded cow crossing, cross the coarse cross cow across the crowded cow crossing carefully.

Does this shop stock short socks with spots?

The sixth sheik's sixth sheep's sick.

"The bun is better buttered," Betty muttered.

Seven sleek sleepless sleepers seek sleep.

Sixty-six sickly chicks.

The sun shines on shop signs.

The shady shoe shop shows sharp sharkskin shoes.

A noise annoys an oyster, but a noisy noise annoys an oyster more

Rush the washing, Russel!

The seething sea ceaseth seething.

Awful old Ollie oils oily autos.

Mummies munch much mush.

This is a zither.

Ike ships ice chips in ice chip ships.

She says she shall sew a sheet.

Feed the flies fly food, Floyd!

Miss Smith dismisseth us.

Ted threw Fred thirty-three free throws.

Rex wrecks wet rocks.

THE STORY OF WALL STREET

Why is Wall Street the financial center in the U.S.? For that matter, why is it even called Wall Street? Glad you asked that question.

HISTORY. In the early 1600s, the southern tip of Manhattan Island was a Dutch settlement known as New Amsterdam. In 1653, the governor of the colony decided the best way to protect his thriving trading post from Indians and the British was to build a wall from the Hudson River to the East River.

However, the wall did little to deter the British. They attacked by ship in 1664, easily overwhelmed the Dutch, and renamed the city New York. Thirty years later, they tore down the wall and used it for firewood.

NAME. The dirt road that ran alongside the wall was—naturally enough—known as Wall Street. When the wall was destroyed, the road became a main thoroughfare in New York.

MAIN INDUSTRY. Wall Street has been a commercial center ever since the British took over.

• They immediately set up a number of "exchanges"—open, shed-like buildings used for trading commodities like furs, molasses, and tobacco—on Wall Street.

• About 100 years later the first stocks and bonds were sold on the street. At the end of the Revolutionary war the Colonies were so deeply in debt that the first Congress of the U.S. issued $80 million in bonds (government IOUs). Stocks were added two years later, when Alexander Hamilton (then Secretary of the Treasury) established the nation's first bank, the Bank of the United States, and offered shares to the public.

The New York Exchange. Stocks and bonds soon became a booming business, and in 1792 a group of 24 brokers decided to create an informal exchange to specialize in these "paper transactions."

Ohio has 22 roller coasters—the most of any state.

They signed a document known as the "Buttonwood Agreement" (named after the tree on Wall Street where the group met), in which they agreed to trade only among themselves and to charge customers a minimum 25% commission. These men are considered the original members of the New York Stock Exchange.

• When conditions on the street got too crowded, the exchange moved into a coffeehouse, then rented a room at 40 Wall Street. New members were required to pay an initiation fee of not less than $25; the amount varied, depending on the location of their seat in the room. This is how traders came to buy "a seat on the exchange."

• By 1848, the prestigious New York Stock Exchange and Board had absorbed all other exchanges on Wall Street and was conducting business in an orderly and unexciting manner: the chairman called the name of each stock twice a day and any trading was completed before moving on.

The American Exchange. Meanwhile, those who couldn't afford to become members continued to trade on the street after-hours, and became known as "curb brokers." For this army of opportunists, the action was in stocks considered too speculative by members of "The Big Board"—especially railroads and mining companies created after the discovery of gold in California.

• By the late 1890s, some of the brokers on "The Curb Exchange" could afford to rent offices in nearby buildings. Telephone clerks took orders and shouted them out the window to the brokers below, who wore loud checkered jackets and hats, from bright green derbies to pith helmets, so their clerks could spot them in the crowded street. When the shouting got out of hand, a system of hand signals (some of which are still used today) was developed to pass on price and volume information.

• This entire scene moved indoors in 1921. And in 1953, the New York Curb Exchange, its name since 1928, became the American Stock Exchange, the second largest exchange on Wall Street.

Miscellany. The term "broker" comes from the french *brochier*, meaning someone who broaches, or breaks, a wine keg. It was originally used to refer to entrepreneurs who bought wine by the barrel, "broke it open," and sold it by the cup.

MALCOLM X SPEAKS

Malcolm X was one of the most controversial—and significant—figures in recent American history.

"You're not supposed to be so blind with patriotism that you can't face reality. Wrong is wrong, no matter who does it or who says it."

"It's easy to become a satellite today without even being aware of it. This country can seduce God. Yes, it has that seductive power—the power of dollarism."

"I for one believe that if you give people a thorough understanding of what confronts them and the basic causes that produce it, they'll create their own program, and when the people create a program, you get action."

"I believe in the brotherhood of man, all men, but I don't believe in brotherhood with anybody who doesn't want brotherhood with me. I believe in treating people right, but I'm not going to waste my time trying to treat somebody right who doesn't know how to return that treatment."

"Power never takes a back step—only in the face of more power."

"Nobody can give you freedom. Nobody can give you equality or justice or anything. If you are a man, you take it."

"After you get your freedom, your enemy will respect you."

"You cannot seperate peace from freedom, because no one can be at peace until he has his freedom."

"Truth is on the side of the oppressed."

"Learn to see...listen...and think for yourself."

"The colleges and universities in the American education system are skillfully used to miseducate."

"There shouldn't be bars. Behind bars, a man never reforms. He will never forget. He will never get completely over the memory of the bars."

Survey Results: 70% of high school students try cigarettes, but only 13% smoke regularly.

BOX-OFFICE BLOOPERS

We all love bloopers. Here are a bunch of movie mistakes to look for in popular films. You can find more in a book called Film Flubs *by Bill Givens.*

Movie: *The Wizard of Oz* (1939)
Scene: Dorothy, the Tin Woodsman, and the Scarecrow dance down the Yellow Brick Road singing, "We're Off to See the Wizard."
Blooper: A crew member can be seen in the background among the trees. (For years, rumors circulated in Hollywood that the crew member had committed suicide and hung himself from one of the trees on the set. The rumors were false.) *Note:* Also pay close attention to the length of Dorothy's hair. Because the scenes were filmed out of sequence, her hair changes from mid-length to long to short as the movie progresses.

Movie: *Spartacus* (1960)
Scene: Peter Ustinov gets off of his horse.
Blooper: His jockey shorts are visible under his tunic as he climbs down.

Movie: *The Alamo* (1960)
Scenes: The battle sequences.
Bloopers: Though the movie is a Western, you can see several mobile trailers in the distance. (And in another scene, you can see a stuntman falling into a mattress.)

Movie: *Children of a Lesser God* (1986)
Scenes: Several occasions in which Marlee Matlin (who is deaf and portrays a deaf character) and co-star William Hurt sign to each other during conversations in which Hurt is speaking.
Blooper: The sign language has nothing to do with the movie—it's about Matlin's and Hurt's private life. (At the time the movie was made, Matlin and Hurt were having an affair.)

Movie: *Rambo III* (1988)
Scene: Rambo steals a "Russian" helicopter.
Blooper: A small American flag is clearly visible on the helicopter's rotor housing.

SENATE FIGHTS

*You've heard of floor fights in Congress...but you probably never imagined
the kind where people get bloody noses and pull guns on each other.
Here are a few instances when that's exactly what happened.*

FOOTE VS. BENTON

Background: Senator Henry Foote of Mississippi had a reputation as a hothead and a fighter; he'd been injured in no less than three duels. His temper reached legendary proportions on April 17, 1850, when he drew a pistol on Thomas Hart Benton of Missouri in the Senate chamber.

What Happened: Benton had just finished delivering a stinging attack on Foote's recently deceased mentor, former Vice President John C. Calhoun of South Carolina. Suddenly Foote leaped to his feet and denounced Benton as a coward. When Benton advanced toward the offending senator, Foote retreated and pulled a pistol from his coat. Benton replied: "I have no pistols. Let him fire. Stand out of the way. Let the assassin fire."

Result: Chaos ensued. Finally, Senator Daniel Dickinson of New York took Foote's pistol away. Foote was later reprimanded for his behavior but no other charges were pressed.

BROOKS VS. SUMNER

Background: Civil War tensions boiled over in Congress on May 22, 1856, when South Carolina Representative Preston Brooks brutally attacked and injured Massachusetts Senator Charles Sumner with a cane. The incident followed a heated address by the antislavery Sumner, who had specifically attacked Brooks's relative, Senator Andrew Butler of South Carolina.

What Happened: When the Senate adjourned, Brooks approached Sumner—who was sitting at his desk—and began striking him on the head with a cane. Sumner was trapped. To avoid the blows, he tried to rise from his bolted-down desk. His effort was so great that he literally ripped the screws from the floor.

Result: Sumner was so badly injured that he spent the next three years recovering. Efforts to punish Brooks—who became a hero in the South—were unsuccessful. He died shortly after the attack.

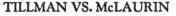

TILLMAN VS. McLAURIN

Background: On February 28, 1902, the Senate was debating a bill relating to government aid for the Philippines.

What Happened: Senator Benjamin Tillman of South Carolina charged that "improper influences" had influenced his colleague, John McLaurin—also from South Carolina—to change his vote on the legislation. When McLaurin heard Tillman's charges, he ran back to the Senate chambers "pale with anger" and accused Tillman of lying. Tillman lunged at McLaurin and punched him in the eye. McLaurin came back with a blow to Tillman's nose.

Result: A doorkeeper and several senators intervened and the gallery was immediately cleared. Later that day, both were suspended for six days for "disorderly conduct." The fight eventually led to Senate Rule 19, which says "no Senator in debate shall, directly or indirectly, by any form of words impute to another Senator or to other Senators any conduct or motive unworthy or unbecoming a Senator."

ENGLE VS. THE FILIBUSTER

Background: On June 10, 1964, one of the most dramatic votes in Senate history took place. Democratic Senator Clair Engle of California, terminally ill with a brain tumor, cast a vote from his wheelchair that led to the passage of the Civil Rights Act of 1964.

A Southern filibuster had stalled the bill on the floor of the Senate. Ending the filibuster required a two-thirds majority, and it looked like the Democrats were one vote short.

What Happened: "Then came the moment few had expected," *The New York Times* reported. "Seconds before his name was called, Senator Clair Engle of California was pushed into the chamber in a wheelchair. He was smiling slightly. 'Mr. Engle,' the clerk called. There was a long silence. Senator Engle, recuperating from two brain operations, tried to speak. He could not. Finally he raised his left arm, as though trying to point toward his eyes. He nodded his head, signaling that he was voting 'aye.' He was wheeled out of the chamber minutes later and taken by ambulance back to his home."

Result: The resolution passed by one vote. Nine days later, on June 19, 1964, the Senate passed the final version of the Civil Rights Act, again with Engle's vote. A month later, "Congressman Fireball"—as Engle had once been called—died at the age of 52.

Beauty Fact: Most lipstick contains fish scales.

WISE GUY

*You've probably never heard of him, but in the 1920s H.L.
Mencken was one of America's most famous newspaper
columnists. His claim to fame was his acid-tongued
social commentary...as these examples demonstrate.*

"Imagine the Creator as a low comedian, and at once the world becomes explicable."

"Jury: a group of twelve men who, having lied to the judge about their hearing, health, and business engagements, have failed to fool him."

"Lawyer: one who protects us against robbery by taking away the temptation."

"The best years are the forties; after fifty a man begins to deteriorate, but in the forties he is at the maximum of his villainy."

"If I had my way, any man guilty of golf would be ineligible for any office of trust in the United States."

"Conscience is a mother-in-law whose visit never ends."

"Criticism is prejudice made plausible."

"A cynic is a man who, when he smells flowers, looks around for a coffin."

"Democracy is the art of running the circus from the monkey cage."

"On one issue, at least, men and women agree: they both distrust women."

"Every man is thoroughly happy twice in his life: just after he has met his first love, and just after he has left his last one."

"Wife: a former sweetheart."

"To die for an idea; it is unquestionably noble. But how much nobler it would be if men died for ideas that were true!"

"An idealist is one who, on noticing that a rose smells better than a cabbage, concludes that it will also make better soup."

Mike Wallace, investigative reporter on "60 Minutes," was once a game show host.

FAMILIAR NAMES

*Some people achieve immortality because their names
become commonly associated with an item or activity.
You already know the names—now here are the people.*

Alfredo di Lellio. A Roman restaurateur. His fettucine with butter, cream, and Parmesan cheese became famous in the '20s after Hollywood stars Mary Pickford and Douglas Fairbanks ate in his restaurant every day during their honeymoon.

John Langon-Down. An English doctor of the late 19th century. He was the first doctor to describe, in medical literature, the genetic defect now known as Down's Syndrome. Down called it "mongolism," because physical characteristics related to the condition reminded him of the features of people of Mongolia.

Queen Mary I of England and Ireland. A fanatical Catholic, she brutally repressed Protestants in her realm. Her reputation earned her the nickname "Bloody Mary," and inspired a cocktail made with vodka and tomato juice.

Vyacheslav Mikhailovich Molotov. Soviet foreign minister, 1939-1949 and 1953-1956, and rabid Stalinist. Finnish resistance fighters battling Russian tanks in the 1940s named their primitive gasoline-filled bottle bombs "Molotov cocktails" in his "honor."

Sir George Everest. The surveyor-general of India from 1830 to 1843, he named the country's (and the world's) tallest mountain after himself.

Dr. A. M. Latan. A quack dentist and peddler of health tonics in Paris during the 1840s. He traveled the city in an opulent coach—usually with a man marching in front, blowing a horn to attract attention—selling his wares as he went. Parisians shouted "Voila, le char (car) de Latan"—later shortened to "charlatan."

Mickey Finn. A 19th-century San Francisco saloon keeper who ran a bar popular with sailors. When customers got too rowdy, he slipped drugs into their drinks to knock them out. Today, giving someone a knockout drink is called "Slipping them a Mickey."

The London Bridge has never fallen down.

Sam Ellis: A tavern keeper on what was later called Ellis Island.

Edward Stanley, twelfth earl of Derby. A British nobleman of the late 1700s and early 1800s. An avid horse lover, he hosted a 1.5-mile horse race in 1780 that he called the "Derby Stakes." Today the term "derby" is used to represent any horse race or other sporting event that has a strong local following.

Gabriel Daniel Fahrenheit. German scientist of the late 17th and early 18th centuries. Invented a new thermometer that used mercury instead of alcohol. Its new scale—which marks water's freezing point at 32° and its boiling point at 212°—was named Fahrenheit after him and became popular in English-speaking countries.

Anders Dahl. In 1789 Alexander von Humboldt, a German explorer, discovered a new species of flower while on an expedition to Mexico. He sent some of the plant's seeds to the Botanic Garden in Madrid, where the curator promptly named the plants *Dahlias*—after his close friend Anders Dahl, a famous Swedish botanist who had died earlier that year.

George Nicholas Papanicolaou. Pioneered the use of cervical tissue smear samples in detecting uterine cancer. Today that test is known as a "Pap smear."

Josiah Wedgwood. An English potter of the late 1700s. He developed a line of china famous for its white designs on a blue background, which later became known as "Wedgwood" china.

David Douglas. A 19th-century Scottish botanist and explorer of the western United States. He discovered a new species of tall evergreen trees that bear his name: Douglas firs.

Draco. A magistrate and lawmaker who wrote the first code of laws of ancient Athens in the 7th century B.C. The code was one of the strictest set of laws ever written; it gave the death sentence for nearly every crime—even petty theft. Today any punishment that seems too severe for the crime can be labeled "draconian."

Caspar Wistar. A professor of "anatomy and midwifery" who held regular Sunday tea parties for a wide variety of scientists. One of his frequent guests was Thomas Nuttall, curator of the Harvard University Botanical Garden. In appreciation, Nuttall named a species of climbing plant "wistarias" in Wistar's honor. But because of a spelling mistake, the plants became known as "wisterias."

There are almost as many chickens in the world as there are people.

THE TRUTH ABOUT THE PANAMA CANAL

The Panama Canal was a triumph of engineering—but it was also a triumph of political conspiracy. As one political wit said in the 1970s: "The Panama Canal belongs to us. We stole it fair and square."

THE MYTH: The Panama Canal was an American idea.

THE TRUTH: The idea of a building a canal through the Panama Strait was more than three centuries old before anybody actually did anything about it.

The possibility was first discussed just decades after Columbus landed in the New World, when the Spaniards realized how far around South America they had to go to get to the Pacific Ocean. Panama seemed to be an ideal spot for a canal, since it measured only 50 miles from coast to coast.

But the issue was put to rest in 1552 by King Philip, whose religious advisors reminded him that the scriptures warned: "What God has joined together let no man put asunder." Philip agreed. "If God had wanted a Panama Canal," he announced, "He would have put one here."

America's First Effort. In the 1850s, during the Gold Rush, President Ulysses Grant sent a survey team to Panama to see if it was possible to build a canal. But he gave up on the idea when they reported that there wasn't "the slightest hope that a ship canal will ever be found practicable across any part of it."

The French Effort. That didn't stop the chief promoter of the Suez Canal from trying. In 1880 Ferdinand de Lesseps, backed by a group of French investors, began building a canal across the Isthmus of Panama. American President Rutherford Hayes was outraged that this was happening in "our" territory and decreed that France should cede control of the canal to the United States.

Before the issue became an international incident, however, the French project collapsed under the weight of corruption, poor planning and the harsh Central American jungle environment: floods, earthquakes, yellow fever, and malaria. The French abandoned their partly dug canal and most of their heavy machinery to rust in the jungle.

THE MYTH: The U.S. signed a treaty with the legitimate government of Panama to build and lease the Canal Zone.

THE TRUTH: Panama wasn't even a country when the U.S. decided to build a canal there—it was a territory of Colombia.

Background. In 1898, the battleship *Oregon*, stationed off the California coast, was ordered to Cuba to prepare for battle in the Spanish American War. The voyage around South America took two months. Clearly, a faster route was needed.

When the war was over, President Theodore Roosevelt began pushing for a canal. He was partial to a canal through Nicaragua: Even though that route was longer, it appeared to be an easier dig, since it would run through Lake Nicaragua.

But Panama had its partisans in the fierce Senate debate about the canal. When the French—who wanted to unload the canal they'd begun—dropped the price for their unfinished assets from $109 million to $40 million, America decided on Panama.

The Colombia Problem. There was just one problem: Roosevelt found that the people he called "Dagos" in Colombia were asking too much for using their territory.

He decided the solution was simple—if the existing country was a problem, create a new country that would be more willing to compromise. The U.S. Army teamed up with a former director of the French canal company, who stirred up a "revolt" against Colombia. Meanwhile, the American battleship *Nashville* positioned itself off the Colombian coastline with guns ready, in case Colombia objected.

Friendly Nation. As soon as a new revolutionary government was announced, the U.S. recognized it and pushed through a deal: for $10 million, an annual fee of $250,000, and a guarantee of "independence," the United States received rights to the ten-mile wide canal zone "in perpetuity." Since the new country of Panama was not much wider than that ten-mile zone, the U.S. effectively controlled the country. Colombia did protest, but there wasn't much it could do. The canal was finished in 1914.

Couch Potatoes: 25% of American adults say they never exercise.

FREE ADVICE

Here are a handful of helpful hints from high-profile heavyweights from Friendly Advice, *by Jon Winokur.*

"Never go out to meet trouble. If you will just sit still, nine cases out of ten someone will intercept it for you."
—Calvin Coolidge

"Don't put no restrictions on the people. Leave 'em the hell alone."
—Jimmy Durante

"The best way to keep money in perspective is to have some."
—Louis Rukeyser
(*Wall Street Week in Review*)

"The only way to keep your health is to eat what you don't want, drink what you don't like, and do what you'd rather not."
—Mark Twain

"If four or five guys tell you that you're drunk, even though you know you haven't had a thing to drink, the least you can do is lie down a while."
—Joseph Schenck

"A man is a fool if he drinks before he reaches fifty, and a fool if he doesn't drink afterward."
—Frank Lloyd Wright

"Never go to a doctor whose office plants have died."
—Erma Bombeck

"A woman's dress should be like a barbed-wire fence: serving its purpose without obstructing the view."
—Sophia Loren

"Never underestimate a man who overestimates himself."
—Franklin D. Roosevelt

"My father gave me these hints in speechmaking: Be sincere ...be brief...be seated."
—James Roosevelt
(FDR's son)

"The secret of dealing successfully with a child is not to be its parent."
—Mell Lazarus

"Saving is a very fine thing. Especially when your parents have done it for you."
—Winston Churchill

"Never put off until tomorrow what you can do the day after tomorrow."
—Mark Twain

Lee Harvey Oswald's cadaver tag sold at auction for $6,600 in 1992.

THE PLUMBER'S HELPER

While you're sitting on the john, take a moment to examine it. Do you notice a problem? If so, you're in luck: the B.R.I. plumber's helper is here. We can't guarantee or even recommend this advice, of course (we're writers, not plumbers), but at least it sounds good.

The problem: Running water

What it usually means: The chain connecting the handle to the flush valve—the hole at the bottom of the tank where the water enters the bowl— is too long. Remove a few links of the chain so that it hangs with only a little slack.

Other possible causes:

• The "float mechanism" that shuts off the water isn't working; it's letting water leak into the overflow pipe. If your mechanism is a "float ball" attached to a horizontal rod, bend the rod so that the ball hangs lower in the tank. If it's a plastic cylinder called a "float cup," adjust it so that it hangs lower in the tank.

• Your "flush valve" is leaking. This is most likely the problem if you have to jiggle the toilet handle a lot, or if the toilet hisses regularly. Your best bet is to replace the rubber bulb mechanism. Replace the flush valve with one that's the same size.

The Problem: A wet floor around the base of your toilet.

How to Fix It: Add several tablespoons of food coloring to the water in the bowl and in the tank. Wipe the floor around the toilet dry, and then wait for the moisture to reappear.

Mop up the area again, this time using white paper towels. If the moisture is colored, your toilet is leaking. If it isn't, you probably have a condensation problem, or a leak from another fixture.

• To fix a leaky toilet tank, drain it and use a wrench or screwdriver to tighten the nuts at the base of the tank (If the washers around the bolts look worn, replace them). Don't overtighten; if you do you'll risk cracking the tank.

• If the toilet still leaks, the flush valve may be loose. The only way to fix it: remove the tank from the bowl and tighten the valve.

A FAMILY AFFAIR

Did TV's "Brady Bunch" seem like a close family to you?
According to actor Barry Williams (Greg Brady) in his new book,
Growing Up Brady, *they were a lot closer than you think.*

"At some point throughout the five years of filming, every Brady (kid) paired up romantically with the opposite sex counterpart," Williams confesses, although as far as he knows, none of the encounters "went all the way." Still, here's the juicy details of some of the closer encounters of the Brady clan:

The Couple: Greg and Mrs. Brady (Williams and Florence Henderson)
The Place: The Coconut Grove Club in Los Angeles
Kiss and Tell: After sharing a dirty joke about lollypops with her on the set, "I got a case of the hots for my mom," Williams confesses, "I just couldn't control myself anymore and wound up asking her out. Amazingly, she accepted." Williams describes their first kiss: "No tongue, but nice."
Why It Ended: They just never hit it off. Henderson later told Williams: "You were really cute, and I was tempted a few times. I think we're lucky Carol never slept with Greg, but...uh...it coulda been."

The Couple: Greg and Marcia (Maureen McCormick and Barry Williams)
The Place: Waikiki beach, when the cast was in Hawaii filming the show's first Hawaiian special
Kiss and Tell: "I kissed her, and the floodgates opened; warm and hard and packed with the kind of osculatory excitement only teenagers can transmit....Years later, I'd find out that this had been Mo's first kiss."
Why It Ended: While on a cruise on the *Queen Elizabeth II*, Williams snuck into McCormick's bedroom, climbed into bed with her, and started caressing her. McCormick woke up and kicked him out of her room. According to Williams: "My desperate groping killed something between us that night."

The Couple: Jan and Peter (Eve Plumb and Christopher Knight)

The Place: Aboard the *Queen Elizabeth II*, and later in Knight's truck

Kiss and Tell: Unlike Williams, Knight didn't have to sneak into his female counterpart's stateroom in search of action—Plumb came to him. And Knight had better luck than Williams did: "Finally, as she nibbled on my ear, something clicked...I thought to myself, 'Oh, my God—now I understand what all the fuss is about!' I was 14."

A year after the show was canceled, Knight and Plumb had another encounter, an attempted "quickie" in Knight's truck. Says Knight: "*This* time, we quickly moved beyond the sensory pleasures of just making out."

Why It Ended: Before they could get very far, a police officer walked up to the truck and shined his flashlight in the window. The interruption killed the romance.

The Couple: Cindy and Bobby (Susan Olsen and Michael Lookinland)

The Place: Tiger's doghouse, Lookinland's dressing room

Kiss and Tell: "During our first season, Michael got the notion that he had a major crush on me. And he'd put his arm around me, and he'd kiss me, and...uh...I kinda liked it."

Why It Ended: "A couple years later...he seemed to have a kinda 'boob thing'...This is at like age 10 or 11....I of course had none, so he decided it was time to get rid of me and chase after Eve for a while. So we got a divorce."

• • •

WHAT ABOUT MR. BRADY?

According to *USA Today*, Robert Reed was "too busy firing off angry memos to the show's creators about how asinine the scripts were" to indulge in the pleasures of Brady flesh: "To blow off steam over crummy storylines, he sometimes went to a nearby bar and came back to work loaded." Alice the maid (Ann B. Davis), now a born-again Christian, also remained Brady-celibate. No word on Tiger the dog (who was run down by a florist's truck one day after he wandered off the set "looking for a place to relieve himself").

Before killing Lincoln, actor John Wilkes Booth was so popular he got 100 fan letters a week.

LAST WISHES

*You've got plenty of time in the bathroom for thinking. So here's something
to ponder: What's the one special thing you'd want to be sure took place
after you died? To give you ideas, we've provided
a few well-known people's last requests.*

Eleanor Roosevelt: Fearful of being buried alive, the former first
lady requested that her major veins be severed to eliminate the
possibility of regaining consciousness after burial.

Harry Houdini: The famous escape artist asked to be buried in the
"trick" coffin he used in his magic act—with letters from his mother
tucked beneath his head.

William Shakespeare: Wanted his oldest daughter, Susanna, to inherit his favorite bed. He left his wife "my second best bed."

President Andrew Johnson: The president who came closest to impeachment asked to be wrapped in an American flag, with a copy of
the U.S. Constitution placed beneath his head.

J. Paul Getty: Requested a burial on the property of the Getty Museum in Malibu. However, his lawyers never applied for burial permits,
so his remains had to be refrigerated and stored in a nearby mausoleum
for *three years* until the necessary paperwork was completed. (Getty
left his son J. Paul, Jr. "the sum of $500, and nothing else.")

W. C. Fields: Wanted a portion of his estate to be used for a "W. C.
Fields College for orphan *white* boys and girls." (The request was never
honored.)

P. T. Barnum: Wanted to keep the Barnum name from dying with
him...so he left his grandson, Clinton Seeley, $25,000—on the condi-
tion that he change his middle name to Barnum. Seeley did.

Janis Joplin: Asked friends to have a farewell party for her at her favorite pub, the Lion's Share, in California—and left $2,500 in her will
to finance it.

Albert Einstein: No one knows what his last wishes were. On his
deathbed, he said something in German to his nurse—but she didn't
speak German.

Leonardo da Vinci painted only 17 paintings—and some of them were unfinished.

THE "WILD THING" STORY

"Wild Thing" is one of those ridiculously catchy tunes you can't forget.
It's been a hit in three different decades and performed by some of the
greatest—and some of the most forgettable—artists. This tale of how it
was written comes from Behind the Hits *by Bob Shannon.*

AN OPPORTUNITY

In 1966 Chip Taylor—actor Jon Voight's brother—was a songwriter working for a music publisher in New York City. One day he got a phone call from a friend who was producing a record by a group called Jordan Christopher and the Wild Ones. The friend explained that the songs he was supposed to use on the album weren't good enough. He wondered if Taylor had "something different, something unique."

Taylor said he'd work on it and send something over.

"It was around one o'clock when I spoke to my friend," Taylor recalls. "I was planning to go into the studio at five o'clock, so between that time and five, I had to figure out what I was gonna do. I didn't come up with anything until around four o'clock...and then I started to get this little riff on the guitar."

IMPROVISING AT THE STUDIO

It was almost 5:00, so Taylor headed for the recording studio. He says: "Between my office and the studio, which was about four blocks, I was humming this crazy little thing, 'Wild Thing, you make my heart sing,' and just had this groove going.

"I got to the studio and I asked the engineer just to let the tape roll, and I told him not to stop me, I was gonna do this nonsense thing and see what came out. I basically had the chorus already, so I just sang it over and over again, and every once in a while I stopped and said some things. What came out was exactly what you've heard on records.

"The next morning, I listened to this [terrible song]. I said, 'All right, send it over to my friend'—because I promised I'd send something over to him—[but] don't let anybody else hear this demo. I was really embarrassed."

Walruses get bald as they age.

THE FIRST VERSION

Eventually, Jordan Christopher and the Wild Ones did make the first recording of "Wild Thing."

"But they did it very differently, with horns," Taylor explains, "and they changed the rhythm and stuff like that. I didn't think it [was very] good, and I was kind of glad that it wasn't a hit. I was glad they recorded it, but I was a little embarrassed anyway."

IT'S A HIT

The music publisher Taylor worked for had a deal with a music company in England—they had to send everything they published to the British company. Taylor was horrified. "I asked them not to send it over," he says, "but somehow it was included with the other material they sent."

To his surprise, a few months later "Wild Thing," by a little-known group called the Troggs (from the word "troglodytes"), hit #2 in England and #1 in the U.S. Even more surprising to Taylor, it later became a rock classic, recorded by everyone from Jimi Hendrix to X. Taylor himself got in on the fun in 1967 when he produced a "Wild Thing" satire performed by "Senator Bobby," a Robert Kennedy soundalike. Even *that* version was a Top 20 hit.

FOR THE RECORD

• How did the Troggs pick "Wild Thing"?

√ Taylor says: "The story I hear is that when they were presented the package to choose what songs to do, they were given a stack of about fifty tapes. They just kept listening to them until they got to 'Wild Thing,' and decided they wanted to do it."

√ The leader of the Troggs, Reg Presley, tells a different tale. He recalls that their manager picked the song—and that he couldn't stand it. "I looked at the lyrics—'Wild thing, you make my heart sing...You make everything groovy'...and they seemed so corny and I thought, 'Oh God, what are they doing to us?' "

• The ocarina solo on the Troggs' record was copied from Taylor's demo tape. But it was originally played on someone's hands, not an instrument. Taylor explains: "While the engineer, Ron Johnson, was playing the tape back in the studio, I heard him playing this little thing on his hands. I said to him, 'Go on out and do that in the middle part.' If you play my demo against the Troggs' record, you'll see it's almost exactly the same."

The index finger is the most sensitive finger on your hand.

LUCKY STRIKES

Some of the most important historical discoveries
have been complete accidents. Here are four examples.

The Discoverer: A peasant farmer digging a well
What He Found: The lost cities of Pompeii & Herculaneum
Lucky Strike: In 1709 a peasant who was digging in the area that had been destroyed when Mount Vesuvius erupted in 79 A.D. brought up several pieces of sculpted marble from statues and other objects. When word of his discovery spread, an Italian prince bought the land and began the first large-scale excavation of the site. Today more than three quarters of ancient Pompeii has been uncovered; the rest remains buried underneath the modern city of Pompeii.

The Discoverers: Some quarrymen digging in a cave
What They Found: Neanderthal man
Lucky Strike: In 1856 workers excavating a cave in Germany's Neander Valley unearthed a human skeleton more than 100,000 years old. The remains provided some of the earliest evidence supporting the theory that modern humans evolved from apes.

The Discoverers: A group of French army engineers in Egypt
What They Found: The Rosetta stone
Lucky Strike: In July 1799 French army engineers working near the Egyptian town of Rosetta noted that a section of the wall they were about to demolish had both Greek script and hieroglyphics carved into it. On a hunch, they saved it. The stone turned out to be the first Egyptian hieroglyphic document ever found that was accompanied by a translation into a modern language. With the aid of this "Rosetta stone," scientists finally cracked the code of the hieroglyphics—which had been indecipherable for more than 1,300 years.

The Discoverer: A Bedouin boy looking for a lost goat
What He Found: The Dead Sea Scrolls
Lucky Strike: In 1947 a Bedouin boy looking for a lost goat on cliffs near the Dead Sea idly tossed a rock into a cave. He heard some pottery shatter. Investigating, he found a number of large clay jars containing hundreds of scrolls, many of which were early versions of the Bible at least 1,000 years older than any other known copy.

Sweet Tooth: 48% of Americans feel guilty after eating candy.

THE ADVENTURES OF SUPERMAN

*"Look! Up in the sky...It's a bird...It's a plane...No, it's Superman!"
The Adventures of Superman, a syndicated TV show filmed from
1951 to 1957, has been on the air sporadically for almost 40 years.
Compared to Superman: the Movie, the special effects (and even the
hero himself) are laughable. But if you've never seen the show, or don't
remember it, you're missing a great slice of 1950s Americana. Check it out.*

HOW IT STARTED
"The Adventures of Superman" was actually just part of
the Man of Steel's leap into every existing entertainment
medium. In the early 1940s, Superman was the star of a popular radio show and a movie cartoon series. In 1948 and 1950, he became
the star of movie serials. ("Now the one and only Superman at his
mightiest as a real live hero on the serial screen!")

In 1951, DC comics agreed to a deal for a feature film and a TV
series. The star of the serials, Kirk Alyn, was offered the lead role,
but he declined. So the producers conducted an extensive—and
unsuccessful—search for a new hero. They interviewed more than
200 actors; they became so desperate that they even checked out
the 1951 Mr. America contest. They weren't impressed. They
wanted brains, not just beef.

It wasn't until George Reeves strolled into their office one day
that Our Hero was ready to fly again. Reeves, who'd played Brett
Tarleton in *Gone with the Wind,* had been stuck in "B" films like *Sir
Galahad* during the 1940s. Now he was hired to star in the first full-
length Superman movie, *Superman and the Mole Men* ("Amer-ica's
favorite hero! His latest . . . his greatest!") not because of his acting
ability, but because of his profile and—most important—his chin,
which looked like Superman's. Reeves wasn't particularly excited
about the part, either. "I've played about every type of part you can
think of," he said at the time. "Why not Superman?"

The low-budget film became the pilot episode of the TV series,
which went on the air in 1953, sponsored by Kellogg's.

American hens lay enough eggs each year to circle the equator 100 times.

CHEAP SHOTS
• "Superman" was filmed like an assembly-line product. Each episode cost only $15,000 to make, and four episodes were shot every 10 days. The cast always wore the same clothes, because several episodes were filmed at the same time; this way they didn't have to keep track of when they were supposed to change costumes.

SUPER SUITS
• Reeves had naturally sloping shoulders, and Superman had big, broad ones—so the Superman costume had rubber and sponge padding built into it (which made it unbearably hot).

MAN AND SUPERMAN
• The show almost cost Reeves his life. In 1953, while Reeves was making an appearance as Superman in Detroit, a youngster aimed his father's loaded pistol at Reeves. (He wanted to watch bullets bounce off Superman.) George calmly talked the kid into giving up the gun, but stopped wearing the Superman suit in public.
• Reeves tried to give up smoking, believing he'd be setting a bad example if kids spotted him with cigarettes. He also tried to avoid being seen in public with women, a tall order for a bachelor TV star. In 1953 he toured the country speaking to kids about the dangers of jaywalking, bicycling...and trying to fly.

UP IN THE SKY
• Special effects have come a long way since Superman flew in 1951. For takeoffs, Reeves jumped off a springboard so he'd look like he was propelled into the air.
• If he was jumping out a window, he just leaped onto a mattress.
• If he was flying, he was pulled into the air by a system of wires and pulleys, and in later episodes by a hydraulic system.
• For Superman's dramatic landings, Reeves simply jumped from an off-screen stepladder.

TYPECASTING
• Sadly, *Superman*'s success ruined Reeves's chances for other acting parts. He had a role in the Oscar-winning film *From Here to Eternity* (1953), for example...but his scenes were cut because audiences shouted "Superman!" every time he appeared in the film. In 1959, after trying singing and directing, he put a gun to his head and pulled the trigger. The headlines blared: "Superman Kills Self."

Until 1850, most golf balls were stuffed with feathers.

THE DEATH OF WARREN G. HARDING

Did Warren Harding die of a heart attack or a poisoned relationship? This examination of the question is from It's a Conspiracy!, *by the National Insecurity Council.*

T he Deceased: Warren G. Harding, 29th president of the United States (1921-1923)

How He Died: In the summer of 1923, President Harding was visiting Vancouver when he became gravely ill. He was rushed to San Francisco and seemed to recover. But then, on August 2, 1923, he suddenly died of a heart attack. *The New York Times* reported: "Mrs. Harding was reading to the President, when utterly without warning, a slight shudder passed through his frame; he collapsed....A stroke of apoplexy was the cause of his death."

Although initial newspaper accounts didn't mention it, the White House physician, General Sawyer, was probably in the room as well when the president died.

SUSPICIOUS FACTS

Warren and the Duchess

• Harding owed his political success to his ambitious wife, Florence (nicknamed "the Duchess"). But his marriage wasn't a happy one; he strayed often. During the 1920 campaign, for example, the Republican National Committee paid a former lover of Harding's $20,000 for incriminating letters, paid her $2,000 a month for her silence, and sent her to Europe to keep her away from reporters.

• Harding had a child by Nan Britten, the daughter of a friend. In fact, they had regular trysts in a large White House closet.

• According to former Treasury agent Gaston Means, who worked for Mrs. Harding, the president's wife despised her husband for his affairs and his ingratitude. In his bestselling book about Harding's death, Means reported that when the president's wife found out Harding had fathered Britten's baby, she got hysterical and vowed revenge. "I made him, I made him president!" she raved. When she confronted her husband, there was a nasty scene. He roared that he had never loved her, was sick of the whole presidential charade, and wanted to live with Britten and his child.

After Harding's Death

• To everyone's surprise, Mrs. Harding refused to allow either an autopsy or a death mask.

• The *New York World* reported: "There will be no death mask made of President Harding....Although it is the usual custom, when a Chief Executive dies, to have a mask made that his features may be preserved for posterity, Mrs. Harding demurred."

• About a year later, while the president's widow was visiting General Sawyer, the former White House physician unexpectedly died in his sleep.

• According to the account in *The New York Times*: "General Sawyer's death was almost identical with the manner of death of the late Warren G. Harding when General Sawyer was with the President in San Francisco. Mrs. Harding was at White Oaks Farm (Sawyer's home) when General Sawyer was found dead. Members of his family had no intimation of the seriousness of the General's condition up to the moment he expired."

POSSIBLE CONCLUSIONS

• **Harding really did have a heart attack.** His administration was riddled with scandals, and people were calling for his impeachment. The president, who'd previously had 5 nervous breakdowns, was said to be despondent. He may have succumbed to the stress.

• **Harding was poisoned by his wife.** If Harding was really ready to give up his political career and marriage, then the Duchess may have poisoned him either to avoid disgrace or to exact revenge. She may have tried first in Vancouver; when Harding didn't die, the attempt was dismissed as food poisoning. Five days later, in San Francisco, she may have succeeded.

√ Refusing a death mask and an autopsy is consistent with this scenario. (Poison victims sometimes die with horrible grimaces.)

√ Sawyer's death is either a remarkable coincidence or proof of Mrs. Harding's guilt. Even if he wasn't involved in killing the president, as a physician Sawyer may have guessed what had happened and helped to cover it up. Mrs. Harding could have poisoned him to keep her secret safe.

STATE YOUR NAME

You know the names of all 50 states...but do you know where even one of them comes from? Since you're not about to get up and go anywhere right now, here's a chance to learn.

LABAMA. Possibly from the Creek Indian word *alibamo*, meaning "we stay here."

ALASKA. From the Aleutian word *alakshak*, which means "great lands," or "land that is not an island."

ARIZONA. Taken either from the Pima Indian words *ali shonak*, meaning "little spring," or from the Aztec word *arizuma*, meaning "silver-bearing."

ARKANSAS. The French somehow coined it from the name of the Siouan *Quapaw* tribe.

CALIFORNIA. According to one theory, Spanish settlers named it after a Utopian society described in a popular 16th-century novel called *Serged de Esplandian*.

COLORADO. Means "red" in Spanish. The name was originally applied to the Colorado River, whose waters are reddish with canyon clay.

CONNECTICUT. Taken from the Mohican word *kuenihtekot*, which means "long river place."

DELAWARE. Named after Lord De La Warr, a governor of Virginia. Originally used only to name the Delaware River.

FLORIDA. Explorer Ponce de Leon named the state "Pascua Florida"—"flowery Easter"—on Easter Sunday in 1513.

GEORGIA. Named after King George II of England, who chartered the colony in 1732.

HAWAII. An English adaptation of the native word *owhyhee*, which means "homeland."

IDAHO. Possibly taken from the Kiowa Apache word for the Comanche Indians.

ILLINOIS: The French bastardization of the Algonquin word *illini*, which means "men."

INDIANA: Named by English-speaking settlers because the territory was full of Indians.

IOWA: The Sioux word for "beautiful land," or "one who puts to sleep."

KANSAS: Taken from the Sioux word for "south wind people," their name for anyone who lived south of Sioux territory.

KENTUCKY: Possibly derived from the Indian word *kan-tuk-kee*, meaning "dark and bloody ground," or *kan-tuc-kec*, "land of green reeds," or *ken-take*, meaning "meadowland."

LOUISIANA: Named after French King Louis XIV.

MAINE: The Old French word for "province."

MARYLAND: Named after Queen Henrietta Maria, wife of English King George I.

MASSACHUSETTS: Named after the Massachusetts Indian tribe. Means "large hill place."

MICHIGAN: Most likely from the Chippewa word for "great water," *micigama*.

MINNESOTA: From the Sioux word for "sky tinted" or "muddy water."

MISSISSIPPI: Most likely taken from the Chippewa words *mici* ("great") and *zibi* ("river").

MISSOURI: From the Algonquin word for "muddy water."

MONTANA: Taken from the Latin word for "mountainous."

NEBRASKA: From the Otos Indian word for "broad water."

NEVADA: Means "snow-clad" in Spanish.

NEW HAMPSHIRE: Captain John Mason, one of the original colonists, named it after his English home county of Hampshire.

NEW JERSEY. Named after the English Isle of Jersey.

NEW MEXICO. The Spanish name for the territory north of the Rio Grande.

NEW YORK. Named after the Duke of York and Albany.

NORTH AND SOUTH CAROLINA. From the Latin name *Carolus*; named in honor of King Charles I of England.

NORTH AND SOUTH DAKOTA. Taken from the Sioux word for "friend" or "ally."

OHIO. Means "great," "fine," or "good river" in Iriquois.

OKLAHOMA. The Choctaw word for "red man."

OREGON. Possibly derived from *Ouaricon-sint*, the French name for the Wisconsin River.

PENNSYLVANIA. Named after William Penn, Sr., the father of the colony's founder, William Penn. Means "Penn's woods."

RHODE ISLAND. Named "Roode Eylandt" (Red Island) because of its red clay.

TENNESSEE. Named after the Cherokee *tanasi* villages along the banks of the Little Tennessee River.

TEXAS. Derived from the Caddo Indian word for "friend" or "ally."

UTAH. Means "upper" or "higher," and was originally the name that Navajos called the Shoshone tribe.

VERMONT. A combination of the French words *vert* ("green") and *mont* ("mountain").

VIRGINIA AND WEST VIRGINIA. Named after Queen Elizabeth I of England, the "virgin" queen, by Sir Walter Raleigh in 1584.

WASHINGTON. Named in tribute to George Washington.

WISCONSIN. Taken from the Chippewa word for "grassy place."

WYOMING. Derived from the Algonquin word for "large prairie place."

The story of Cinderella has been made into a movie 58 times.

WHO WERE HARLEY & DAVIDSON?

*They're two of the best-known names in America. But who were they?
No need to prolong the suspense…read on.*

The first motorcycle was developed by Gottlieb Daimler, one of the founders of Daimler-Benz (maker of the Mercedes Benz) in Germany in 1885. Ten years later two German brothers, Hildebrand and Alois Wolfmuller, began manufacturing motorcycles to sell to the public.

In 1901 news of the Wolfmullers' motorcycles reached Milwaukee, Wisconsin. Four young friends—21-year-old William Harley and the Davidson brothers, William, Walter, and Arthur—decided to build a small engine in the Davidsons' backyard and attach it to one of their bicycles. Legend has it that the engine was made from household castoffs, including a carburetor made of a tomato can.

After working out the bugs on their prototype, they built three more motorized bicycles in 1903 and began riding them around town. Their bikes were simple but reliable—one of them ultimately racked up 100,000 miles. People began asking if they were for sale.

The Harley-Davidson Motorcycle Company legally incorporated in 1909. More than 150 U.S. manufacturers eventually followed suit, but Harley-Davidson has outlasted them all. It's now the only American motorcycle company and sells more than 50,000 motorcycles a year.

THE HARLEY IMAGE

In the mid-1980s, Harley's "rough rider" image began hurting sales. So the company took steps to change it. They encouraged Harley execs to wear white or red shirts to biker rallies to dispel the notion that Harley riders wear only black. They formed the Harley Owner's Group (H.O.G.) and the "Ladies of Harley" club to offset outlaw biker clubs. And they licensed the Harley name and logo to $100 million worth of products as diverse as wine coolers, cologne, and removable tattoos for women. Still, the company prefers customers with permanent Harley tattoos: "If you can persuade the customer to tattoo your name on their chest," one company executive admits, "they probably will not switch brands."

THE HONEYMOONERS

When TV critics are asked to pick the best sitcom in history, many select Jackie Gleason's 1955 one-season wonder, "The Honeymooners." Here are some facts about that classic program from Cult TV *by John Javna.*

HOW IT STARTED

In the early days of TV, the three networks were CBS, NBC...and Dumont. This third network was founded in 1946 by the Allen Dumont Laboratories and limped along for nine years before finally disappearing in 1955. Its main contribution to television history was making Jackie Gleason a star.

In 1950 Gleason wasn't welcome on the major networks—he'd done poorly as star of NBC's sitcom *The Life of Riley* the previous season, and network executives were wary of his excessive lifestyle. But on Dumont, he flourished. As host of its 1950 variety show, "Cavalcade of Stars"—performing his own comedy sketches as well as emceeing—he was a smash. His first two shows attracted a large audience and got rave reviews.

For the third one, Gleason wanted to come up with something special. So he invented a husband/wife comedy sketch based on his childhood environment. "I knew a thousand couples like these in Brooklyn," Gleason said. "It was like the loudmouth husband... with the wife who's a hell of a lot smarter than [him]. My neighborhood was filled with them."

His writers wanted to call the skit "The Beast," but Gleason didn't like it. The husband might be a windbag, Gleason said, but he wasn't an animal—he and his wife really loved each other. So the writers suggested "The Lovers"—which was close, but not right. Finally, Gleason came up with "The Honeymooners."

The sketch, which featured Jackie as bus driver Ralph Kramden and Pert Kelton as his wife, Alice, was only on for a few minutes. But it elicited an enormous response from viewers. In fact, it was so popular that it became a regular feature on Gleason's show. Gleason added two neighbor characters: sewer worker Ed Norton and his wife, Trixie.

When Gleason moved to CBS in 1952, he brought "The Honeymooners" with him, and in 1955 it became a series. Thirty-nine episodes aired. Although it was a popular program, Gleason didn't

---

Spotted skunks do handstands before they spray.

want to continue it. He preferred variety shows, where "The Honeymooners" periodically surfaced. The last "Honeymooners" special aired in 1978. Gleason unveiled 75 "lost episodes" in the 1980s.

INSIDE FACTS

Belly Laughs. Gleason never rehearsed, and generally didn't need to because he had a photographic memory—one look at the script and he had it down. Nonetheless, he occasionally forgot his lines, which was a potential disaster in the days of live TV. When he did forget, Gleason would pat his stomach—a sign for someone else to think of something...quick. Once Alice snapped, "If you get any bigger, gas bag, you'll just float away." That wasn't in the script.

Another time, Gleason forgot to make an entrance. Art Carney (Ed Norton), who was onstage at the time, calmly went to the icebox, pulled out an orange, and began peeling it until Gleason realized his mistake.

On one evening Art Carney showed up for a performance completely plastered. Gleason, who'd memorized Carney's part as well as his own, did the whole show by asking a sitting (and incoherent) Carney yes or no questions.

Heeere's Alice. Pert Kelton, the first actress to play Alice Kramden on the show, fell ill with a heart condition and could not continue in the role when Gleason moved to CBS. When another actress, Audrey Meadows, was asked if she knew anyone who could play the part of Alice, she said, "Me." Gleason turned her down because she was too pretty. That made her want the part more. She sent Gleason photos of herself as a "frumpy" housewife, and Gleason triumphantly announced he'd found the right actress—not realizing she was the same woman he'd already rejected.

You Can Do Better. Joyce Randolph played Ed Norton's wife, Trixie. But Randolph's mother didn't like her daughter playing the part—she thought Joyce "could do better than marrying a sewer worker."

Ice Cold. One of the few pieces in the Kramdens' living room was an old-fashioned icebox. A refrigerator company once offered to sponsor "The Honeymooners" if Gleason would replace it with a refrigerator. He refused.

At his heaviest, President James Madison weighed 98 pounds.

ONE-HIT WONDERS

You're listening to the radio, and you hear this great (or terrible) song by a new group. It rockets all the way to #1 and sells 5 million copies...but then you never hear anything by the artists again. They're one-hit wonders—part of a pop music phenomenon no one can explain. Here are a few case studies for B.R.I. members to ponder.

The Artist: The Monotones

The Song: "The Book of Love" (1958, #5)

The Story: In 1955 six kids from Newark, New Jersey, formed a doo-wop band called The Monotones. One day a member of the group was looking at the sheet music for a song called "Book of Love," when he heard a Pepsodent toothpaste commercial on the radio: "You'll wonder where the yellow went, when you brush your teeth with Pepsodent." It inspired him to write: "Oh I wonder, wonder who...who wrote the book of love."

He and the group turned it into a song. "It was a joke to us," he explains. But when a rival group wanted to record it, The Monotones quickly made a demo and sold it to a record company. It became a rock classic and a Top 10 hit. Unfortunately, The Monotones didn't bother putting out a follow-up record until 3 months after "Book of Love" peaked. By then, their fans had moved on.

The Artist: David Soul

The Song: "Don't Give Up On Us, Baby" (1977, #1)

The Story: David Solberg dropped out of college in the 1960s to become a folk singer. He decided he needed a gimmick to get attention, so he wrote a song called "The Covered Man"—which he sang while wearing a ski mask. The stunt got him on "The Merv Griffin Show" more than 20 times, but he still couldn't sell any records. Solberg (now renamed Soul) did, however, get enough exposure to land a starring role on the TV show "Starsky & Hutch." The program's popularity encouraged him to try music again. He released "Don't Give Up On Us Baby" in 1977. It hit #1...but none of his follow-ups made it into the Top 40. He gave up recording about the same time "Starsky & Hutch" went off the air.

The Artist: Steam

The Song: "Na-Na, Hey, Hey, Tell Him Goodbye" (1969, #1)

The Story: In 1969 a singer named Gary DeCarlo recorded his first single for Mercury Records. Then he went back to the studio to record a throwaway "flip side"—something so bad no disc jockey would accidentally play it instead of the "A" side.

A few friends were at the studio that night; they suggested a tune they'd performed in a band in 1961. It was called "Kiss Him Goodbye," and it was perfect for the "B" side of the record...except that it had no chorus. No problem—they made one up on the spot, with "na-nas" instead of lyrics. They described it as "an embarrassing record...an insult."

But to everyone's horror, Mercury thought it was great and decided to release it as a single. No one wanted to be identified with the record, so it was credited to "Steam."

"Na-Na" sold more than a million copies, but DeCarlo wouldn't make another Steam record. Mercury got a different group to do the follow-ups, but the best they could come up with was "I've Gotta Make You Love Me," which reached #46 on the charts in 1970.

The Artist: Zager and Evans

The Song: "In the Year 2525 (Exordium & Terminus)" (1969, #1)

The Story: In 1968 Denny Zager and Rick Evans were playing folk music in a motel lounge in Lincoln, Nebraska. One of their most popular songs was "In the Year 2525," an up-tempo apocalyptic vision Evans had written four years earlier. They decided to record it. For $500, they got recording studio time and 1,000 copies of their single—which they sold to local record stores and passed out to Nebraska radio stations.

Zager and Evans were delighted when the song began getting airplay in Lincoln...and flabbergasted when it drew the attention of a hotshot management firm in Los Angeles. An executive with the firm flew to Lincoln and signed Zager and Evans to a personal contract; then he signed them to a recording contract with RCA.

A few weeks later, "In the Year 2525" was released nationally ....and a few weeks after that, it was #1 in America. However, Denny Zager had never really liked the song and wasn't interested in doing any more tunes in the same style. None of the pair's subsequent records even made it into the Top 100.

A restaurant in Mississippi called *Hello, I'm Jello* serves over 400 dishes made from Jell-O.

FREE ADVICE

Here are more helpful hints from high-profile heavyweights.
From Friendly Advice, *by Jon Winokur.*

"Never kick a fresh turd on a hot day."
—*Harry S Truman*

"Never say anything on the phone that you wouldn't want your mother to hear at the trial."
—*Sydney Biddle Barrows, the "Mayflower Madam"*

"You can get much further with a kind word and a gun than you can with a kind word alone."
—*Al Capone*

"Never trust a man unless you've got his pecker in your pocket."
—*Lyndon Baines Johnson*

"To succeed with the opposite sex, tell her you're impotent. She can't wait to disprove it."
—*Cary Grant*

"Sleeping alone, except under doctor's orders, does much harm. Children will tell you how lonely it is sleeping alone. If possible you should always sleep with someone you love. You recharge your mutual batteries free of charge."
—*Marlene Dietrich*

"Anything worth doing is worth doing slowly."
—*Gypsy Rose Lee*

"Don't try to take on a new personality; it doesn't work."
—*Richard Nixon*

"There's nothing to winning, really. That is, if you happen to be blessed with a keen eye, an agile mind, and no scruples whatsoever."
—*Alfred Hitchcock*

"Rise early. Work late. Strike oil."
—*J. Paul Getty*

"Don't let your mouth write a check that your tail can't cash."
—*Bo Diddley*

"Never eat at a place called Mom's. Never play cards with a man named Doc. And never lie down with a woman who's got more troubles than you."
—*Nelson Algren*

"What is worth doing is worth the trouble of asking someone to do it."
—*Ambrose Bierce*

NIXON'S THE ONE?

*Did Richard Nixon undermine LBJ's peace talks and keep the
Vietnam War going in 1968, just to get elected? Here are some facts to
consider from It's a Conspiracy!, by the National Insecurity Council.*

Although President Lyndon Johnson wasn't running for re-
election in 1968, he was still obsessed with ending the war
in Vietnam. His decision was partly political, since any
resolution would help the Democrats hold on to the White House.
But more important, by finding an "honorable" settlement to the
conflict, Johnson could avoid becoming the first American president to lose a foreign war.

In June Johnson came up with a plan: he proposed a halt to the
U.S. bombing of North Vietnam, to be followed by negotiations
with all parties. At first the proposal was rejected by the Communists. Then, after several months of secret meetings, the North
Vietnamese suddenly agreed to his terms. The U.S. allies, the
South Vietnamese, also accepted the plan—in fact, they insisted
that talks begin immediately after the cease-fire went into effect.

Peace talks were scheduled to begin on November 2, three days
before the presidential election. Democrats were sure the talks
would help defeat Richard Nixon.

WHAT HAPPENED

• Suddenly, on October 29, South Vietnam—whose defense had
already cost 29,000 American lives—backed out of the peace talks.
According to former Defense Secretary Clark Clifford, South Vietnamese President Nguyen Van Thieu "reneged on everything he
had previously agreed to," saying the peace talks were "too soon."

• Thieu said he would need "materially more time" to prepare for
talks in Paris and that he "needed to consult the South Vietnamese
National Security Council again."

• Johnson and his aides were livid. But they could do nothing to
bring Thieu back to the negotiating table. When the peace talks
were aborted, so was Democratic nominee Hubert Humphrey's bid
for the presidency. On November 2, Richard Nixon won by

510,645 votes, or less than 1 percent of the total votes cast.

SUSPICIOUS FACTS

• On July 12, 1968, Nixon, Bui Diem (the South Vietnamese ambassador to the U.S.), and Anna Chennault (a prominent rightwing Republican) met secretly in New York City.

• Chennault was an important figure in both Asian and American politics and had access to highly placed officials on the two continents. She was one of the mainstays of the China Lobby, a Taiwan-based group that fought to keep Red China out of the United Nations, and was the chairwoman of Republican Women for Nixon.

• At Nixon's request—perhaps made at the July 12 meeting—Ambassador Diem began regular and secret communications with Nixon's campaign manager, John Mitchell, and other senior members of the Nixon team.

• The White House knew what was going on. "Gradually," Defense Secretary Clark Clifford wrote later, "we realized that President Thieu's growing resistance to the agreement in Paris was being encouraged—indeed, stimulated—by the Republicans, and especially by Anna Chennault." (*The New Yorker*)

• According to former Assistant Secretary of State William Bundy: "Johnson and his inner circle...learned through intercepted South Vietnam Embassy cables, particularly one of October 27, that Anna Chennault was conveying via Bui Diem apparently authoritative 'Republican' messages urging Mr. Thieu to abort or cripple the deal by refusing to participate. That 'smoking gun' cable included promises of later favor from Mr. Nixon, including a possible visit to Saigon before the inauguration if he were elected." (*The New York Times*)

• Bundy also said that "on November 3, two days before the election, Mr. Johnson [confronted] Mr. Nixon with Mrs. Chennault's activities, and Mr. Nixon categorically denied any connection or knowledge—almost certainly a lie in light of later disclosures." (ibid.)

• Clifford reported that, on the day after the election, South Vietnamese Vice President Nguyen Ky "almost contemptuously" told U.S. Ambassador Ellsworth Bunker "that it might take two months—just about the length of time left to the Johnson administration—to resolve his government's problems with the negotiating format." President Thieu finally agreed to resume peace negotiations on January 25, 1969—just days after Richard Nixon's inauguration.

WAS IT A CONSPIRACY?

Clark Clifford thought so. He said the secret Republican effort was "a plot—there is no other word for it—to help Nixon win the election by a flagrant interference in the negotiations."

• Clifford adds: "No proof…has ever turned up linking Nixon [himself] directly to the messages to Thieu….On the other hand, this chain of events undeniably began with Bui Diem's meeting with Richard Nixon in New York, and Nixon's closest adviser, John Mitchell, ran the Chennault channel personally, with full understanding of its sensitivity." (*The New Yorker*)

• "The activities of the Nixon campaign team," Clifford wrote, "went far beyond the bounds of justifiable political combat. They constituted direct interference in the activities of the executive branch and the responsibilities of the Chief Executive—the only people with authority to negotiate on behalf of the nation. [They] constituted a gross—and potentially illegal—interference in the national-security affairs by private individuals." (ibid.)

FOOTNOTE

Why didn't LBJ or Hubert Humphrey turn Nixon's alleged interference with the peace talks into a campaign issue? Bundy says that "in the circumstances, Mr. Johnson and Mr. Humphrey decided, separately, not to raise what would surely have been a highly divisive issue so late in the campaign."

RECOMMENDED READING

"Annals of Government: The Vietnam Years," by Clark Clifford and Richard Holbroke (*The New Yorker* magazine; May 6, May 13, and May 20, 1991). *A three-part article.*

Note: It's a Conspiracy! *is a 256-page book full of amazing, entertaining stories. Highly recommended as bathroom reading.*

THE MYTH-ADVENTURES OF THOMAS EDISON

Most Americans believe that Thomas Edison invented the light bulb. He didn't. In fact, although he was a great inventor, there are a number of myths we commonly believe about Edison. Let's puncture a few.

THE MYTH: Edison was the father of electric light.

THE TRUTH: Electric lighting had been made practical decades before Edison began his famous research. Although incandescent light (the kind that's made by charging a wire filament until it glows white hot with energy) had not yet been perfected, by the 1870s *arc* lighting (light that's created when a spark "arcs" across two highly charged electric rods) was already in use in lighthouses and in the street lamps of some major cities.

The only problem was, they used too much energy and generated too much light (300 times as much as the household gas lights of the day) to be practical in homes. A less powerful source of light was needed.

THE MYTH: Edison invented the incandescent light bulb.

THE TRUTH: Incandescent light bulbs had been around as a laboratory curiosity since 1823, and the first incandescent bulb was patented by Joseph Swan, an English inventor, in 1845.

By the time Edison began experimenting with light bulbs in 1878, scientists around the world had already spent 55 years trying to perfect them. Edison wasn't trying to invent the light bulb; he was trying to find a long-lasting *filament* that would make the light bulb practical for the first time.

Incandescent light bulbs operate on the principle of electrically heating a tiny filament until it glows white hot with energy, creating light in the process. The main problem at the time: most substances either melted or burned up when heated to such a high temperature, causing the bulb to burn out after only a few seconds.

Vacuum bulbs, which had some of their air removed, solved part of the problem; by reducing the amount of oxygen in the bulb, they

---

Riding Hazards: 40% of people killed from falling off a horse are drunk.

lengthened the time it took for the filament to burn up. Even so, in 1878 even the best bulbs only only lasted a short time...and *that's* where Edison came in.

THE MYTH: He perfected the incandescent bulb by himself.

THE TRUTH: He failed on his own, and had to bring in experts.
Edison thought the secret to building a better light bulb was to design a switch inside the bulb that would function like a heater thermostat, turning off the electricity when the filament got too hot, and turning it on again as soon as the filament cooled off—a process that would take only a fraction of a second.

Edison thought (and announced) that he could develop the switch in a few weeks—but he guessed wrong. It didn't work at all.

More a scientific tinkerer than a scientist, his strategy had always been to blindly build prototype after prototype. He ignored work that other researchers had done and, as a result, often unwittingly repeated their failed experiments. That's what happened with the light bulb. After a month of trying on his own, he threw in the towel and hired Francis Upton, a Princeton physicist, to help him.

As soon as Upton signed on, he had the lab's researchers study old patents, electrical journals, and the work of competing inventors to see what progress they had made. He also shifted the focus of the work from testing prototypes to methodically experimenting with raw materials (in order to understand their scientific properties and see which ones made the best filaments). Without this important shift in strategy, Edison's lab might never have developed a practical bulb at all...and certainly would have fallen behind competing labs.

THE MYTH: Edison made his critical breakthrough on October 21, 1879—known for many years as "Electric Light Day"—when he kept a light bulb lit for more than 40 hours.

THE TRUTH: The story is a fake. According to lab notes, nothing important happened on October 21—and it took another full year to produce a 40-hour bulb. The October 21 date was made up in late December 1879—by a newspaper reporter who needed a good story for the Christmas season.

Couch Potato Fact: 80% of people who own VCRs don't know how to program them.

INNOVATIONS IN YOUR HOME

You probably have some of these products around the house. Here's how they were created.

COPPERTONE SUNTAN LOTION

Background: In the early part of the 20th century, suntans were the mark of the lower classes—only laborers who worked in the sun, like field hands, had them. But as beaches became more popular and bathing suits began revealing more skin, styles changed. Suntans became a status symbol that subtly demonstrated that a person was part of the leisure class.

Innovation: The first suntan lotion was invented in the 1940s by Dr. Benjamin Green, a physician who'd helped develop a petroleum-based sunblock for the military to protect soldiers from the sun. After the war, Green became convinced civilians would buy a milder version of his product—one that protected them from the sun while letting them tan. He called his lotion Coppertone, because it produced a copper-colored tan on the people who used it.

RUNNING SHOES WITH "WAFFLE" SOLES

Background: In the late 1950s Phil Knight was a track star at the University of Oregon. His coach, Bill Bowerman, was obsessed with designing lightweight shoes for his runners. "He figured carrying one extra ounce for a mile," Knight recalls, "was equivalent to carrying an extra thousand pounds in the last 50 yards."

When Knight began his graduate work at the Stanford Business School, he wrote a research paper arguing that lightweight running shoes could be manufactured cheaply in Japan and sold at a low price in the United States. Then he actually went to Japan and signed a distribution deal with a Japanese shoe company called Tiger. He and Bowerman each invested $500 to buy merchandise, and the Blue Ribbon Sports Company (later Nike) was founded.

Innovation: Bowerman developed Nike shoes to meet runners' needs. *Swoosh: The Story of Nike* describes the origin of the celebrated "waffle" shoe: "It occurred to Bowerman to make spikes out of rubber....One morning while his wife was at church, Bowerman sat at the kitchen table staring at an open waffle iron he had seen hundreds of times. But now, for some reason, what he saw in the familiar pattern was square spikes. Square spikes could give traction to cross-country runners sliding down wet, muddy hills.

"Excited, Bowerman took out a mixture of liquid urethane... poured it into about every other hole of the waffle iron in...just the right pattern, and closed the lid to let it cook. Legend had it that he opened the waffle iron and there was the waffle sole that became Nike's first signature shoe. But what really happened that morning is that when he went to open the smelly mess, the waffle iron was bonded shut....[He] switched to a plaster mold after that."

THERMOS JUGS

Background: In the 1890s British physicist Sir James Dewar invented a glass, vacuum-walled flask that kept liquids hot longer than any other container in existence. Dewar never patented his invention, however; he considered it his gift to the scientific world.

Innovation: Reinhold Burger, a German glass blower whose company manufactured the flasks, saw their potential as a consumer product. Dewar's creations were too fragile for home use, so Burger built a sturdier version, with a shock-resistent metal exterior. He patented his design in 1903 and held a contest to find a name for the product. The contest was more of a publicity stunt than anything else, but Burger liked one entry so much that he used it: "Thermos," after the Greek word for heat.

S.O.S. SOAP PADS

Background: In 1917 Edwin W. Cox was peddling aluminum cookware door to door in San Francisco. He wasn't making many sales, though; aluminum cookware was a new invention, and few housewives would even look at it.

Innovation: In desperation, Cox began offering a free gift to any housewife who'd listen to his presentation—a steel-wool soap pad he made in his own kitchen by repeatedly soaking plain steel-wool pads in soapy water. (His wife used them in their own kitchen and loved them; she called them "S.O.S." pads, meaning Save Our Saucepans.) The gimmick worked—sort of. Housewives still weren't interested in the cookware, but they loved the soap pads. Eventually he dropped pots and pans and began selling soap pads full-time.

American chickens are direct descendants of the ones brought over by Columbus.

THE S&L SCANDAL: TRUE OR FALSE?

"I think we've hit the jackpot."
—Ronald Reagan to assembled S&L executives, as he signed the Garn-St. Germaine Act deregulating the savings and loan industry.

You, your children and your grandchildren are going to be paying for the savings & loan scandal for years, but how much do you know about it? See if you can tell which of the following statements are true:

1. The S&L scandal is the second-largest theft in the history of the world.

2. Deregulation eased restrictions so much that S&L owners could lend money to themselves.

3. The Garn Institute of Finance, named after Senator Jake Garn—who co-authored the S&L deregulation bill—received $2.2 million from S&L industry executives.

4. For his part in running an S&L into the ground, Neil Bush, George's son, served time in jail and was banned from future S&L involvement.

5. Rep. Fernand St. Germain, House banking chairman and co-author of the S&L deregulation bill, was voted out of office after some questionable financial dealings were reported. The S&L industry immediately sent him back to Washington...as its lobbyist.

6. When asked whether his massive lobbying of government officials had influenced their conduct, Lincoln Savings president Charles Keating said, "Of course not. These are honorable men."

7. The S&L rip-off began in 1980, when Congress raised federal insurance on S&L deposits from $40,000 to $100,000, even though the average depositor's savings account was only $20,000.

8. Assets seized from failed S&Ls included a buffalo sperm bank, a racehorse with syphilis, and a kitty-litter mine.

9. Working with the government in a bailout deal, James Fail invested $1 million of his own money to purchase 15 failing S&Ls. In return, the government gave him $1.85 billion in federal subsidies.

10. Federal regulators sometimes stalled as long as seven years before closing hopelessly insolvent thrifts.

11. When S&L owners who stole millions went to jail, their jail sentences averaged about five times the average sentence for bank robbers.

12. The government S&L bailout will cost taxpayers as much as $500 billion.

13. If the White House had admitted the problem and bailed out failing thrifts in 1986, instead of waiting until after the 1988 election, the bailout might have cost only $20 billion.

14. With the money lost in the S&L rip-off, the federal government could provide prenatal care for every American child born in the next 2,300 years.

15. With the money lost in the S&L rip-off, the federal government could have bought 5 million average houses.

16. The authors of *Inside Job*, a bestselling exposé of the S&L scandal, found evidence of criminal activity in 50% of the thrifts they investigated.

ANSWERS
(1) F; it's the *largest*. (2) T (3) T (4) F (5) T (6) F; actually he said: "I certainly hope so." (7) F; all true, except the average savings account was only $6,000. (8) T (9) F; it was only $1,000 of his own money. (10) T; partly because of politics, partly because Reagan's people had fired 2/3 of the bank examiners needed to investigate S&L management. (11) F; they served only a fifth of the time. (12) F; it may hit $1.4 *trillion*. (13) T (14) T (15) T (16) F; they found criminal activity in *all* of the S&Ls they researched.

SCORING
13-16 right: Sadder, but wiser.
6-12 right: Just sadder.
0-5 right: Charlie Keating would like to talk to you about buying some bonds.

This quiz is from *It's a Conspiracy!* by the National Insecurity Council. Thanks to *The Nation* and *Inside Job* for the facts cited.

DIRTY TRICKS

*Why should politicians have all the fun? You can pull off some
dirty tricks, too. This "dirty dozen" should inspire you to new lows.*

P OUND FOOLISH
Pay a visit to the local dog pound or SPCA, wearing a chef's
hat and an apron. Ask to see one of the kittens or puppies
that are available for adoption. Pick it up and act as if you're weighing it, then set it down and ask to see one that's "a little more
plump."

SOCK IT TO 'EM
Tired of looking for that one sock you lost in the laundry? Pass on
your anxieties: Stick the leftover sock in with someone else's washload. Let them look for the missing sock for awhile.

SOMETHING FISHY
If you have a (clean) aquarium, toss some thin carrot slices into the
tank. Later when you have guests over, grab the slices out of the
tank and eat them quickly. If you do it quick enough, your victims
will assume you're eating a goldfish. (If you accidentally grab a *real*
goldfish, toss it back in, grab the carrot slice, and complain to your
victims that the first fish was "too small.")

LOST YOUR MARBLES?
Pry the hubcap off a friend's car, drop 2 or 3 steel ball bearings inside, and replace the hubcap. Then watch them drive off. The ball
bearings will make an enormous racket for a few seconds, until they
become held in place by centrifugal force. They'll stay silent until
the victim applies the brakes, and then they'll shake loose again.

TV GUIDE
Got a friend who's a couch potato? Carefully remove the cover of
their *TV Guide* (or weekly newspaper TV schedule), then glue it to
an older schedule, so the TV listings are wrong. It'll drive a true
TV fanatic crazy.

RETURN TO SENDER

Embarrass a coworker by buying a magazine they would *never* read (*High Times*, *Guns & Ammo*, and *Easy Rider* work well), and glue the mailing label from one of their regular magazines to the cover. Then stick it in the cafeteria or restroom where other coworkers can see it.

PRACTICE DRILLS

The next time you visit the dentist, scream really loud the minute you get seated in the dentist's chair. You'll send the patients in the waiting room running for cover.

MAD HATTER

If your friend wears a favorite hat, find out the manufacturer and buy two or more others of varying sizes. Then periodically switch them with your friend's hat. He'll be convinced his head is changing sizes. (Another hat trick: fill your victim's hat with baby powder.)

AT A WEDDING

If you're a close friend of the groom, paint a message on the sole of his shoes (the raised part near the heel that doesn't touch the ground) without telling him. When he kneels at the altar, the message will be visible for everyone to see.

PARK PLACE

The next time you're walking through a crowded parking lot, pull out your car keys and act as if you're looking for your car. Walk in between cars across the rows; motorists looking for a parking space will race to keep up with you.

PARTY IDEA

Using superglue, glue someone's drink to the bar or to a table.

WAKE UP CALL

Gather as many alarm clocks as you can find and hide them in different places in your victim's room. Set one alarm so it goes off very early in the morning, and set the others so they go off every five minutes afterward. Guaranteed to make your victim an early riser.

There are approximately 720 peanuts in every pound of peanut butter.

THE ROCK 'N' ROLL RIOTS OF 1956

Were there really rowdy rockers in 1956 at Bill Haley and the Comets concerts? Did DJs really accuse him of being "a menace to life, limb, decency, and morals"? Believe it or not, they did. By the mid-'50s, parents were already sure rock and roll had ruined their kids.

TEENS RIOT IN MASSACHUSETTS
Boston, Mass., March 26, 1956 (Wire service report)

"Record hops by disc jockeys featuring 'rock and roll' tunes were banned in Boston today after a riot at Massachusetts Institute of Technology's annual charity carnival.

"The disturbance involved nearly 3,000 students. It began when hundreds of teenagers who paid the 99¢ admission fee to see WCOP disc jockey Bill Marlowe discovered the carnival wasn't a record hop, and they couldn't dance.

"More than 20 officers were summoned to the scene, but they were unable to cope with the surging mob of teenagers who overturned booths, smashed records, and battled M.I.T. students who tried to keep order.

" 'Some of that music is crazy,' commented Mary Driscoll of the Boston licensing board. 'Teenagers have no business listening to disc jockeys at 12:00 at night.

The way they're going, they'll have high blood pressure before they're 20.' "

WASHINGTON MELEE
Newsweek, June 18, 1956

"Even before the joint began to jump, there was trouble at the National Guard Armory in Washington, D.C. As 5,000 people, mostly teenagers, poured in for some rock'n'roll, knives flashed and one young man was cut in the arm. Inside the auditorium, 25 officers waited tensely for Bill Haley and his Comets to swing into the 'big beat.'

"Haley gave the downbeat, the brasses blared, and kids leaped into the aisles to dance, only to be chased back to their seats by the cops. At 10:50, the Comets socked into their latest hit, 'Hot Dog, Buddy, Buddy!' and the crowd flipped.

"Some of the kids danced, some scuffled, fights broke out, a chair flew. William Warfield, 17, a high school junior, was hit. Suffering from a concussion and a severe cut over one eye, he was rushed to the hospital. 'Before I knew it, everybody was pounding everybody,' he said later.

"The fight overflowed into the street. A 19-year-old was struck over the head, and a 16-year-old was cut in the ear. Two cars were stoned and one exuberant teenager turned in a false alarm.

" 'It's the jungle strain that gets 'em all worked up,' said Armory manager Arthur (Dutch) Bergman, surveying the damage."

THEATER ATTACKED
Hartford, Ct., March 28, 1956
"Hartford police have instituted action to revoke the license of the State Theater, as a result of a series of riots during rock'n'roll shows. The latest took place this weekend during performances of an Alan Freed show.

"The 4,000-seat theater has had five police riot calls since last November. Over this past weekend alone, a total of 11 people were arrested. Practically all arrests have been teenagers."

ROCK, ROLL, AND RIOT
Time magazine, June 18, 1956
"In Hartford city officials held special meetings to discuss it....In Minneapolis a theater manager withdrew a film featuring the music after a gang of youngsters left the theater,

snake-danced around town and smashed windows....At a wild concert in Atlanta's baseball park one night, fists and beer bottles were thrown, and four youngsters were arrested.

"The object of all this attention is a musical style known as 'rock'n'roll,' which has captivated U.S. adolescents.

"Characterisics: an unrelenting syncopation that sounds like a bullwhip; a choleric saxophone honking mating-call sounds; an electric guitar turned up so loud that its sound shatters and splits; a vocal group that shudders and exercises violently to the beat while roughly chanting either a near-nonsense phrase or a moronic lyric in hillbilly rhythm....

"Psychologists feel that rock'n'roll's appeal is to teenagers' need to belong; [in concert], the results bear passing resemblance to Hitler mass meetings."

QUEEN SCREENS
Scholastic Magazine, Oct. 4, 1956
"In England, over 100 youths were arrested in 'rock and roll' riots that broke out during showing of a 'rock and roll' film. Queen Elizabeth II, disturbed by the growing number of such arrests, has scheduled a private screening of the film at her palace for official study."

Termites can't hear.

WILDE ABOUT OSCAR

Wit and wisdom from Oscar Wilde, one of the 19th century's most popular—and controversial—writers.

"The only way to get rid of temptation is to yield to it."

"It is better to have a permanent income than to be fascinating."

"The soul is born old but grows young. That is the comedy of life. And the body is born young and grows old. That is life's tragedy."

"Seriousness is the only refuge of the shallow."

"Children begin by loving their parents. After a time they judge them. Rarely, if ever, do they forgive them."

"There's no sin...except stupidity."

"Experience is the name everyone gives to their mistakes."

"Formerly we used to canonize our heroes. The modern method is to vulgarize them. Cheap editions of great books may be delightful, but cheap editions of great men are absolutely detestable."

"All women become like their mothers. That is their tragedy. No man does. That's his."

"Society often forgives the criminal; it never forgives the dreamer."

"It is better to be beautiful than to be good, but it is better to be good than to be ugly."

"The only portraits in which one believes are portraits where there is very little of the sitter and a very great deal of the artist."

"The youth of America is their oldest tradition. It has been going on now for three hundred years."

"One should always play fairly—when one has the winning cards."

"Discontent is the first step in the progress of a man or a nation."

"The well-bred contradict other people. The wise contradict themselves."

The three best-known western names in China: Jesus Christ, Richard Nixon, and Elvis Presley.

INSIDE STORY: THE FIRST VIDEO GAME

Where do video games come from? Who invented them? Here's the inside story on what's probably the only completely "safe" technology ever to come from a nuclear laboratory.

BACKGROUND

In the 1950s, Americans were becoming increasingly paranoid about the atomic bomb. But they weren't just scared of weapons, they were nervous about the "peaceful" use of atomic energy as well. In 1958, to combat this perception, the U.S. government began holding "open houses" at non-secret nuclear labs. The public was invited to visit and see for themselves what scientists were up to.

One of the facilities scheduled to hold an open house was Brookhaven National Laboratory in Upton, New York. And one of the men who was organizing the event was Willy Higinbotham, a distinguished scientist who had worked on the Manhattan Project. Higinbotham thought the standard displays of radiation detectors and black-and-white photos would be too boring for the public to enjoy. To provide a little entertainment, he decided to hook up an oscilloscope to a computer and build a TV-like game from spare parts and equipment he found lying around the lab.

TENNIS, ANYONE?

Author Ira Flatow describes what happened next in his book, They All Laughed: The Fascinating Stories Behind the Great Inventions That Have Changed Our Lives.

"We looked around and found that we had a few pieces we could throw together and make a game," recalled Willy years later, "which would have a ball bouncing back and forth, sort of like a tennis game viewed from the side."

Two hours of scratching a design on paper and two weeks of wiring and debugging, and the game was complete. The tennis game was displayed on a tiny, five-inch screen. It involved two players, each having a box with a button and a knob. If you pushed the

button, you hit the ball to the opponent's court. The knob controlled how high the ball was hit.

"You could actually hit the ball into the net," recalled Dave Potter, Willy's associate, "see it bounce into the net and see it bounce onto the floor back to you. So it was a very cleverly designed game Willy came up with."

Set up on a table in the gym right under the basketball hoop on the far wall, the tennis game was practically lost among the other electronic gadgets on display. But when the doors to the gym were opened, the public had no trouble finding the video game. Willy and Dave could hardly believe their eyes.

"Willy's tennis game was a hit," remembered an astonished Potter, "there were long lines. People wanted to play."

Willy was shocked. What was so attractive about a dot bouncing around an oscilloscope screen?

"It never occurred to me that I was doing anything very exciting. The long line of people I thought was not because this was so great but because all the rest of the things were so dull."

For the following year's (1959) open house, Willy improved the game. The picture tube was enlarged to ten or fifteen inches and a novel feature was added: Visitors could play tennis on the moon with very low gravity or on Jupiter with very intense gravity. Again the game was a great success; hundreds stood in line to play.

Most fathers of such a success might have immediately set out to cash in on their invention. But not Willy. Despite the game's popularity, Willy never made a nickel off his invention. He never saw any commercial value in it. The idea seemed too obvious. Anybody with simple equipment bought at Radio Shack could make the game. So Willy never patented the idea. [*B.R.I. note: The first commercial video game, Pong, was a copy of Willy's game.*]

Years later, Willy told me, "My kids complained about this and I keep saying: Kids, no matter what, even if I patented it, I wouldn't have made any money." Because he worked at a government institution, Uncle Sam would have owned the patent and Willy might have collected a ten-dollar royalty. And anybody wanting to market a video game would have had to pay the U.S. Treasury royalties.

"I never realized it until many years later," Willy said in 1983, "when the first dumb games came out about 1970-71, that these games would be as popular as they have turned out to have been."

TV THEME SONG TRIVIA

For your bathroom-reading pleasure: 10 facts you don't know about classic TV themes, from John Javna's TV Theme Song Sing-Along Songbook.

JUST THE FACTS

The first TV theme ever to become a Top 40 hit was the theme from "Dragnet." It was recorded by band leader Ray Anthony as "The Dragnet March" in 1953, and reached #3 on the national charts. At the time, "Dragnet" was the second-most popular TV program in America, behind "I Love Lucy."

HEY LOOOSY!

The theme song from "I Love Lucy" was also released as a single in 1953. But despite the fact that "Lucy" was the #1 program on TV at the time, the record flopped—perhaps because America knew it as an instrumental, and this version had *lyrics*. Desi Arnaz had commissioned Oscar-winner Harold Adamson to write words to the song ("I love Lucy, and she loves me / We're as happy as two can be"), and then sang it on the air. Arnaz and Columbia Records thought they had a sure smash, but America wasn't buying. It wasn't until 24 years later—20 years after "Lucy" had gone off the air—that it finally made the charts...as a *disco song*. (Performed by the Wilton Place Band, it reached #24 in 1977.)

THAT'S TER-R-RIBLE, WILBUR-R-R

The "Mr. Ed" theme song ("A horse is a horse, of course, of course") is one of the all-time classics. But for the strangest of reasons, it was almost dumped before the show aired.

To save money, the music for the "Mr. Ed" pilot episode was done in Italy...and the Italians who scored the show picked an opera singer to perform the theme song. His version was so bad that the show's producers planned to replace the whole song.

"They thought it was the song, not the singer," explains the theme's composer, Jay Livingston. To prove the song was usable, he recorded his own version. The producers liked it so much they had Livingston sing the final version. That's him you hear on reruns.

NO, NO, NOT AGAIN!

"Bonanza" was one of the most popular TV shows of the '60s. Its theme song—an instrumental by guitarist Al Caiola— hit #19 on the *Billboard* charts in 1961.

Most fans never knew that the theme song had lyrics, and that the Cartwright family had actually sung it once on the show: At the end of the "Bonanza" pilot episode, Ben, Adam, Little Joe, and Hoss rode into the sunset singing its ludicrous lyrics, "We got a right to pick a little fight, Bonanza..."

The rendition was so awful that it's been shown on TV blooper shows...but it was never sung on the show again.

HAPPY DAYS ARE HERE AGAIN

When the '50s nostalgia show "Happy Days" made its debut in 1974, it didn't have a theme song. Instead, the producers used "Rock Around the Clock," by Bill Haley and the Comets—which had been #1 in 1955 but hadn't been on the charts since then. Such is the power of TV that "Rock Around the Clock" became a Top 40 hit again in 1974, and Haley—a "has-been"—was briefly resurrected as a star.

In 1976, a new theme was introduced. "Happy Days," sung by a duo named Pratt and McClain, immediately went to #5 on the national charts.

HERE ON GILLIGAN'S ISLE

"Gilligan's Island" creator Sherwood Schwartz had a hell of a time selling his show to CBS. Network executives insisted that while the basic idea was okay, it had one major flaw: viewers who turned in for the first time wouldn't understand what seven people were doing on an island together. They wanted Schwartz to turn "Gilligan" into a sitcom about a charter boat instead.

Schwartz desperately wanted to keep the original premise...and came up with a solution: He wrote a theme song that described who the characters were and how they wound up on the island. Then, in the middle of a formal meeting with CBS execs, he abruptly got up and performed the tune. They bought the show.

WE'RE #1

The first TV theme to hit #1 on the charts was "Davy Crockett," in 1955. The second was "Welcome Back Kotter," in 1976.

IT'S A MIRACLE!

The tabloids are full of stories of people who see images of Jesus in everything from a lima bean to a smudge on a car window. Could they be real? Here are the details of 5 actual sightings. Judge for yourself.

The Sighting: Jesus in a forkful of spaghetti, Stone Mountain, Georgia

Revelation: Joyce Simpson, an Atlanta fashion designer, was pulling out of a gas station in Stone Mountain when she saw the face of Jesus in a forkful of spaghetti on a billboard advertising Pizza Hut's pasta menu. Simpson says at the time she was trying to decide whether to stay in the church choir or quit and sing professionally. (She decided to stick with the choir.)

Impact: Since the sighting, dozens of other people called Pizza Hut to say that they, too, had seen someone in the spaghetti. But not all the callers agreed that the man in the spaghetti was Jesus; some saw Doors singer Jim Morrison; others saw country star Willie Nelson.

The Sighting: Jesus in a tortilla, Lake Arthur, New Mexico

Revelation: On October 5, 1977, Maria Rubio was making burritos for her husband when she noticed a 3-by-3-inch face of Jesus burned into the tortilla she was cooking. Local priests argued that the image was only a coincidence, but the Rubio family's faith was unshaken. They saved the tortilla, framed it, and built a shrine for it in their living room.

Impact: To date more than 11,000 people have visited it.

The Sighting: Jesus on a soybean oil tank, Fostoria, Ohio

Revelation: Rita Rachen was driving home from work along Ohio Route 12 one night in 1986 when she saw the image of Jesus with a small child on the side of an Archer Daniels Midland Company oil tank containing soybean oil. She screamed "Oh, my Lord, my God," and nearly drove off the side of the road, but recovered enough to continue driving.

Impact: She spread the word to other faithful, and the soybean tank became a popular pilgrimage site. (Since then, however, the oil tank has been repainted. Jesus is no longer visible.)

The Sighting: Jesus on the side of a refrigerator, Estill Springs, Tennessee

Revelation: When Arlene Gardner bought a new refrigerator, she had the old one dragged out onto her front porch. A few nights later, she noticed several of her neighbors were standing around staring at the old fridge. They told her that the reflection from a neighbor's porch light had created an image of Jesus on the side of the fridge. Gardner took a look and agreed.

Impact: Soon thousands of faithful were making pilgrimages to the site—so many, in fact, that Gardner's neighbors had their porch light disconnected, so Jesus could be seen no more. (Note: Not everyone agreed that Jesus had really made an appearance; as one local skeptic explained to a reporter, "When the good Lord comes, he won't come on a major appliance.")

The Sighting: A 900-foot Jesus at the City of Faith, Tulsa, Oklahoma

Revelation: This vision—one of the most publicized Jesus sightings ever—came to famed televangelist Oral Roberts on May 25, 1980 ...but he inexplicably kept it secret for more than 5 months. Then one day he shared his vision and explained what he'd seen to reporters: "He reached down, put His hand under the City of Faith (a city Roberts had built), lifted it, and said to me, 'See how easy it is for me to lift it?' "

On January 4, 1987, Roberts told his followers God had appeared again, this time demanding $8 million. Roberts warned that if the money wasn't sent in by March 31, "God would call me home."

Impact: Roberts's followers coughed up $9.1 million.

• • • •

Royal Gossip
Queen Elizabeth likes to do crossword puzzles. She also likes to read mysteries by Dick Fancis and play parlor games like charades.

Canada's official animal is the beaver.

IT WAS A DARK AND STORMY NIGHT

According to San Jose State University's Bulwer-Lytton Fiction Contest,
"It was a dark and stormy night..." is the worst sentence ever used to begin
a novel. But every year they have a contest to see if anyone can top it.
Can you? It's a creative way to spend your bathroom time.

B ACKGROUND.
Have you ever tried to write the Great American Novel and failed? Don't give up. There may still be a literary goal within in your grasp: You can compete in the Bulwer-Lytton Fiction Contest, tying to write the worst opening sentence for a novel. The erudite competition is named after Edward George Earle Bulwer-Lytton, whose 1830 novel *Paul Clifford* began with the following classic sentence:

"It was a dark and stormy night; the rain fell in torrents—except at occasional intervals, when it was checked by a violent gust of wind which swept up the streets (for it is in London that our scene lies), rattling along the housetops, and fiercely agitating the scanty flame of the lamps that struggled against the darkness."

Think you can write worse than that? It's not easy. Here's a sample of some entertaining entries, from the books *It Was a Dark and Stormy Night: The Best from the Bulwer-Lytton Contest, Son of It Was a Dark and Stormy Night,* and *Bride of It Was a Dark and Stormy Night.*

BAD FICTION

"When I walked into the room and saw the twisted, dead corpse lying lifeless on the blood-soaked carpet, I wanted and needed to cry in the worst sort of way, but I couldn't—a sort of lachrymal constipation—so I lightly stepped over the body in its gruesome repose and walked over to the desk to play with the adding machine until help arrived."

—Pamela Wylder, Bloomington, Illinois

"It didn't matter to Gordon that he couldn't outrun the enraged mother grizzly; all he had to do was outdistance his chubby hiking partner, Fred."

—David Willingham, Georgetown, Tennessee

"On their wedding night 230-pound but svelte Gloria, her gnarled toe caught in her greasy pantyhose, fell gushing onto the waterbed while Buford, lovesick with Ripple, felt his prostate swell in anticipation of the delights to come."

—Dennis E. Minor, Ruston, Louisiana

"In the Mexican town of Texacallo sits a fat woman at her door staring moodily at the chickens; it is she who best of all recalls Enrico Prumbello."

—Y. David Shulman, Brooklyn, New York

" 'Mein Gott im Himmel,' murmured Der Führer, 'I was commanding the immediate presence of Goebbels, not gerbils!" as he waded through the now chest-high throng of rodents, his purposeful pinpoint pupils quickly regaining their customary expression of almost saintly Teutonic benevolence."

—Andy Oates, Sydney, Australia

"His coat bulging like a rotting cat with maggots, Kevy Honeyman, his too-pretty lips involuntarily pouted, stumbled up to a border guard in that two-bit, fourth-class, third-world banana-land country, beads of Roman-candle sweat popping from his brows as he nervously eyed the guard's open shirt, which revealed a mat of jungle-musky hair that Kevy would come to know all too well in the ensuing months, and trying to act casual, he squeaked out in a crackling Freudian falsetto slip-of-doom, 'Golly, it's raining cats and hashish out there!' "

—Glen Bering, Ann Arbor, Michigan

HOW TO ENTER

Got a winning sentence to send in? For a copy of the contest rules write to: The Bulwer-Lytton Fiction Contest, Department of English, San Jose State University, San Jose, CA 95192-0090.

"MADAM, I'M ADAM"

A palindrome is a word or phrase that spells the same thing backward and forward. Here are the best that B.R.I. members have sent us. Try your own. If you come up with a good one, send it to us and we'll publish it in the next edition.

TWO-WORD PHRASES

No, Son.

Sue us!

Pots nonstop.

Dump mud.

Go, dog!

Stack cats.

Worm row.

Party trap.

LONGER PHRASES

Wonder if Sununu's fired now.

Never odd or even.

Ed is on no side.

Step on no pets.

Rise to vote, sir!

Naomi, did I moan?

"Desserts," I stressed.

Spit Q-Tips.

Roy, am I mayor?

A car, a man, a maraca.

Are we not drawn onward, we few, drawn onward to new era?

A man, a plan, a canal… Panama!

Live not on evil.

If I had a Hi-Fi…

A slut nixes sex in Tulsa.

Put Eliot's toilet up.

Pull up, Bob, pull up!

Pa's a sap.

Ma is as selfless as I am.

NONSENSE PHRASES

Did mom poop? Mom did.

We panic in a pew.

Yawn a more Roman way.

Mr. Owl ate my metal worm.

Airlines in America spend an average of $5.73 on food per passenger.

THE TV SPEECH THAT MADE A PRESIDENT

John Kennedy owed his 1960 nomination for the presidency to a carefully planned campaign...starting with the 1956 TV speech that made him a national political figure.

BACKGROUND. In 1956 John F. Kennedy—an ambitious freshman senator from Massachusetts—wanted the Democratic nomination for vice president. But his chances were slim; the favorite was Senator Estes Kefauver of Tennessee.

On the first night of the Democratic convention, Kennedy narrated a film on the history of the Democratic party, called *The Pursuit of Happiness*. It was well received, and when JFK went to take a bow, the applause "was surprisingly loud and long."

Adlai Stevenson, the Democrats' presidential candidate, was impressed. He asked JFK to give his nomination speech—a peace offering that meant JFK wasn't going to be his running mate. But Kennedy didn't give up. He saw the speech as an opportunity. "One last possibility remained," writes Herbert Parmet in *The Struggles of John F. Kennedy*, "—going before the convention with a performance...so effective that even Stevenson and the other skeptics would have no choice but to recognize Kennedy's attractions as a running mate."

Although Stevenson gave Kennedy a prepared speech, JFK discarded it and spent the next 10 hours working on a new one.

THE SPEECH. On August 16, 1956, JFK made his first nationally televised speech ever, placing Stevenson's name in nomination. A few excerpts:

• "We here today are selecting a man who must be more than a good candidate, more than a good politician....We are selecting the head of the most powerful nation on Earth—the man who will hold in his hands the power of survival or destruction, of freedom or slavery."

• "We must, therefore, think beyond the balloting of tonight and tomorrow to seek, beyond even the election of this November, and think instead of the four years ahead and of the crises that will come in them....Let us be frank about the campaign in the days ahead. Our party will be up against two of the toughest, most skilled campaigners in American political history—one who takes the high road (Eisenhower) and one who takes the low road (Nixon)."

• "These are critical times—times that demand the best we have, times that demand the best America has. We have, therefore, an obligation to pick the man best qualified not only to lead our party but to lead our country....Ladies and gentlemen, it is now my privilege to present to the convention as a candidate for the president of the United States...the man from Libertyville...Adlai Stevenson."

THE REACTION. The speech, described as "Kennedy's second success of the convention," put Stevenson in a quandary: Should he pick Kennedy, Kefauver, Sen. Albert Gore, or Sen. Hubert Humphrey?

In the end, Stevenson decided not to pick anyone. He announced to the convention that *they* could select the vice presidential candidate with a roll-call vote. "The choice will be yours," he told them. "the profit will be the nation's."

Kennedy came within about 30 votes of the nomination on the second ballot. But in a wild scene on the convention floor, he eventually lost to Kefauver. On learning the news, he rushed to the convention center and pushed his way onto the stage. The chairman saw him and brought him up to the microphone.

THE CONCESSION. "TV coverage of conventions was still something fresh and new in 1956, and a hundred million Americans were watching," writes historian Ralph G. Martin. "They saw this freshman senator on the podium before a packed national political convention, listening to the roar, picking at some invisible dust on his boyish, handsome face, nervously dry-washing his hands, waving to yelling friends nearby, his smile tentative, but warmly appealing, his eyes slightly wet and glistening. He spoke without notes, and his words were short, gallant, and touching. For the TV audience, it was a moment of magic they would not forget."

AFTERMATH. The Stevenson/Kefauver ticket went down in a landslide, but JFK emerged as the Democrats' rising star. His performance on TV made him the most sought-after political speaker in America and opened the door for a 1960 presidential run.

WHO WROTE SHAKESPEARE'S PLAYS?

We include this to inspire you to add the Bard's writing to your bathroom reading. B.R.I. members have a lofty image to uphold, after all.

B ACKGROUND. William Shakespeare authored 36 plays, 154 sonnets, and 2 narrative poems between 1588 and 1616. Though his works are among the most influential literature of Western civilization, little is known about the man himself— and no manuscripts written in his own hand have ever been found.

• This fact has inspired speculation by pseudoscholars, cranks, and English society snobs that Shakespeare—the commoner son of a glovemaker—couldn't have been intelligent or educated enough to write "his own" works.

• Why would the real author have given the credit to Shakespeare? One theory: Many of the plays dealt with members of the English royal family and were politically controversial. It may have been too dangerous for the real author to take credit for the radical ideas they contained.

• The *real* William Shakespeare, according to this theory, was a 3rd-rate actor, playwright, and theatre gadfly who was more than happy to take credit for work he was not capable of producing.

• Whatever the case, more than 5,000 other authors (including Queen Elizabeth I and a Catholic pope) have been proposed as the *real* Shakespeare. Here are five of the more popular candidates:

1. SIR FRANCIS BACON. An English nobleman, trusted advisor to Queen Elizabeth I, and renowned writer, scholar, and philosopher.

Background: The Sir Francis Bacon-as-Shakespeare theory was popularized in 1852 by Delia Bacon (no relation), a 41-year-old Connecticut spinster who detested William Shakespeare, referring to him as "a vulgar, illiterate...deer poacher" and "stableboy."

• Bacon believed that Shakespeare had been buried with docu- ments that would prove her theory. She spent much of her life struggling to get permission to open the crypt. She never succeeded and died insane in 1859.

Evidence: According to some theorists, a number of Shakespeare's plays demonstrate "profound legal expertise." But Shakespeare was not a lawyer—and according to one theorist, "A person of Shakespeare's known background could not have gained such knowledge." Sir Francis Bacon, on the other hand, was so gifted as a lawyer that he eventually became Lord Chancellor of England.

• Shakespeare's plays also show a strong familiarity with continental Europe, though there's no evidence the Bard himself ever left England. Bacon, an aristocrat, was well traveled.

• Bacon had a reason for hiding his authorship: in the 17th century poetry and playwriting was considered frivolous and beneath the dignity of a nobleman. Bacon may have kept his identity a secret to protect his reputation (as well as his standing in the royal court, since a number of the plays dealt with English monarchs). So he paid William Shakespeare, a nobody, to take the credit.

2. CHRISTOPHER MARLOWE. An accomplished playwright of the 1500s. Author of such works as *Edward the Second* and *The Tragical History of Doctor Faustus,* Marlowe was considered as talented as Shakespeare by audiences of the day.

Background: Unlike most candidates for the Shakespearean crown, Marlowe was already dead by the time most of Shakespeare's plays were written; according to the official story, he was stabbed to death during a drunken brawl in a pub in 1593. Marlowe theorists disagree—they believe he *faked* his death:

• Marlowe had a reputation for rowdiness, was an alleged homosexual and atheist, and may have even been an English spy.

• His wild life and radical beliefs eventually got him into trouble, and in 1593 a warrant was put out for his arrest. Marlowe theorists believe that his alleged lover, Sir Thomas Walsingham, staged the pub fight, had someone else murdered, and then bribed the coroner to report that Marlowe was the man who'd been killed. Marlowe escaped to France to continue his writing career, and Sir Thomas hired Shakespeare to publish—under his own name—the manuscripts Marlowe sent back from France.

Evidence: Though the theory was first suggested by W. G. Zeigler, a California lawyer, in 1895, it wasn't until the early 1900s that an

Ohio professor, Thomas C. Mendenhall, checked to see if the claims were credible. He spent months analyzing more than 400,000 individual words from Shakespeare's plays and comparing them with words from Marlowe's known works.

• His stunning conclusion: The two men had similar writing styles, and for both Marlowe and the Bard, "the word of greatest frequency was the four-letter word." (One problem with the research: Mendenhall studied *contemporary* editions of Shakespeare's plays, which spelled many words differently than they had appeared in the original plays.)

• Other researchers dug up Sir Thomas's grave to see if it held any clues to whether Marlowe really was a homosexual. The search turned up nothing—not even Sir Thomas.

3. EDWARD DE VERE, 17th Earl of Oxford. Though none of his plays survive, de Vere was an accomplished author in his own right. He's also been described as a "hot-tempered youth, a spendthrift, and a philanderer specializing in the queen's maids-of-honor."

Background: J. Thomas Looney, father of the de Vere-as-Shakespeare theory, was an English schoolmaster and Bard buff in the early 1900s. Over time he came to believe that Shakespeare's descriptions of Italy in *The Merchant of Venice* could only have been made by someone who'd actually been there, and Shakespeare had not. Looney began researching the lives of other writers of Shakespeare's day to see if he could find the real author. He eventually settled on de Vere.

Evidence: De Vere had traveled abroad. After emitting "an unfortunate flatulence in the presence of the Queen," he was compelled to leave England and spent several years traveling in Europe. During his travels he spent a great deal of time in Italy and gained the knowledge Looney alleges he needed to write *The Merchant of Venice* and other plays.

• According to Looney, many of de Vere's relatives had names that were similar to the names of characters in Shakespeare's plays—too many relatives to be a coincidence.

4. SIR WALTER RALEIGH. Raleigh, an "author, adventurer, and explorer," was the founding father of the state of Virginia and, like Bacon, was popular in Queen Elizabeth's court. But he fell out of favor when James I took the throne, and was beheaded in 1618.

Background: George S. Caldwell, an Australian, first advanced the theory that Raleigh wrote Shakespeare's plays in 1877. The theory later became popular with U.S. Senator Albert J. Beveridge, who made speeches supporting it in the 1890s. In 1914 Henry Pemberton, Jr., a Philadelphia writer, gave the theory new life in his book *Shakespeare and Sir Walter Raleigh.*

Evidence: Raleigh was familiar with the traditions of the royal court and the military, which were central themes in a number of Shakespeare's plays.

• Unlike Shakespeare, who was not known for being emotional, Raleigh was a passionate man, much like the characters in Shakespeare's plays.

5. MICHEL ANGELO FLORIO.
Florio, an Italian, was a defrocked Franciscan monk who converted to Protestantism. A Calvinist, he lived in exile in England for much of his life. His son John Florio most likely knew William Shakespeare; many historians speculate that the two men were close friends.

Background: In 1925 Santi Paladino, a writer, visited a fortune-teller and was told that he would someday shock the world with an amazing discovery. Within four years he had published his book *Un Italiano Autore Delle Opere Shakespeariane*, which claimed that Michel Angelo Florio was the true author of Shakespeare's works.

Evidence: Again, the main body of circumstantial evidence is that Florio had an intimate knowledge of Italy that Shakespeare could not have possessed. Florio-as-Shakespearists believe that the elder Florio, whose experience as an exile made him leery of publishing in his own name, wrote Shakespeare's plays in *Italian*, had his son translate them into English, and paid Shakespeare to publish them under his own name.

• Shakespeare's supporters disagree, arguing that the Bard wrote the plays himself, but got a lot of his information on Italy from the Florios, who were writers themselves and owned a large library of Italian books. Shakespeare may have even borrowed from some of the Florio's writings, they say, but there's no hard evidence anyone other than Shakespeare wrote the plays.

CARNIVAL TRICKS

*Do the booths at carnivals and traveling circuses seem rigged to you?
According to Matthew Gryczan in his book* Carnival Secrets,
*many of them are. Here are some booths to look out for—
and some tips on how to beat them.*

The Booth: "Ring a Bottle"
The Object: Throw a small ring over the neck of a soft-drink bottle from a distance of about five feet.
How It's Rigged: The game isn't rigged, but it doesn't have to be—it's almost impossible to win.

• In 1978 researchers stood 6 feet away from a grouping of 100 bottles and tossed 7,000 rings at it. They recorded 12 wins—an average of one shot in every 583 throws. What's more, the researchers found that all of the 12 winning tosses were ricochets; not a single *aimed* shot had gone over the bottles. In fact, the light, plastic rings wouldn't stay on the bottles even if dropped from a height of three inches directly over the neck of the bottle.

How to Win: It appears that the only way to win is to throw two rings over a bottle neck at the same time. However, carnival operators usually won't let you throw more than one ring at a time.

The Booth: "The Bushel Basket"
The Object: Toss softballs into a bushel basket from a distance of about six feet.
How It's Rigged: The bottom of the basket is connected to the baseboard in such a way that it has a lot of spring to it, so the ball will usually bounce out.

• In addition, carnies sometimes use balls that weigh as little as 4 ounces, rather than the 6-1/4-ounce minimum weight of an official softball. The lighter ball makes the game harder to win.

• Some carnies use a heavier ball when demonstrating the game or to give to players for a practice shot. Then, when play begins, they switch to a lighter ball that's harder to keep in the basket.

How to Win: Ask to use the same ball the carny used.

- The best throw is to aim high, so that the ball enters the basket from a vertical rather than a horizontal angle. The worst place to put the ball is directly on the bottom of the basket.

- Aim for the lip or the sides of the basket. If the rules prohibit these shots, the game will be tough to win.

The Booth: "Shoot Out the Dots"
The Object: Using soft graphite bullets, shoot out all the red in three to five dots printed on a paper target.

How It's Rigged: The bullet, called an "arcade load," is discharged from the rifle barrel in little chunks. Propelled by a low-powder charge that ranges from a .22 cap to a .22-short, the chunks barely penetrate the target.

- Even if the bullet remained intact, it would not be able to take out all of the red of the .22-caliber-sized dots, because its diameter ranges from .15 caliber to .177 caliber. Besides, the chunks of graphite *tear* the paper target instead of punching out a clean hole. So there's always some red left on the target, even with a direct hit.

How to Win: In many cases, winning is impossible. During a trial, one carny testified that she'd never had one winner in 365,000 plays over five and a half years—despite the fact the game was frequented by U.S. naval personnel with experience in shooting guns.

The Booth: "The Milk Can"
The Object: Toss a softball into a 10-gallon milk can.

How It's Rigged: Most carnival cans aren't ordinary dairy cans. For the midway game, a concave piece of steel is welded to the rim of the can's opening, reducing the size of the hole the ball must travel through to anything from 6-1/2 inches in diameter down to 4-3/8 inches in diameter.

- At one game played at a state fair in 1987, there were 15 wins out of a total of 1,279 tries—one win for every 86 balls thrown.

How to Win: Carnies say the best way to win is to give the ball a backspin and try to hit the back edge of the can.

- Another way: Toss the ball as high as you can, so that it drops straight into the hole. This isn't always easy; operators often hang prizes from the rafters of the booth to make high tosses difficult.

THEY WENT THAT-A-WAY

Malcolm Forbes wrote a fascinating book about the deaths of famous people. Here are some of the wierdest stories he found.

FRANCIS BACON

Claim to Fame: One of the great minds of the late 16th century. A statesman, philosopher, writer, and scientist. Some people believe he's the real author of Shakespeare's plays (see page 114).

How He Died: Stuffing snow into a chicken.

Postmortem: One afternoon in 1625, Bacon was watching a snowstorm. He began wondering if snow might be as good a meat preservative as salt...and decided to find out. With a friend, he rode through the storm to a nearby peasant's cottage, bought a chicken, and had it butchered. Then, standing outside in the cold, he stuffed the chicken with snow to freeze it. The chicken never froze, but Bacon did. He caught a serious chill and never recovered. He died from bronchitis a few weeks later.

WILLIAM HENRY HARRISON

Claim to Fame: Ninth president of the U.S.; elected in 1841 at the age of 67.

How He Died: Pneumonia.

Postmortem: Harrison's advanced age had been an issue in his race against incumbent president Martin van Buren. Perhaps because of this—to demonstrate his strength—he rode on horseback in his inaugural parade without a hat, gloves, or overcoat. Then he stood outside in the snow for more than one and a half hours, delivering his inaugural address.

The experience weakened him, and a few weeks later he caught pneumonia. Within a week he was delirious, and on April 4—just one month after his inauguration—he died. He served in office long enough to keep only one campaign promise: not to run for a second term.

AESCHYLUS

Claim to Fame: Greek playwright in 500 B.C. Many historians consider him the father of Greek tragedies.

How He Died: An eagle dropped a tortoise on his head.

Postmortem: According to legend, an eagle was trying to crack open a tortoise by dropping it on a hard rock. It mistook Aeschylus's head (he was bald) for a rock and dropped it on him instead.

TYCHO BRAHE

Claim to Fame: An important Danish astronomer of the 16th century. His groundbreaking research enabled Sir Isaac Newton to come up with the theory of gravity.

How He Died: Didn't get to the bathroom on time.

Postmortem: In the 16th century it was considered an insult to leave a banquet table before the meal was over. Brahe, known to drink excessively, had a bladder condition—but failed to relieve himself before the feast started. He made matters worse by drinking too much at the dinner, and was too polite to ask to be excused. His bladder finally burst, killing him slowly and painfully over the next 11 days.

JEROME IRVING RODALE

Claim to Fame: Founding father of the organic food movement, creator of *Organic Farming and Gardening* magazine. Founded Rodale Press, a major publishing company.

How He Died: On the "Dick Cavett Show," while discussing the health benefits of organic food.

Postmortem: Rodale, who bragged "I'm going to live to 100 unless I'm run down by a sugar-crazed taxi-driver," was only 72 when he appeared on the "Dick Cavett Show" in January 1971. Partway through the interview, he dropped dead in his chair. Cause of death: a heart attack. The show was never aired.

ATTILA THE HUN

Claim to Fame: One of the most notorious villains in history. By 450 A.D., Attila's 500,000-man army conquered all of Asia—from Mongolia to the edge of the Russian empire—by destroying villages and pillaging the countryside.

How He Died: He got a nosebleed on his wedding night.

Postmortem: In 453 Attila married a young girl named Ildico. Despite his reputation for ferocity on the battlefield, he tended to eat and drink lightly during large banquets. But on his wedding night he really cut loose, gorging himself on food and drink. Sometime during the night he suffered a nosebleed, but was too drunk to notice. He drowned in his own blood and was found dead the next morning.

JIM FIXX

Claim to Fame: Author of the bestselling *Complete Book of Running*, which started the jogging craze of the 1970s.

How He Died: A heart attack...while jogging.

Postmortem: Fixx was visiting Greensboro, Vermont. He walked out of his house and began jogging. He'd only gone a short distance when he had a massive coronary. His autopsy revealed that one of his coronary arteries was 99% clogged, another was 80% obstructed, and a third was 70% blocked—and that Fixx had had three other heart attacks in the weeks prior to his death (when he'd competed in 12-mile and 5-mile races).

HORACE WELLS

Claim to Fame: Pioneered the use of anaesthesia in the 1840s.

How He Died: Used anaesthetics to commit suicide.

Postmortem: While experimenting with various gases during his anaesthesia research, Wells became addicted to chloroform. In 1848 he was arrested for splashing sulfuric acid on two women outside his home. In a letter he wrote from jail, he blamed chloroform for his problems, claiming he'd gotten high before the attack. Four days later he was found dead in his cell. He'd anaesthetized himself with chloroform, then slashed open his thigh with a razor.

• • • •

And Now for Something Completely Different

• Elvis Presley was a big Monty Python fan; he saw *Monty Python and the Holy Grail* at least 5 times.

• The King's favorite board games were Monopoly and Scrabble. Neutrogena was his favorite soap.

Memo to Uncle Walt: The original Cinderella was Egyptian and wore fur slippers.

THE ELVIS SIDESHOW

Hurry, hurry, step right up! See the amazing Elvis freaks!

Richard Tweddell III. Inventor of the Elvis Vegiform, a plastic garden mold that fits over young vegetables and gets them to grow into the shape of the King. He says, "[Elvis-shaped] vegetables are more weighty, and the flavor is enhanced."

Nicholas "S&L-vis" D'Ambra. An Elvis impersonator with a social conscience. "S&L-vis" takes on the savings and loan scandal with songs like "Tax-break Hotel." Sample lyrics: "The deal the bank board gave them; was too good to be true; for every dollar they put in there; there's 15 from you."

"Major" Bill Smith. Believes the King is still alive and claims to have regular phone conversations with him. Smith, a 68-year-old Texan, is a religious man; he sees Elvis as a sort of mini-messiah: "Elvis is coming back in the spirit of Elijah....Praise God, he's coming back....This thing's about to bust right open." He has devoted his life to paving the way for the Second Coming of Elvis, which he considers the Lord's work. "Like Elvis told me, 'I'm walkin' the line God has drawn for me.' It's what the Holy Spirit told me to do."

Peter Singh. A Sikh living in Wales, England, he croons Elvis hits, Indian-style, to customers at his pub. Favorites include "Who's Sari Now," "My Popadum Told Me," and "Singh, Singh, Singh."

Uri Yoali. An Israeli Arab, owner of a roadside diner called The Elvis Inn, located in the Holy Land just 7,000 miles from Memphis. "It's not just for tourists," Yoali says, "Elvis is my life." The diner is decorated with 728 pictures and posters of the King. It boasts a 12-foot, 500-pound, epoxy-and-plaster likeness of Presley outside its entrance. "I've always dreamed of seeing Elvis big," Yoali says, "In my mind he is so large, bigger even than this."

Danny Uwnawich. Owner of Melodyland, a small, 3-bedroom version of Graceland in California's San Fernando Valley. Highlight: a white wrought-iron gate surrounding his home. Like the gate at Graceland, it's shaped like an open music book. According to Uwnawich, "The only people who have those gates is me and Him."

A strong bolt of lightning can contain as much as 100 million volts of electricity.

COWBOY TALK

Well, Hoss, maybe you can't be a cowboy, but you can still talk like one. Here are a few phrases to practice. Save 'em until you can find a way to use 'em in conversation. And smile when you say them, son.

"He's crooked enough to sleep on a corkscrew": He's dishonest.

"Raised on prunes and proverbs": A religious person.

"Coffin varnish": Whiskey.

"Fat as a well-fed needle": Poor.

"Deceitful beans": Beans that give you gas. (They talk behind your back.)

"Got a pill in his stomach that he can't digest": Shot dead.

"She's like a turkey gobbler in a hen pen": She's proud.

"He's like a breedin' jackass in a tin barn": He's noisy.

"Fryin' size but plumb salty": A senior citizen.

"Quicker 'n you can spit 'n holler 'Howdy!' ": Very fast.

"Studying to be a half-wit": Stupid or crazy.

"Built like a snake on stilts": Tall.

"Shy on melody, but strong on noise": A bad singer.

"Weasel smart": Very crafty.

"Scarce as bird dung in a cuckoo clock": Hard to find.

"Dry as the dust in a mummy's pocket": Very dry.

"In the lead when tongues was handed out": Talks too much.

"If he closed one eye he'd look like a needle": Very skinny.

"He lives in a house so small he can't cuss his cat without getting fur in his mouth": He's a tightwad.

"He died of throat trouble": He was hung.

DUBIOUS ACHIEVERS

Here are some of the stranger people
listed in the Guiness Book of World Records:

R andy Ober, Bentonville, Arkansas
Achievement: Spit a wad of tobacco 47 feet, 7 inches in 1982.

Joe Ponder, Love Valley, North Carolina
Achievement: Lifted a 606-pound pumpkin 18 inches off the ground
with his teeth in 1985.

Neil Sullivan, Birmingham, England
Achievement: Carried a large bag of "household coal" 34 miles on
May 24, 1986. It took him 12 hours and 45 minutes.

Travis Johnson, Elsberry, Missouri
Achievement: Held 9 baseballs in his hand "without any adhesives"
in 1989.

David Beattie and Adrian Simons, London, England
Achievement: Rode up and down escalators at the Top Shop in London for 101 hours in 1989. Estimated distance of travel: 133.19 miles.

Pieter van Loggerenberg, Hoedspruit, South Africa
Achievement: Played the accordion for 85 hours during a wildlife festival in 1987.

Michel Lotito, Grenoble, France
Achievement: Has been eating metal and glass since 1959; currently
he eats more than 2 pounds of metal every day. Since 1966 he has
eaten 10 bicycles, a supermarket food cart, 7 televisions, 6 chande-
liers, a coffin, and a Cessna airplane.

"Country" Bill White, Killeen, Texas
Achievement: Buried alive in a coffin, more than 6 feet underground,
for 341 days in July 1981. Only connection to the outside world: a 4-
inch tube used for feeding and breathing.

King Taufa'ahau, Tonga
Achievement: World's fattest king; weighed 462 pounds in 1976.

Alfred West
Achievement: Split a human hair into 17 different pieces "on eight different occasions."

Remy Bricka, Paris, France
Achievement: In 1988, using 13-foot-long floating "skis," he "walked" across the Atlantic Ocean from Tenerife, Spain, to Trinidad (a distance of 3,502 miles). The trip took 60 days.

Steve Urner, Tehachapi, California
Acheivement: Threw a dried, "100% organic" cow chip more than 266 feet on August 4, 1981.

N. Ravi, Tamil Nadu, India
Acheivement: Stood on one foot for 34 hours in 1982.

"Hercules" John Massis, Oostakker, Belgium
Achievement: Used teeth to stop a helicopter from taking off, 1979.

Zolilio Diaz, Spain
Achievement: Rolled a hoop from Mieres to Madrid, Spain, and back—a distance of more than 600 miles. It took him 18 days.

Nine employees of the Bruntsfield Bedding Centre, Scotland.
Achievement: Pushed a wheeled hospital bed 3,233 miles between June 21 and July 26, 1979.

Fred Jipp, New York City, New York
Achievement: Most illegal marriages: Between 1949 and 1981, using over 50 aliases, married 104 women in 27 states and 14 foreign countries. Sentenced to 34 years in prison and fined $336,000.

Octavio Guillen and Adriana Martinez, Mexico City, Mexico
Acheivement: Longest engagement: 67 years. They finally tied the knot in 1969. Both were age 82.

Sisters Jill Bradbury and Chris Humpish, London, England
Achievement: Made a bed (2 sheets, 1 undersheet, 1 blanket, 1 pillow, and a bedspread) in 19 seconds flat on October 8, 1985.

YOU ANIMAL!

A number of B.R.I. members have written to suggest we report on some of the more unusual ways animals reproduce or give birth. Okay, you've got it. Some of these are so weird they're hard to believe.

SQUID
The male squid's sperm are contained in 1/2-inch-long pencil-shaped "packages" called spermatophores, which are located in a pouch near his gills. When the male is ready to reproduce, he grabs some of the spermatophores with one of his tentacles and deposits them deep inside the gill chamber of a female squid. The spermatophores remain inside the female until she ovulates, when they explode into a cloud of sperm and fertilize the egg. (In some species the male's arm breaks off inside the female and remains there until it is absorbed by her body.)

SLOTHS
Sloths are the only land animals besides humans that regularly mate face to face. One important difference: they do it while hanging from tree branches by their arms.

SEA URCHINS
Sea urchins expel their semen directly into the surrounding seawater, doing nothing to ensure that it ever reaches an unfertilized egg. If the current is right, the semen will eventually be carried to an egg, and reproduction will take place.

"NOSE," OR "VAQUERO," FROGS
When the female is ready to reproduce, she lays 20-30 unfertilized eggs. Nearby male frogs surround the eggs, fertilize them, and then guard them for as long as two weeks. As soon as they can see tadpoles forming within the eggs, each frog immediately tries to "swallow" as many eggs as possible, depositing them in a large throat sac that extends from their chins to their thighs. The eggs remain there until the tadpoles metamorphosize completely into frogs, when they enter the world by crawling out of the father's mouth.

The gorilla's scientific name is "Gorilla gorilla gorilla."

MUD TURTLES

The female mud turtle has a pair of bladders connected to her intestines that she uses to build a nesting pit for her eggs. When she is ready to lay her fertilized eggs, she fills the bladders with water, and then partially empties them over the patch of dirt she wants to use for her nest. Then she starts digging, emptying the rest of the water in her bladders as she digs. When the bladders are empty, she returns to the water to refill them, then returns to the nest and continues digging. When she finishes, she kicks her eggs into the hole with her feet or tail, and covers the nest with fresh mud.

EUROPEAN CUCKOOS

Like all species of cuckoos, the European cuckoo does not build its own nest. Instead, it lays its eggs in the nests of other species of birds. Some types of cuckoos remove the original eggs from the nest, other types leave them in the nest, and the host mother raises all the young as if they were her own. But the offspring of the European cuckoo are more aggressive than most: a few hours after one is born it begins kicking uncontrollably, an involuntary response that lasts about four days. By that time, the fledgling has usually kicked everything out of the nest—including any other baby birds.

SNAILS

Snails practice a form of foreplay in which they shoot chalky "love darts" at each other to determine if they are members of the same species. Because snails are hermaphrodites—they have male and female sex organs—each snail will impregnate the other.

GREAT GREY SLUGS

Like snails, grey slugs are hermaphrodites and engage in foreplay. But grey slug foreplay consists of circling one another for hours, generating lots of slime in the process. Then they mate while hanging from ropes of slime.

DUCKS

According to one study, young male ducks are often disinterested in sex—even to the point of resisting the advances of females who are "in the mood." Sometimes the ducks appear to make elaborate excuses for why they cannot have sex, such as chasing away an imaginary enemy, taking an unneeded bath, etc. But the male ducks make up for it in later life: once they select a mate, they become "thoroughgoing lechers."

AFRICAN ELEPHANTS

According to at least one study, female elephants act as midwives for one another when the hour of birth draws near. One researcher reported observing three female elephants leaving their herd and approaching a thicket. One of the females went into the thicket, while the other two stood guard outside, driving away any elephant or other animal that tried to approach. After a while the sentries returned to the herd, followed shortly afterwards by the third elephant and her newborn.

SPIDERS

Because the male spider has no sex organ, he has to squeeze sperm from his belly onto his web, which he then picks up with his antennae before going off in search of a female spider. Male spiders also have to be careful once they find a female; if they aren't careful, the female will bite their head off during sex.

PRAYING MANTISES

As soon as the male praying mantis mounts the female, the female bites his head off. Undeterred, the male continues mating while the female eats his shoulders and upper abdomen. Unlike most other creatures, the male mantis's brain *prevents* him from releasing sperm, so the female *has* to bite his head off.

BEES

Only one male bee in a hive has the right to mate with the Queen, a process that takes about two seconds. When the male bee pulls away, his penis breaks off and remains inside the Queen, while he falls to the bottom of the hive and bleeds to death.

SNAKES

Female snakes mate with several male snakes during each mating cycle and can store sperm in their bodies for months. According to one theory, snakes do this in order to have a "sperm contest" inside their bodies, somehow allowing only the healthiest sperm to fertilize their eggs. This increases the number of live births per season, increasing the chance that the species will survive.

Secret Stash: FBI Director J. Edgar Hoover kept a collection of pornography locked in his desk.

THE CANDIDATE WHO NEVER STOPPED RUNNING

*Harold Stassen almost won the GOP nomination for president in 1948.
Did something "snap" when he lost? No one knows for sure,
but he kept on running...and running...and running...*

BACKGROUND. Harold Stassen was the Republican "Boy Wonder" of Minnesota politics in the 1930s. He was elected governor of the state in 1937 at the age of 31, and re-elected in 1940 and 1942. He was widely regarded—by friends *and* foes—as presidential timber.

THE SURE THING: 1948 was the presidential election Republicans had been waiting for: FDR was dead, and Harry Truman's approval rating had slipped below 30%. The Republican nominee—whoever he was—was a shoo-in to claim the Oval Office. And Harold Stassen was a front-runner for the nomination.

Stassen steamrolled through the Nebraska, Wisconsin, and Pennsylvania primaries. And he lost New Jersey by only 600 votes, despite the fact that Governor Thomas E. Dewey of New York was the favorite son of a neighboring state. Next, he stormed West Virginia, winning 117,000 of the state's 139,000 votes. He looked unstoppable—until he got to Oregon.

HOW HE LOST: Stassen had agreed to debate Dewey on May 17, 1948—only days before the Oregon primary—on the single issue of whether or not the Communist Party should be banned in the U.S. Stassen debated in favor of the ban; Dewey opposed it.

Stassen was the first candidate to speak, and he ripped into the Reds. "These Communist organizations are not really political parties. They actually are fifth columns....Governor Dewey's position in effect means a soft policy towards Communism...we must not coddle Communism with legality." One broadcaster later described Stassen's delivery as being the "assured and authoritative delivery of a man comfortable with command."

Next came Dewey's turn to reply. He didn't defend Communism, but he urged restraint in dealing with it: "The people of this country are being asked to outlaw Communism. That means this: Shall we in America, in order to defeat a totalitarian regime which we detest, voluntarily adopt the methods of that system?...I am unalterably, wholeheartedly, unswervingly against any scheme to write laws outlawing people because of their religious, political, social, or economic ideas."

Dewey was an experienced district attorney, and his defense of his position was eloquent and masterful. In fact, he took such command of the debate that Stassen began to panic. Tom Swaford, a broadcaster who was there, described Stassen's reaction:

> The Minnesotan was a different man. As he responded, he was wearing the kind of half smile a boxer puts on after taking a damaging blow when he wants the judges to think it didn't hurt. The radio audience couldn't see that, of course, but it could hear the uncertain, diffident delivery that had replaced the earlier booming confidence. The smooth flow was gone. I thought at the moment that we were watching a man who had not done his homework and was now aware of it.

Stassen's rebuttal was so weak that Dewey shot back: "I gather from Mr. Stassen's remarks that he has completely surrendered." In a way, Stassen had. And in doing so, he lost more than just the debate: he lost the Oregon primary...and he lost his momentum. In the end, Dewey edged Stassen out for the Republican nomination.

WORLD-CLASS LOSER: Some politicians would have retired gracefully after such a humiliating defeat, but not Stassen. He showed the form that makes him a truly *world-class* loser, continuing to run in races he had no chance to win for the next 45 years! He ran for president in 1952, 1964, 1968, 1976, 1980, 1984, 1988, and 1992. He lost races for Mayor of Philadelphia (1962), senator of Minnesota (1978), another term as governor of Minnesota (1982), and a bid for Congress (1986).

Stassen became a national joke, usually referred to as "the perennial candidate." In the 1992 Republican National Convention, delegates made fun of him with their "Stop Stassen" buttons. "The ridicule bothers me," said the 85-year-old candidate, "but it doesn't stop me....Every one of the ten times [I've run], there has been some solid result." Besides, he adds, "Winning is not the primary concern. My primary concern is to move America."

Pop singer Michael Jackson collects mannequins.

ONE NUCLEAR BOMB CAN RUIN YOUR WHOLE DAY

*We don't want to make you paranoid, but
all of these incidents really happened.*

1. In July 1956 a B-47 aircraft plowed into a storage igloo 20 miles outside of Cambridge, England. The plane's jet fuel burst into flames almost immediately, but for some reason didn't ignite the contents of the igloo. A lucky thing, too—it contained three Mark 6 nuclear bombs.

2. In 1958 a B-47E accidentally dropped a nuclear bomb into a Mars Bluff, South Carolina, family's vegetable garden. The bomb didn't explode, but it did damage five houses and a church. Air Force officials apologized.

3. In 1961 a B-52 dropped two 24-megaton bombs on a North Carolina farm. According to one physicist: "Only a single switch prevented the bombs from detonating."

4. In 1966 another B-52 carrying four 20-megaton bombs crashed in Palomares, Spain—with one of the bombs splashing into the Mediterranean Sea. It took the U.S. 6th fleet—using 33 ships and 3,000 men—several weeks to find the missing bomb.

5. In 1980 a repairman working on a Titan II missile in Arkansas dropped a wrench—which bounced off the floor, punctured the missile, and set off an explosion that blew the top off the silo and threw the warhead 600 feet into the air.

6. Did June 3, 1980, seem tense to you? It did to the Strategic Air Command in Omaha, Nebraska. Their computers detected a Soviet submarine missile attack in progress. Within minutes, more than 100 B-52s were in the air, but the SAC soon called off the counterattack—the computers had made a mistake. The culprit: a 46¢ computer chip. Three days later the same mistake happened again.

According to the FBI, most burglaries occur in winter.

FAMILY HOLIDAYS

Every year, Americans celebrate holidays honoring our fathers, our mothers, our grandparents, and even our mothers-in-law. Whose idea were these events? Are they sponsored by florists and card companies?

THE HOLIDAY: Mother's Day (Second Sunday in May)

ORIGIN: The result of a one-woman crusade launched in 1908 by Anna Jarvis, a West Virginia schoolteacher whose mother had died three years earlier. On May 10, 1908, she persuaded pastors in nearby Grafton, West Virginia, and Philadelphia, Pennsylvania, to hold Mother's Day services in their churches. (They handed out carnations, Anna's mother's favorite flower.) From there she launched a letter-writing campaign to U.S. governors, congressmen, clergy, media, etc. She wasn't immediately successful, but by 1914 Congress endorsed the idea. On May 9, 1914, President Wilson issued a proclamation establishing the holiday.

COMMERCIALISM: Jarvis—who had no children—grew to hate the holiday she had created. She railed against the commercialism that surrounded it, and especially loathed flowers and Mother's Day cards. "Any mother would rather have a line of the worst scribble from her son or daughter," she complained, "than any fancy greeting card." She became a recluse who never left her house, posting "Warning—Stay Away" signs on her front lawn. She refused to give interviews, but a reporter posing as a deliveryman managed to speak with her. "She told me with terrible bitterness that she was sorry she had ever started Mother's Day," he wrote.

THE HOLIDAY: Father's Day (Third Sunday in June)

ORIGIN: Anna Jarvis's "success" inspired a number of other Americans to begin work for a Father's Day. First among them was Sonora Smart Dodd, a Spokane, Washington, housewife whose father had raised six children alone after her mother died in childbirth. She proposed making Father's Day the *first* Sunday in June (the month of her father's birthday), but local religious leaders vetoed the date; they needed more time to prepare sermons on fatherhood. So they settled on the third Sunday. The holiday was first celebrated in Spokane on June 19, 1910.

It took the all-male U.S. Congress longer to acknowledge Father's Day than it took them to recognize Mother's Day: The reason: They feared voters would think it was too self-serving. Although President Wilson personally observed the holiday, he refused to issue a proclamation making it official. In 1924 Calvin Coolidge encouraged state governments to enact their own Father's Days, but he too declined to make it a federal holiday. Finally in 1972, Father's Day was proclaimed a federal holiday by President Nixon.

COMMERCIALISM: Although she turned down many offers to endorse products, Dodd had nothing against giving gifts on Father's Day. "After all," she said, "why should the greatest giver of gifts not be on the receiving end at least once a year?" When the day's commercialism was decried in the 1950s, Dodd defended it again: "I'm convinced that giving gifts is a sacred part of the holiday, as the giver is spiritually enriched in the tribute paid his father." Dodd died in 1978, but she'd probably be happy to know that 15% of the 7 million electric shavers sold in the U.S. every year are bought for Father's Day, and Americans annually spend some $20 million on Father's Day ties.

THE HOLIDAY: Grandparent's Day (First Sunday after Labor Day)

ORIGIN: Michael Goldgar, a grandparent himself, came up with the idea after visiting his aunt in an Atlanta, Georgia, nursing home. Using $11,000 of his savings, he made 17 trips to Washington, D.C. over the next 7 years to lobby for a national holiday. President Carter signed the holiday into law in 1978.

COMMERCIALISM: Today Americans send more than 4 million Grandparent's Day cards a year.

THE HOLIDAY: Mother-in-Law's Day (Fourth Sunday in October)

ORIGIN: In 1981 the U.S. House of Representatives passed a resolution establishing Mother-in-Law's Day. But the Senate never passed a similar resolution, and the bill hasn't been signed into law.

COMMERCIALISM: Some 800,000 Americans mail Mother-in-Law's Day cards annually.

THE DUKE

Some people call John Wayne an American hero, others call him a Neanderthal right-winger. Neither side really knows much about him, but the B.R.I. does. Here are some facts about the Duke.

As a boy, Wayne learned to handle a gun by shooting rattlesnakes while his father plowed the land. But, according to one biographer, the experience gave Wayne nightmares of "slithering, disembodied snake heads coming at him. [He] often awoke in a cold sweat in the middle of the night—but he kept these fears to himself."

After finishing high school, Wayne tried to get into the U.S. Naval Academy...but was turned down. In later years, referring to the Academy's rejection, Wayne claimed "I'd probably be a retired admiral by now." (However, during World War II, he received an exemption for being the father of four children.)

Wayne created his tough-guy image only because he didn't think he could act. Later in his career he explained to *The New York Times*: "When I started, I knew I was no actor and I went to work on this Wayne thing. It was as deliberate a projection as you'll ever see. I figured I needed a gimmick, so I dreamed up the drawl, the squint, and a way of moving meant to suggest that I wasn't looking for trouble but would just as soon throw a bottle at your head as not. I practiced in front of a mirror."

After attending Governor Ronald Reagan's inauguration in 1971, the Duke spotted a group of Vietnam War protesters waving Vietcong flags. Enraged, he charged into the crowd screaming, "You dirty no–good bastards," and punching wildly. Police intervened, and the scuffle quickly ended; however, the next day, one of the protesters filed a complaint with the local police, claiming Wayne had disturbed the peace. Police refused to prosecute.

Wayne died in 1979. His funeral was held at 5 a.m., and his body was buried in an unmarked grave to prevent fans from mobbing the burial site. Four fresh "decoy" graves were also dug to prevent anyone from positively identifying the real one.

Calling Mr. Sartre: 27% of U.S. male college students believe life is "a meaningless existential hell."

A SLICE OF LIFE

A slice of the history of the most popular "ethnic" food in America.

ORIGIN. The ancient Greeks invented pizza. The most accomplished bakers of the ancient world, they made a variety of breads topped with spices, herbs, and vegetables. Their first pizza was designed as a kind of "edible plate," with the thick crust around the edge serving as a handle.

How did pizza become Italian? The Greeks occupied part of Italy for 6 centuries; one of their legacies is the popularity of pizza there.

TOMATOES
• Early pizzas featured cheese, herbs, vegetables, and fish or meat—but no tomatoes. Tomatoes, a New World food, didn't reach Italy until the mid-1500s—and weren't popular until the late 19th century because people believed they were poisonous.
• In 1889 pizza maker Raffaele Esposito added tomatoes to pizza for the first time. The reason: He wanted to make a pizza for Italian Queen Margherita in the colors of the Italian flag—red, white, and green—and needed something red to go with white mozzarella cheese and green basil.

PIZZA IN THE U.S.
• The first American pizzeria was opened in New York in 1905. By the early 1920s, family-run pizzerias were popping up all over the American Northeast...but it was still considered an exotic food.
• American G.I.s returning from Italy after World War II made pizza popular throughout the U.S. But it wasn't until the '60s that it became a fad...and a movie may have been responsible. In the controversial 1961 film *Splendor in the Grass*, Warren Beatty asks a waitress, "Hey, what is pizza?" The waitress takes him "out back," introducing him to pizza and a bit more.
• Today Americans eat more than 30 million slices of pizza per day—or 350 slices a second—and spend as much as $25 billion a year on pizza.
• Pepperoni is the most popular pizza topping nationwide; anchovies are the least favorite.

MEET THE BEATLES

The Beatles were personalities, as entertaining at press conferences as they were on record. To prove it, here are excerpts from Beatle press conferences held in the mid-1960s, when the group had become popular. At the time, rock bands were still considered vacuous non-artists. It's interesting to see how the Beatles changed that.

Reporter: Beethoven figures in one of your songs. What do you think of Beethoven?
Ringo: He's great. Especially his poetry.

Reporter: Ringo, why do you wear two rings on each hand?
Ringo: Because I can't fit them through my nose.

Reporter: When you do a new song, how do you decide who sings the lead?
John: We just get together and whoever knows most of the words sings the lead.

Reporter: Do you think it's wrong to set such a bad example to teenagers, smoking the way you do?
Ringo: It's better than being alcoholics.

Reporter: What do you think of the criticism that you are not very good?
George: We're not.

Reporter: What do you believe is the reason you are the most popular singing group today?
John: We've no idea. If we did, we'd get four long-haired boys, put them together and become their managers.

Reporter: You've admitted to being agnostics. Are you also irreverent?
Paul: We are agnostics...so there's no point in being irreverent.

Reporter: Why do teenagers stand up and scream piercingly and painfully when you appear?
Paul: None of us know. But we've heard that teenagers go to our shows just to scream. A lot of them don't even want to listen be-

---

Not Tonight, Dear: An estimated one in five American adults—some 38 million—don't like sex.

cause they have our records. We kind of like the screaming teenagers. If they want to pay their money and sit out there and shout, that's their business. We aren't going to be like little dictators and say, "You've got to shut up." The commotion doesn't bother us anymore. It's come to be like working in a bell factory. You don't hear the bells after a while.

Reporter: Ringo, why do you think you get more fan mail than anyone else in the group?
Ringo: I don't know. I suppose it's because more people write me.

Reporter: Do you date much?
Ringo: What are you doing tonight?

Reporter: How do you like this welcome [in the U.S.]?
Ringo: So this is America. They all seem out of their minds.

Reporter: What do you do when you're cooped up in a hotel room between shows?
George: We ice skate.

Reporter: How did you find America?
Ringo: We went to Greenland and made a left turn.

Reporter: Would you like to walk down the street without being recognized?
John: We used to do this with no money in our pockets. There's no point in it.

Reporter: Are you scared when crowds scream at you?
John: More so in Dallas than in other places perhaps.

Reporter: Is it true you can't sing?
John (pointing to George): Not me. Him.

Reporter: Why don't you smile George?
George: I'll hurt my lips.

Reporter: What's your reaction to a Seattle psychiatrist's opinion that you are a menace?
George: Psychiatrists are a menace.

Reporter: Do you plan to record any anti-war songs?
John: All our songs are anti-war.

Ronald Reagan is the only U.S. president to have performed in Las Vegas.

Reporter: Does all the adulation from teenage girls affect you?
John: When I feel my head start to swell, I look at Ringo and know perfectly well we're not supermen.

Reporter: Do you resent fans ripping up your sheets for souvenirs?
Ringo: No I don't mind. So long as I'm not in them while the ripping is going on.

Reporter: Do you follow politics?
John: I get spasms of being intellectual. I read a bit about politics but I don't think I'd vote for anyone. No message from any of those phony politicians is coming through to me.

Reporter: What's the most unusual request you've had?
John: I wouldn't like to say.

Reporter: What do you plan to do next?
John: We're not going to fizzle out in half a day. But afterwards I'm not going to change into a tap dancing musical. I'll just develop what I'm doing at the moment, although whatever I say now I'll change my mind next week. I mean, we all know that bit about: "It won't be the same when you're twenty-five." I couldn't care less. This isn't show business. It's something else. This is different from anything that anybody imagines. You don't go on from this. You do this and then you finish.

Reporter: Do you like topless bathing suits?
Ringo: We've been wearing them for years.

Reporter: Girls rushed toward my car because it had press identification and they thought I met you. How do you explain this phenomenon?
John: You're lovely to look at.

Reporter: How do you add up success?
John, Paul, George, Ringo: Money.

Reporter: What will you do when Beatlemania subsides?
John: Count the money.

Reporter: What do you think of the Bomb?
Paul: It's disturbing that people should go around blowing us up, but if an atom bomb should explode I'd say, "Oh well, no point in saying anything else, is there." People are so crackers. I know the

bomb is ethically wrong but I won't go around crying. I suppose I could do something like wearing those "ban the bomb" things, but it's something like religion that I don't think about. It doesn't fit in with my life.

Reporter: What do you think of space shots?
John: You see one, you've seen them all.

Reporter: What do you think about the pamphlet calling you four Communists?
Paul: Us, Communists? Why, we can't be Communists. We're the world's number one capitalists. Imagine us. Communists!

Reporter: What's your biggest fear?
John: The thing I'm afraid of is growing old. I hate that. You get old and you've missed it somehow. The old always resent the young and vice-versa.

Reporter: What about the recent criticism of your lyrics?
Paul: If you start reading things into them you might as well start singing hymns.

Reporter: You were at the Playboy Club last night. What did you think of it?
Paul: The Playboy and I are just good friends.

Reporter: George, is the place you were brought up a bit like Greenwich Village?
George: No. More like The Bowery.

Reporter: Ringo, how do you manage to find all those parties?
Ringo: I don't know. I just end up at them.
Paul: On tour we don't go out much. Ringo's always out, though.
John: Ringo freelances.

Reporter: There's a "Stamp Out the Beatles" movement underway in Detroit. What are you going to do about it?
Paul: We're going to start a campaign to stamp out Detroit.

Reporter: Who thought up the name, Beatles?
Paul: I thought of it.
Reporter: Why?
Paul: Why not?

Some 4% of Americans are more likely to vote *for* a candidate who has an extramarital affair.

WORDPLAY

We use these words all the time, but most of us have no idea where they came from. Fortunately, the B.R.I. is on the job, ready to supply their history and make your brief (?) stay in the john an educational one.

POTLUCK. In the Middle Ages, cooks threw all their leftovers into a pot of water that was kept boiling most of the time. This makeshift stew was eaten by the family or fed to strangers when no other food was available. Since food was thrown in at random, its quality and taste depended entirely on luck.

JUKE BOX. The term "juke" was originally a New Orleans slang expression meaning "to have sex." Juke boxes got their name because they were popular in houses of prostitution known as juke joints.

SLUSH FUND. "Slush" was originally the name for kitchen grease from the galleys of naval sailing ships. Most of this sludge was used to lubricate masts of the ship; the rest was sold with other garbage whenever the ship entered port. Money made from the sale was kept in a "slush fund," used to buy items for enlisted men.

HAYWIRE. Bales of hay are held together with tightly strung wire. If the wire snaps, it whips around wildly and can injure people standing nearby.

BROKE. Many banks in post-Renaissance Europe issued small, porcelain "borrower's tiles" to their creditworthy customers. Like credit cards, these tiles were imprinted with the owner's name, his credit limit, and the name of the bank. Each time the customer wanted to borrow money, he had to present the tile to the bank teller, who would compare the imprinted credit limit with how much the customer had already borrowed. If the borrower was past the limit, the teller "broke" the tile on the spot.

BOMB. The term "bomb," long in use as a name for explosive devices, was first used to describe a bad theater play by Grevile Corks, theater critic for the *New York Standard* in the 1920s. When one

---

Sherlock Holmes kept his tobacco in the toe of a Persian slipper.

particularly bad play closed after only two performances, Corks wryly observed: "Since the producers were so eager to clear the theater, they might have tried a smoke bomb instead. It would have been quicker for the audience, and less painful." The column was so popular that Corks started the "Bomb of the Year" award for the worst play on Broadway.

OUTSKIRTS. As medieval English towns grew too big to fit inside town walls, houses and other buildings were built outside them. These buildings surrounded the wall the same way a woman's skirt surrounds her waist—and became known as the town's "skirts." People living on the outer fringes of even thesebuildings were considered to be living in the outskirtsof the town.

BANGS. In the early 19th century, it was common for English noblemen to maintain elaborate stables for their horses. But hard times in following years made stables an expensive luxury. Many nobles were forced to reduce their staffs—which meant that the remaining grooms had less time to spend on each horse. One innovation that resulted: instead of spending hours trimming each horse's tail, grooms cut all tail hair the same length, a process they called "banging off." Eventually the "banged" look became popular as a woman's hairstyle, too.

HUSBAND. Comes from the German words hus and bunda, which mean "house" and "owner." The word originally had nothing to do with marital status, except for the fact that home ownership made husbands extremely desirable marriage partners.

WIFE. Comes from the Anglo-Saxon words wifan and mann, which mean "weaver" and "human." In ancient times there were no words that specifically described males or females; one way Anglo-Saxons denoted the difference was to use the word wifmann or "weaver-human," since weaving was a task traditionally performed by women.

PEN KNIFE. One problem with quill pens was that their tips dulled quickly and needed constant sharpening. Knife makers of the 15th century produced special knives for that purpose; their sharp blades and compact size made them popular items.

ON A CAROUSEL

*Wow! Here's more fascinating, but useless,
information—a B.R.I. specialty. This batch was
contributed by B.R.I. member Jack Mingo.*

THE CAROUSEL

The name *carousel* originated with a popular 12th-century Arabian horseman's game called *carosellos*, or "little wars." The rules were simple: teams rode in circles throwing perfume-filled clay balls from one rider to another. If a ball of perfume broke, the team lost. Their penalty: they carried the smell of defeat with them for days after.

The game was brought to Europe by knights returning from the Crusades, and it evolved into elaborate, colorful tourneys called *carrousels*.

Making the Rounds. In the 17th century, the French developed a device to help young nobles train for carrousels. It featured legless wooden horses attached to a center pole. As the center pole turned (powered by real horses, mules, or people), the nobles on their wooden steeds would try to spear hanging rings with their lances. (This later evolved into the "catching the brass ring" tradition.) The carousel device gradually evolved into a popular form of entertainment. The peasants rode on barrellike horses; the nobles rode in elaborate chariots and boats.

The Machine Age. Until the 1860s carousels, which had become popular all over Europe, were still dependent on horses and mules for power. But that changed when Frederick Savage, an English engineer, designed a portable steam engine, which could turn as many as four rows of horses on a 48-foot diameter wheel. Later, Savage also patented designs for the overhead camshafts and gears that moved the wooden horses up and down. This new type of carousel—called a "round-about" (later, merry-go-round)—was a huge success throughout Europe.

In the U.S. Ads for carousels first appeared in America as early as 1800. Typically, offering fun was not enough—carousel owners

---

Stargazer: Galileo believed in astrology.

also felt obliged to claim that doctors recommended the rides to improve blood circulation.

THE FERRIS WHEEL

A 33-year-old American engineer named George Washington Ferris designed a giant "observation wheel" for Chicago's World's Columbian Exhibition in 1893, as an American counterpart to the Eiffel Tower (which had been unveiled four years earlier). At 250 feet in diameter, this first Ferris wheel could carry more than 2,000 passengers high above the city...and bring them smoothly back down. It was the hit of the fair; some 1.5 million people rode in it.

It was such a success, writes Tad Tuleja in *Namesakes*, that "it fostered many imitators at the turn of the century, the most notable being a 300-foot wheel constructed for the 1897 London Fair and a 197-foot one built for Vienna's Prater Park in 1896....These giants proved impractical, of course, for the many carnival midways where Ferris's invention now prospers; the average traveling wheel today is about 50 feet in diameter."

In 1904 Ferris's original wheel, which cost $385,000 to build, was dismantled and sold for scrap. It brought in less than $2,000.

ROLLER COASTERS

The roller coaster was invented by an enterprising showman in Russia who built elaborate ice slides in St. Petersburg during the 15th century. Catherine the Great enjoyed the ice slides so much that she ordered tiny wheels added to the sleds so she could ride in the summer.

• The first "modern" roller coaster was built in Coney Island in 1884, more than 400 years later.

• Believe it or not, statistically, roller coasters are much safer than merry-go-rounds. One reason: people rarely decide to jump off a roller coaster while the ride is still moving. Also, the safety restraints work better. Despite that, twenty-seven people died on roller coasters between 1973 and 1988.

• Designers purposely create the illusion that your head is in danger of being chopped by a low overhang at the bottom of a hill. Actually there's almost always a nine-foot clearance.

• Americans took an estimated 214 million roller coaster rides last year.

OXYMORONS

*Here's a list of oxymorons sent to us by B.R.I. member Peter McCracken.
Peter writes: "I've been collecting these for a while...and sometimes spend
valuable throne time trying to come up with new ones. In case you
don't know, an oxymoron is a common phrase made of two
words that appear to be contradictory."*

Military Intelligence	Death Benefits
Light Heavyweight	Upside Down
Jumbo Shrimp	Original Copy
Painless Dentistry	Random Order
Drag Race	Irrational Logic
Friendly Fire	Business Ethics
Criminal Justice	Slightly Pregnant
Permanent Temporary	Holy Wars
Amtrack Schedule	Half Dead
Genuine Imitation	Supreme Court
Mandatory Option	Even Odds
Protective Custody	Baby Grand
Limited Nuclear War	Inside Out
Dear Occupant	Fresh Frozen
Standard Deviation	Moral Majority
Freezer Burn	Truth In Advertising
Pretty Ugly	Friendly Takeover
Industrial Park	Good Grief
Loyal Opposition	United Nations
Eternal Life	Baked Alaska
Natural Additives	Plastic Glasses
Student Teacher	Peacekeeping Missiles
Educational Television	Somewhat Addictive
Nonworking Mother	Science Fiction
Active Reserves	Open Secret
Full-Price Discount	Unofficial Record
Limited Immunity	Tax Return

According to zoologists, deer like to play tag. They tag each other using their hooves.

IT'S IN THE CARDS

*Do you like to play poker?…gin rummy?…bridge…or (in the
bathroom) solitaire? Then maybe we can interest you in
reading a couple of pages on the origin of playing cards.*

H ISTORY
Origin. The first playing cards are believed to have come
from the Mamelukes, people of mixed Turkish and Mongo-
lian blood who ruled Egypt from 1250 to 1517. Like today's standard playing cards, the Mamelukes' deck had 52 cards and four suits
(swords, polo sticks, cups, and coins), with three face cards and 10
numbered cards per suit. Mameluke decks did not include queens
or jacks; they used "Deputy Kings" and "Second," or "Under-
Deputy Kings" instead.

European Popularity. In the mid-1300s the cards were introduced
to Europe, where they spawned a gaming craze similar to the Monopoly or Trivial Pursuit fads of the 20th century. Historians measure their popularity not by how many times people wrote about
them (cards received little or no mention) or by the number of
decks that survive (few did), but by the number of cities that
banned them. Paris was one of the first: it outlawed card-playing
among "working men" in 1377. Other cities soon followed, and by
the mid-1400s anti-card sentiments reached a fervor. During one
public demonstration in Nuremburg, led by the Catholic priest and
saint John Capistran (better known by his Spanish name, San Juan
Capistrano), more than 40,000 decks of cards, tens of thousands of
dice, and 3,000 backgammon boards were burned in a public bon-
fire. None of the attempts to eliminate card-playing were successful; in fact, cards are one of only a few items of the 12th century
that survive almost unchanged to this day.

THAT SUITS ME FINE
• The four modern suits—hearts, clubs, spades, and diamonds—
originated in France around 1480, at a time when card makers were
beginning to mass produce decks for the first time.

• The simple single-color designs were easier to paint using stencils and cheaper to produce than the more elaborate designs that had been popular in the past.

• Not all today's cards use diamonds, hearts, spades, and clubs as suit symbols. Traditional German cards use hearts, leaves, acorns, and bells; Swiss cards use roses, shields, acorns, and bells; and Italian cards use swords, batons, cups, and coins.

CARD FACTS

• For more than 500 years, playing cards were much larger than today's versions and didn't have the *indices* (the numbers, letters, and suit marks on the top left corners) that let you read the cards in a tightly held hand. Card players either had to hold their cards in both hands to read them (which made them easy for other players to see), or else had to memorize them and then play with none of the cards showing. In the mid-19th century card makers began adding the indices in decks called "squeezers" (which let you hold the cards closely together).

• It was in "squeezer" decks that the jacks became a part of the deck. Earlier they had been called knaves, which, like kings, started with the letter "K." To avoid the confusion of having two types of cards with the letter "K", card makers changed *knaves* to *jacks* (a slang term for the knaves already) and used the letter "J" instead.

• The first face cards were elaborately painted, full-length portraits. While beautiful, they posed a serious disadvantage: when they were dealt upside down, novice players tended to turn them right-side-up—telling experienced players how many face cards were in their hand. Card makers corrected this in the 19th century, when they began making decks with "double-ended" face cards.

• The joker is the youngest—and the only American—card in the deck. It was added in the mid-19th century, where it was the highest-value card in an American game called Euchre. From there it gained popularity as a "wild" card in poker and other games.

• In November 1742 an Englishman named Edmond Hoyle published a rule book on the popular game of Whist. The book was so successful that dozens of writers plagiarized it, even using the name "Hoyle's" in the pirate editions. Today's "Hoyle's" rule books are descendants of the *plagiarized* versions, not the original.

• The word "ace" is derived from the Latin word *as*, which means the "smallest unit of coinage."

THE SINGING CHIPMUNKS

*Alvin, Simon, and Theodore are the most famous chipmunks
in the world. This mini-biography was taken from* Behind
the Hits, *by Bob Shannon and John Javna.*

THE WITCH DOCTOR

In 1957, a 38-year-old songwriter named Ross Bagdasarian
(stage name: David Seville) was sitting in his study when an
idea for a new song came to him.

"I looked up from my desk and saw a book called *Duel with the
Witch Doctor*," he recalled. "All the teenage records seemed to have
one thing in common back then—you couldn't understand any of
the lyrics. So I decided to create a 'Witch Doctor' who would give
advice to the lovelorn in his own language—a kind of qualified
gibberish."

Bagdasarian quickly wrote and recorded the song…but was
stumped about what kind of voice to use for the witch doctor
(Whose advice consisted of : "Oo-ee, Oo-ah-ah, Ting-tang, Walla-
walla Bing-bang.")

FINDING A VOICE

One day Bagdasarian was fooling around with a tape recorder, playing with the speeds. He sang into the machine while it was running
at half-speed…and then played it back at full-speed. The result: It
sounded like he'd swallowed helium…or played a 45-rpm record at
78 rpm. It was exactly the voice he'd been looking for. (Note: Remember this was 1957; today's sophisticated recording equipment
hadn't been invented yet.)

Bagdasarian brought his finished tape to Liberty Records. "They
flipped," he said. Before 24 hours had elapsed, "The Witch Doctor"
was on its way to record stores. And within weeks it was the #1
song in the nation. In all, it sold about 1.5 million copies.

THE SINGING CHIPMUNKS

A year later, Liberty Records found itself in financial trouble. So
they asked Bagdasarian to come up with another song like "The

Witch Doctor." He agreed to try.

He decided to turn the Witch Doctor's voice into several different characters. As his son recalls: "He didn't know whether to make them into hippos or elephants or beetles or what. He came up with the idea of chipmunks when he was driving in Yosemite National Park and this chipmunk almost dared him and his huge car to drive past. My dad was so taken with their audacious behavior that he decided to make these three singing characters chipmunks. He named them after three executives at Liberty Records. (Alvin: Al Bennett, the label president; Simon: Si Waronker, vice-chairman of the label; Theodore: Ted Keep, Liberty's chief recording engineer.)

"Then he took the song he'd written, 'The Chipmunk Song,' to Liberty and the president, Alvin's namesake, said, 'We need hits, not chipmunks.' My dad said, 'You have nothing to lose, why don't you put it out?' In the next seven weeks they sold 4.5 million records."

Ultimately, the first Chipmunk record sold more than 7 million copies; At the time, it was the fastest-selling record in history.

LIFE AFTER DEATH

The Chipmunks outlived Bagdasarian. He died in 1972 of a heart attack; eleven years later, in 1983, the Chipmunks emerged as stars of their own Saturday morning TV cartoon show. Today they rank as three of the most lucrative characters ever created in a pop song.

• • • •

THE "PURPLE PEOPLE EATER"

In 1958, a friend of actor/singer Sheb Wooley's told him a riddle he'd heard from his kid: "What flies, has one horn, has one eye, and eats people?" The answer: "A one-eyed, one-horned people eater." Wooley thought it was funny, and wrote a song based on it.

A short time later, he met with the president of MGM Records to decide on his next record. Wooley played every song he'd written, but there was nothing the guy liked. "You got anything else?" the president asked. "Well, yeah," Wooley said, "one more thing—but it's nothing you'd want to hear." The president insisted, so Wooley reluctantly played him "Purple People Eater." Three weeks later it was the #1 song in the country.

THE SECRETS OF A HARLEQUIN ROMANCE

Romance novels account for a hefty chunk of the paperback book market. If you're looking for a few extra bucks, writing one may be a way to pick them up. So, for you aspiring "writers," here are some facts and guidelines about Harlequin Romances.

VITAL STATS

History: Harlequin Books was founded in Winnipeg, Manitoba, in 1949 to reprint romance novels put out by the British publisher Mills & Boon. In 1958 Richard and Mary Bonnycastle bought the company, rechristened it Harlequin Enterprises, and set up headquarters in Toronto. Now, with more than 10 billion romances sold, Harlequin is the McDonalds of paperback publishing. They print books in some 17 languages and ships to more than 100 different countries.

Sales: In 1970 Harlequin sold 3 million books. Now it sells more than 200 million a year. The company estimates that every 6 seconds, another Harlequin romance is sold.

Market: Romance is the biggest-selling area of the paperback book market—25-40% of all mass-market paperback sales...and Harlequin has an estimated 80% of that market. Surveys show that romance addicts will spend up to $60 a month on romances (and read them in less than two hours apiece).

Audience: More than 100 million people worldwide read romances regularly—mostly in the U.S., Germany, France, and the U.K. But Harlequin reports that sales are growing steadily in Asia. Company surveys indicate that 50 percent of its North American readers are college-educated, and a third make more than $30,000 a year.

YOU CAN WRITE A ROMANCE

Tired of reading other people's fantasies? Think you've got what it takes to pen prose powerful enough to promote palpitations? Want to try your hand at writing a romance novel? Here are excerpts from the editorial

To avoid being trapped in a burning building, Hans Christian Anderson always carried a rope.

guidelines for a basic Harlequin romance. This is the information Harlequin supplies to all prospective writers, and we provide it here as a service to you.

Guidelines: "What we are looking for are romances with...strong believable characters, not stereotypes; stories that center on the development of the romance between the heroine and hero, with the emphasis on feelings and emotions."

Style: "Keep 'strong' language (swear words) and highly provocative, sensual language to a minimum.

"Descriptions of sex or sexual feeling should be kept to a minimum in Romances. Love scenes are fine, but the descriptions of such, which should not go on for pages, should deal with how the heroine feels (perhaps the hero, too)—her emotional responses, not just purely physical sensations. Leave a lot to the imagination. A kiss and an embrace, if well told, can be just as stimulating to the reader as pages of graphically described sensual scenes."

Heroine: "Generally, younger than the hero, relatively inexperienced sexually, though this fact need not be stressed. She should hold traditional (not to be equated with old-fashioned) moral standards....The heroine need not be a career woman, nor even a woman with a fascinating, different job....She may hold just an average job, earning average income; she may be unemployed. If she works in a traditional woman's job—secretarial, nursing, teaching, etc.—that's okay, too.

Hero: "Try to avoid excessive age difference; for instance, the 17-year-old heroine and the 37-year-old hero. He should be very attractive, worldly and successful in his field and, unlike the heroine, quite sexually experienced, and this fact may be implied."

SEND NOW!

Want more info? Send for complete guidelines. Enclose a self-addressed, stamped envelope to Harlequin Enterprises, Ltd., 225 Duncan Mill Road, Don Mills, Ontario, Canada M3B 3K9. (Don't quit your day job: Publishers receive up to 1,000 unsolicited manuscripts every month. For the few books they do buy, they pay advances between $1,000 and $15,000, with royalties of 7-8%.)

UNSUNG SUPERHEROES

Imagine inventing America's most popular comic character...and getting only $130 for it. That's what happened to these guys.

THE HEROS: Jerry Siegel and Joseph Shuster

WHAT THEY DID: Created Superman, the most popular comic book character in American history.

One night in 1934, 17-year-old Jerry Siegel, an aspiring comic book writer fresh out of high school, came up with the idea for Superman. He was so excited that at dawn he ran twelve blocks to his tell his friend and partner, Joseph Shuster.

The pair began drawing up cartoon panels showing their hero in action. They sent samples to newspaper comic strip editors all over the country, but no one was interested. Finally in 1938 DC Comics agreed to print a Superman comic and paid Siegel and Shuster $130—$10 a page for 13 pages of work. In addition, the two were hired as staff artists to draw future Superman comics.

Superman made his first appearance in June 1938. He was an instant smash. Over the years he inspired a radio show, animated cartoons, a TV series, movies, and licensed products. In the 1970s alone, Superman products grossed about $1 billion.

THE SAD FACTS: When Siegel and Shuster sold the first comic to DC for $130 and signed on as staff artists, they effectively signed away all rights to Superman. From then on, all the money went to DC Comics.

They continued drawing the strip for DC until 1948, when the company fired them for asking for a share of the profits. Both men filed suits against DC...which they ultimately lost. By the 1970s both were broke, living on money made by selling old comic books and other memorabilia they still owned. Shuster was unemployed, nearly blind, and living in a tiny apartment in Queens, New York.

Finally, in 1975, Warner Communications (owner of DC) voluntarily gave them pensions of $20,000 a year. In 1981 these were increased to $30,000—plus a $15,000 bonus after the first *Superman* film grossed $275 million. That was all the compensation the two men ever received for their creation.

PATRON SAINTS

The Roman Catholic Church has more than 5,000 saints, many of whom are "patron saints"—protectors of certain professions, sick people—even hobbies. Here are a few of the more interesting ones:

Saint Matthew: Patron Saint of Accountants. (He was a tax collector before becoming an apostle.)

Saint Joseph of Cupertino: Patron Saint of Air Travelers. (Nicknamed "The Flying Friar," he could levitate.)

Saint Fiacre: Patron Saint of Taxi Drivers, Hemorrhoid Sufferers, and Venereal Disease.

Saint Matrona: Patron Saint of Dysentery Sufferers.

Saint Louis IX of France: Patron Saint of Button Makers.

Saint Adrian of Nicomedia: Patron Saint of Arms Dealers.

Saint Anne: Patron Saint of Women in Labor. (Not to be confused with Saint John Thwing, Patron Saint of Women in *Difficult* Labor.)

Saint Nicholas of Myra (also known as Santa Claus): Patron Saint of Children *and* Pawnbrokers.

Saint Bernardino of Siena: Patron Saint of Advertisers and Hoarseness.

Saint Blaise: Patron Saint of Throats (he saved a child from choking) and Diseased Cattle (he also healed animals).

Saint Joseph: Patron Saint of Opposition to Atheistic Communism.

Saint Sebastian: Patron Saint of Neighborhood Watch Groups.

Saint Joseph of Arimathea: Patron Saint of Funeral Directors.

Saint Eligius: Patron Saint of Gas Station Workers. (He miraculously cured horses, the precursors to automobiles.)

Saint Martin de Porres: Patron Saint of Race Relations, Social Justice, and Italian Hairdressers.

Saint Martha: Patron Saint of Dietitians.

In 1992 former Panamanian pres. Noriega's wife was arrested in Miami for shoplifting buttons.

ACCIDENTAL DISCOVERIES

Not all scientific progress is the product of systematic experimentation. A number of important modern discoveries have been a matter of chance— which means you should keep your eyes and ears open, even while you're just sitting there on the john. You never know what might happen.

The Discovery: Insulin

How It Happened: In 1889 Joseph von Mering and Oscar Minkowski, two German scientists, were trying to understand more about the digestive system. As part of their experiments, they removed the pancreas from a living dog to see what role the organ plays in digestion.

The next day a laboratory assistant noticed an extraordinary number of flies buzzing around the dog's urine. Von Mering and Minkowski examined the urine to see why...and were surprised to discover that it contained a high concentration of sugar. This indicated that the pancreas plays a role in removing sugar from the bloodstream.

Legacy: Von Mering and Minkowski were never able to isolate the chemical that produced this effect, but their discovery enabled John J. R. MacLeod and Frederick Banting, two American researchers, to develop insulin extracts from horse and pig pancreases and to pioneer their use as a treatment for diabetes in 1921.

The Discovery: Photography

How It Happened: The *camera obscura*, designed by Leonardo da Vinci in the early 1500s and perfected in 1573 by E. Danti, was a workable camera. It was widely used in the early 1800s—but not for taking photographs. The reason: the technology for photos didn't exist. People used the camera for tracing images instead, placing transparent paper over its glass plate.

In the 1830s, French artist L. J. M. Daguerre began experimenting with ways of recording a camera's images on light-sensitive photographic plates. By 1838 he'd made some progress; using silver-coated sheets of copper, he found a way to capture an image.

Aztec emperor Montezuma had a nephew, Cuitlahac, whose name meant "plenty of excrement."

However, the image was so faint that it was barely visible. He tried dozens of substances to see if they'd darken it...but nothing worked. Frustrated, Daguerre put the photographic plate away in a cabinet filled with chemicals and moved on to other projects.

A few days later, Daguerre took the plate out. To his astonishment, the plate had mysteriously darkened; now the image was perfectly visible. One of the chemicals in the cabinet was almost certainly responsible...but which one?

He devised a method to find out. Each day he removed one chemical from the cabinet and put a fresh photographic plate in. If the plate still darkened overnight, the chemical would be disqualified. If it didn't, he'd know he'd found the chemical he was looking for. It seemed like a good idea, but even after *all* the chemicals had been removed, the plate continued to darken. Daguerre wondered why. Then, examining the cabinet closely, he noticed a few drops of mercury that had spilled from a broken thermometer onto one of the shelves.

Legacy: Later experiments with mercury vapor proved that this substance was responsible. The daguerrotype's worldwide popularity paved the way for the development of photography.

The Discovery: Safety glass

How It Happened: In 1903 Edouard Benedictus, a French chemist, was experimenting in his lab when he dropped an empty glass flask on the floor. It shattered, but remained in the shape of a flask. Benedictus was bewildered. When he examined the flask more closely, he discovered that the inside was coated with a film residue of cellulose nitrate, a chemical he'd been working with earlier. The film had held the glass together.

Not long afterward, Benedictus read a newspaper article about a girl who had been badly injured by flying glass in a car accident. He thought back to the glass flask in his lab and realized that coating automobile windshields, as the inside of the flask had been coated, would make them less dangerous.

Legacy: Variations of the safety glass he produced—a layer of plastic sandwiched by two layers of glass—are still used in automobiles today.

A typical eggshell takes up 12% of an egg's weight.

BOX-OFFICE BLOOPERS II

Here are a few more movie mistakes to look for in popular films.

Movie: *Rear Window* (1954)
Scene: Jimmy Stewart, in a cast and sitting in a wheelchair, argues with Grace Kelly.
Blooper: His cast switches from his left leg to his right.

Movie: *Raiders of the Lost Ark* (1982)
Scene: German soldiers and Gestapo agents lift the ark.
Blooper: Paintings of C3P0 and R2D2, the androids from *Star Wars* (another George Lucas film), are included among the hieroglyphics on the wall.

Movie: *Close Encounters of the Third Kind* (1977)
Scene: Richard Dreyfus and Teri Garr smash through several road blocks as they near Devil's Tower.
Blooper: The license plate on their station wagon keeps changing.

Movie: *Abbot and Costello Go to Mars* (1953)
Blooper: In the movie they actually go to Venus.

Movie: *Camelot* (1967)
Scene: King Arthur (Richard Harris) praises his medieval kingdom while speaking to some of his subjects.
Blooper: Harris is wearing a Band-Aid on his neck.

Movie: *The Fortune Cookie* (1966)
Scene: Walter Matthau leaves one room and enters another—and appears to lose weight in the process.
Blooper: Matthau suffered a heart attack while this scene was being filmed; only half was completed before he entered the hospital. He returned 5 months later to finish the job—40 pounds lighter than he was in the first part of the scene.

Movie: *Diamonds Are Forever* (1971)
Scene: James Bond tips his Ford Mustang up onto two wheels and drives through a narrow alley to escape from the bad guys.
Blooper: The Mustang enters the alley on its two right wheels—and leaves the alley on its two *left* wheels.

THE TRUTH ABOUT LEMMINGS

You've probably heard that lemmings commit mass suicide when they experience overpopulation. It turns out that isn't true...and you can blame the myth on the Walt Disney Company.

THE MYTH

In 1958 Walt Disney produced *White Wilderness*, a documentary about life in the Arctic. This film gave us the first close look at the strange habits of arctic rodents called lemmings.

• "They quite literally eat themselves out of house and home," says the narrator. "With things as crowded as this, someone has to make room for somebody somehow. And so, Nature herself takes a hand....A kind of compulsion seizes each tiny rodent and, carried along by an unreasoning hysteria, each falls into step for a march that will take them to a strange destiny."

• The film shows a pack of lemmings marching to the sea, where they "dutifully toss themselves over a cliff into certain death in icy Arctic waters." "The last shot," says critic William Poundstone, "shows the sea awash with dying lemmings."

• The narrator says: "Gradually strength wanes...determination ebbs away...and the Arctic Sea is dotted with tiny bobbing bodies."

THE TRUTH

• According to a 1983 investigation by Canadian Broadcasting Corporation producer Brian Vallee, *White Wilderness*'s lemming scene was sheer fabrication.

• Vallee says the lemmings were brought to Alberta—a landlocked province that isn't their natural habitat—where Disney folks put them on a giant turntable piled with snow to film the "migration segment."

• Then, Vallee reports, they recaptured the lemmings and took them to a cliff over a river. "When the well-adjusted lemmings wouldn't jump," writes Poundstone, "the Disney people gave Nature a hand [and tossed them off]....Lemmings don't commit mass suicide. As far as zoologists can tell, it's a myth."

Shocking Fact: 7 times as many men as women are killed by lightning in the U.S.

TRANSLATED HITS

Here are six popular songs that originated in a foreign language and were translated into English—sometimes by people with no idea of what the original lyrics were. From Behind the Hits *by Bob Shannon.*

IT'S NOW OR NEVER—ELVIS PRESLEY

Background: In 1901, Italian composer Eduardo di Capua wrote "O Sole Mio." This operatic theme was eventually popularized in America by Mario Lanza (who sang it in Italian) and again by Tony Martin in 1949. Martin's version, an English "translation," was called "There's No Tomorrow." It hit #2 on the pop charts in 1949.

The Elvis Version: While Elvis was in the Army from 1958 to 1959, he decided to clean up his image by recording a new version of "O Sole Mio" that even teenagers' *parents* could love. (Although his fans didn't know it, Presley had always admired operatic voices like Mario Lanza's.) But Elvis didn't like the Tony Martin version—it "wasn't his style"—so he commissioned a new set of lyrics.

It took two New York writers 20 minutes to write the song. Elvis loved it (it became his favorite of all his records) and recorded it about two weeks after he got out of the Army. It hit #1 all over the globe, selling more than twenty million copies worldwide. For a few years, it was listed in the *Guinness Book* as the largest-selling single in the history of pop music.

MY WAY—FRANK SINATRA

Background: The lyrics of this song were written specifically with Sinatra in mind, but the melody belonged to a French tune called "Comme d'habitude," or "As Usual."

The Sinatra Version: Paul Anka, who felt a growing affinity with Frank Sinatra, decided that if he ever had the chance, he'd write something special for ol' Blue Eyes. And at about three o'clock on a rainy Las Vegas morning, it happened. As he thought of the melody of "Comme d'habitude" (which he'd heard in France), the words of "My Way" spontaneously came to him. "[It was] one of the magic moments in my writing career," he says. "I finished it in an hour and a half." Sinatra loved the song and spent two weeks perfecting it. Within a year it had been recorded by over a hundred different artists. Elvis Presley did a live version in 1977 that sold over a million copies.

VOLARE—DEAN MARTIN, BOBBY RYDELL, & OTHERS

Background: The original Italian version, by Domenico Modugno, was a million-seller in the U.S. and the #1 record of 1958. The original title, however, was not "Volare," but "Nel Blu, Dipinto di Blu" (literal translation: "the blue, painted in blue"). The lyrics told the story of a man dreaming he was flying through the air with his hands painted blue.

The English Version: When Modugno's record started selling in the U.S., American artists clamored for an English-language version they could record. So Mitchel Parish wrote new lyrics, retitling the song "Volare." About a dozen versions were released right away, and combined sales of the song in 1958 alone were estimated at eight million. The best-selling U.S. renditions: Dean Martin's (#12 in 1958), Bobby Rydell's (#4 in 1960), and Al Martino's (#15 in 1975). Chrysler Corp. even named a car after the song.

SEASONS IN THE SUN—TERRY JACKS

Background: The song was originally written as "Le Moribund" (literal translation: "the dying man") by Jacques Brel in 1961.

The English Version: Rod McKuen adapted the song to English in 1964, and Jacks heard it on a Kingston Trio record. In 1972 he took it to a Beach Boys' session he was producing, and the Beach Boys recorded it...but didn't release it. So Jacks, who was distraught over a friend's death, did his own version.

Jacks was playing his year-old recording of it one day at his house when the boy who delivered his newspapers overheard it; the boy liked it so much that he brought some friends over to Jacks's house to listen to it, and their enthusiastic response inspired him to release it on his own Goldfish record label. The result: It skyrocketed to #1 all over the world and sold 11.5 million copies.

THOSE WERE THE DAYS—MARY HOPKIN

Background: It was originally a Russian tune called "Darogoi Dlimmoyo," which means "Dear to Me." The original artist was Alexander Wertinsky, who recorded it in the 1920s.

The English Version: In the '50s a Finnish singer translated it to her native language and recorded it. An American named Gene Raskin heard the record and wrote English lyrics (which were popularized in the U.S. by a folk trio called the Limeliters). In 1965 he and his wife performed the song in a London club called The Blue Angel. Paul McCartney was in the audience.

Three years later, McCartney heard about a 17-year-old Welsh singer named Mary Hopkin, who had appeared on the TV show "Opportunity Knocks" (a London version of "Star Search") and won three times. The Beatles had just formed Apple Records and were looking for people to record—so McCartney asked her if she wanted to audition. She did, and when she sang for Paul, her high soprano made him think of "Those Were the Days." He bought the rights to the song, and Hopkin recorded it. Her record was included in a specially boxed introductory set of the first four Apple releases. It became the second million-seller on Apple. ("Hey Jude" was the first.) Worldwide, it sold five million copies.

THE LION SLEEPS TONIGHT—THE TOKENS, ROBERT JOHN, & OTHERS

Background: The original title of this song was "Mbube" (which means "lion"); the subject was a sleeping lion. Sample lyrics: "Hush! Hush! If we will all be quiet, there will be lion meat for dinner." It was sung with a haunting Zulu refrain that sounded, to English-speaking people, like "wimoweh."

"Mbube" was popular on the boats of what is now Swaziland. In the 1930s a South African singer named Solomon Linda recorded it; then the tune passed into the broad field of folk music. As the '50s arrived, Miriam Makeba recorded the song in its original Zulu...and an American folk group called the Weavers adapted her version into a Top 15 hit called "Wimoweh."

The English Version: In 1961 a Brooklyn doo-wop group called the Tokens were offered a try-out with RCA. Caught up in the folk music boom of the time, they auditioned with "Wimoweh." The RCA executives liked the song, but decided it needed new lyrics...so they wrote "The Lion Sleeps Tonight" for the Tokens—not knowing that the original version had also been about a lion. The Tokens' record hit #1 in 1961, and Robert John's was #3 in 1972.

MEN OF LETTERS

In his entertaining book Dear Wit, *H. Jack Lang chronicles celebrities' humorous correspondence. Here are a few examples.*

GIVE HIM A BRAKE

In 1872, George Westinghouse asked Cornelius Vanderbilt, multimillionaire president of the New York Central Railroad, to listen to his ideas about developing an "air brake." Vanderbuilt wrote back:

I have no time to waste on fools. —*Vanderbilt*

After the brake was successfully tested on another railroad, Vanderbilt wrote Westinghouse asking to see it. Westinghouse wrote back:

I have no time to waste on fools. —*Westinghouse*

FIERY WRITING

The celebrated author Sommerset Maugham once received a manuscript from a young writer, accompanied by a letter that said:

Do you think I should put more fire into my stories?

Maugham replied: No. Vice Versa.

GIVE HIM A SIGN

In the early 1960s columnist Leonard Lyons complained to President John F. Kennedy that JFK's signature was only worth $65 to collectors—compared to $175 for George Washington and $75 for Franklin Roosevelt. Kennedy responded:

Dear Leonard: In order not to depress the market any further, I will not sign this letter.

NO JOKE

A publisher who wanted an endorsement for a humor book sent Groucho Marx a copy and asked for Groucho's comments. Marx wrote back:

I've been laughing ever since I picked up your book. Some day I'm going to read it. —*Groucho*

Joe Louis was the world heavyweight boxing champ for 11 years and 252 days.

MAKING THE BREAST OF IT

At dinner, Winston Churchill asked his American hostess, "May I have a breast?" She replied: "In this country, it is customary to ask for white or dark meat." The next day, as an apology, Churchill sent her an orchid, with a card that said:

> Madam: I would be most obliged if you would pin this on your white meat. —*Winston Churchill*

ARE YOU SURE?

Playwrite Eugene O'Neill received a cable from Hollywood bombshell Jean Harlow asking him to write a play for her. "Reply collect in 20 words," the cable requested. O'Neill cabled back:

> NO NO NO NO NO NO NO NO NO NO
> NO NO NO NO NO NO NO NO NO NO

FANCY FOOTWORK

Jack London's publisher sent him the following letter when the famous novelist missed a publishing deadline:

> My dear Jack London: If I do not receive those stories from you by noon tomorrow, I'm going to put on my heaviest soled shoes, come down to your room, and kick you downstairs. I always keep my promises. —*Editor*

London wrote back:

> Dear Sir: I, too, would always keep my promises if I could fulfill them with my feet. —*Jack London*

WHAT'S THE STORY?

After a news item reported that Rudyard Kipling was paid $5 a word for his magazine articles, an autograph collector sent him a check for $5 and a letter asking for a single word. Kipling wrote back:

> Thanks. —*Rudyard Kipling.*

Afterward the autograph-seeker wrote back:

> Dear Mr. Kipling: I sold the story of your one-word reply to a magazine for two hundred dollars. The enclosed check is your half.

OH, KATE!

Here are a few of Katherine Hepburn's unscripted comments.

"When I started out, I didn't have any desire to be an actress or to learn how to act. I just wanted to be famous."

"Sometimes I wonder if men and women really suit each other. Perhaps they should live next door and just visit now and then."

"If you give audiences half a chance they'll do half your acting for you."

"Being a housewife and a mother is the biggest job in the world, but if it doesn't interest you, don't do it....I would have made a terrible parent. The first time my child didn't do what I wanted, I'd kill him."

"I find men today less manly ...but a woman of my age is not in a position to know exactly how manly they are."

"Great performing in any field is total simplicity, the capacity to get to the essence, to eliminate all the frills and foibles."

"If you survive long enough, you're revered—rather like an old building."

"I don't care what is written about me as long as it isn't true."

"A sharp knife cuts the quickest and hurts the least."

"Life is to be lived. If you have to support yourself, you had bloody well better find some way that is going to be interesting. And you don't do that by sitting around wondering about yourself."

"What the hell—you might be right, you might be wrong... but don't just *avoid*."

"The male sex, as a sex, does not universally appeal to me."

"You can't change the music of your soul."

"Life's what's important. Walking, houses, family. Birth and pain and joy. Acting's just waiting for a custard pie."

OPENING LINES

TV science fiction programs have always had great introductions.
Here are a few memorable ones.

THE ADVENTURES OF SUPERMAN (1953-57)

"Look! In the sky!" "It's a bird!" "It's a plane!" "It's Superman!" "Yes, it's Superman, strange visitor from another planet who came to Earth with powers and abilities far beyond those of mortal men. Superman, who can change the course of mighty rivers, bend steel in his bare hands; and who, disguised as Clark Kent, mild-mannered reporter for a great Metropolitan newspaper, fights a never-ending battle for truth…justice…and the American way!"

CAPTAIN VIDEO (1949-56)

"Captain Video! Master of space! Hero of science! Captain of the Video Rangers! Operating from his secret mountain headquarters on the planet Earth, Captain Video rallies men of good will everywhere. As he rockets from planet to planet, let us follow the champion of justice, truth, and freedom throughout the universe."

ROD BROWN OF THE ROCKET RANGERS (1955-56)

"CBS television presents…'Rod Brown of the Rocket Rangers'! Surging with the power of the atom, gleaming like great silver bullets, the mighty Rocket Rangers' spaceships stand by for blast off!… Up, up, rockets blazing with white hot fury, the man-made meteors ride through the atmosphere, breaking the gravity barrier, pushing up and out, faster and faster and then…outer space and high adventure for…the Rocket Rangers!"

THE TIME TUNNEL (1966-67)

"Two American scientists are lost in the swirling maze of past and future ages during the first experiments on America's greatest and most secret project—the Time Tunnel. Tony Newman and Doug Phillips now tumble helplessly toward a new, fantastic adventure somewhere along the infinite corridors of time!"

STAR TREK (1966-69)

"Space, the final frontier. These are the voyages of the starship Enterprise. Its five-year mission: to explore strange new worlds; to seek out life and new civilizations; to boldly go where no man has gone before."

TOM CORBETT, SPACE CADET (1950-56)

"Space Academy, USA, in the world beyond tomorrow. Here the Space Cadets train for duty on distant planets. In roaring rockets, they blast through the millions of miles from Earth to far-flung stars and brave the dangers of cosmic frontiers protecting the liberties of the planets, safeguarding the cause of universal peace in the age of the conquest of space!"

THE TWILIGHT ZONE (1959-63)

"There is a fifth dimension beyond that which is known to man. It is a dimension as vast as space and timeless as infinity. It is the middle ground between light and shadow, between science and superstition, and it lies between the pit of man's fears and the summit of his knowledge. This is the dimension of imagination. It is an area which we call the Twilight Zone."

SPACE PATROL (1950-56)

"High adventure in the wild, vast regions of space! Missions of daring in the name of interplanetary justice! Travel into the future with Buzz Corey, commander in chief of...the Space Patrol!"

THE OUTER LIMITS (1963-65)

"There is nothing wrong with your television set. Do not attempt to adjust the picture. We are controlling transmission. If we wish to make it louder, we will bring up the volume. If we wish to make it softer, we will tune it to a whisper. We will control the horizontal. We will control the vertical. We can roll the image; make it flutter. We can change the focus to a soft blur, or sharpen it to crystal clarity. For the next hour, sit quietly and we will control all you see and hear. We repeat: There is nothing wrong with your television set. You are about to participate in a great adventure. You are about to experience the awe and mystery which reaches from the inner mind to...the Outer Limits."

The U.S. minted 12,837,140 pennies and 2,240,355,488 dimes in 1989.

MORE CARNIVAL TRICKS

*Here's more information about carnival booths to look out for—and some
tips on how to beat them—from Matthew Gryczan's book* Carnival Secrets.

The Booth: "Plate Pitch"
The Object: Players toss dimes onto plates sitting on the
heads of large stuffed animals. If a dime remains on the
plate, the player wins the animal.

How It's Rigged: Some carnival suppliers put their glass plates in a
furnace for 48 hours. The heat makes the sides of the plates droop,
so the surface of the plate is significantly flatter than that of the
same style of plate found in stores. This makes it easier for the
dimes to slip off the plates.
• Some operators polish the dishes with furniture wax to make
them slippery, or set them on an angle so the coins slide off.

How to Win: It helps to practice at home for this one.
• The best pitches are thrown softly, in a low arc. According to
one manufacturer, if the coin lands flat against the back edge of the
plate in Plate Pitch, it will rebound back into the center.
• Toss the coin so it travels in a line to other plates if it skips off
the first plate.

The Booth: "Spill the Milk"
The Object: Throw a ball and knock down a pyramid of three aluminum bottles shaped like old-fashioned glass milk bottles. Knock-
ing all three pins completely off their stand wins you a prize.
How It's Rigged: The bottles look identical, but they don't always
weigh the same amount. Some carnies set a heavier bottle on the
bottom row. That way, the ball will hit the lighter two bottles first,
and won't have enough energy to knock the heavy bottle off.
• Some unscrupulous operators fill the bottles with molten lead, so
they're too heavy to be knocked over with a softball. Other operators cast lead in the *side* of the bottle so it can be knocked down,
but not off the stand.
• If the player is allowed two shots, there may be a different set-up.
One bottle may be unweighted, while the remaining two are

different weights. The carny sets the unweighted bottle on top and gives the player a heavier softball. If the player strikes the center of the pyramid, the top bottle flies off, the lighter lower bottle is knocked over, and the heavier bottle remains standing. Then the player is given an ultralight ball that can't be thrown hard enough to knock over the heaviest bottle.

How to Win: Make sure the game isn't rigged. Ask about the weights of the bottles and the ball and don't play until you get a satisfactory answer. Ask to examine the bottles. Check whether they're all the same weight or if the weight is distributed in each bottle unevenly.

• Carnies say the best way to win at Spill the Milk is a direct hit in the triangular area where the three bottles meet.

The Booth: "High Striker"

The Object: Using an oversized rubber mallet, hit a cast-iron striker to the top of a 21-foot-high tower to ring the bell.

How It's Rigged: Most High Strikers in use today are honest, but, according to one manufacturer, some early models used several "guy wires" that held up the tower. Unknown to players, one of the guy wires led from a stake directly down the front of the tower. The striker traveled along this wire.

• The unscrupulous agent would lean up against the phony guy wire and keep it taut enough so a player could ring the bell on the first and second tries. But on the player's third swing (the one that could win the prize), the agent would stop leaning on the wire. With the wire slack, the striker brushed against the tower as it traveled skyward, and friction prevented it from reaching the gong. The player had no chance to win the grand prize for three rings.

How to Win: "The trade secret is to hit the pad squarely, just as if you were splitting wood," according to the manufacturer.

The Booth: "Basketball"

The Object: Toss the basketball into a hoop while standing behind a designated foul line.

How It's Rigged: Some operators overinflate the balls, so they have more bounce and are tougher to get through the hoop. Others don't attach the hoops securely to the backboard, so the rims vibrate when struck by the ball. This keeps rim shots from going in.

Burger Update: By 1989 McDonald's had sold 75 billion hamburgers.

THE STORY OF LAS VEGAS

Have you ever wondered how Las Vegas became the
gambling capital of the world? Here's the story:

NAME. "Las Vegas" means "the meadows" or "the fertile plains" in Spanish. The city acquired this name in the early 1800s, when it was a peaceful rest stop on the Old Spanish Trail.

HISTORY. Ironically, the Mormans were the first to settle Las Vegas, in 1855. They built the first church, first fort, and first school in Nevada, only to abandon them three years later. Pioneers were still using the site as a watering hole and, as one missionary noted, few could be induced to attend the church. "Only one man attended," he wrote. "The rest of them were gambling and swearing at their camps."

Las Vegas didn't become a real town until almost 50 years later. Because of its central location and ample water supply, the railroad decided it would make an ideal stop on the transcontinental train line. They bought the land and, one scorching hot day in 1905, auctioned it off to 1,200 eager settlers. A few days later, the town appeared: a haphazard assortment of canvas tent saloons, gambling clubs and drinking parlors that quickly established the city's character and reputation.

Despite prohibitionist protests, Las Vegas maintained its early emphasis on night life and continued to flourish throughout the 1920s. "Such places as the Red Rooster, the Blue Goose, the Owl, and Pair-o-Dice were temporarily inconvenienced from time to time by raids from federal agents," writes one local historian. "But they were, of course, as safe as a church from local interference."

In 1931, the Nevada state legislature enacted two well-publicized "reforms": They liberalized divorce laws, changing residency requirements from 6 months to 6 weeks, and officially legalized gambling. Now Las Vegas had two unique attractions. While the rest of the country was suffering through the Great Depression, Las Vegas casinos made a killing catering to the workers constructing nearby Boulder Dam, as well as the 230,000 tourists who came to see it. (Las Vegas also became a significant divorce center after movie star Clark Gable's wife, Rhea, chose it as the place to divorce him.)

The first full-fledged resort, the plush El Rancho Vegas, was built in 1940. Another (the New Frontier) followed, and the notorious Vegas "strip" was established. A military base and a magnesium plant were installed nearby in the early 1940s, and both brought more people to the area and kept the town prosperous through World War II. By 1970 more than half of Nevada's entire population lived in Las Vegas.

MAIN INDUSTRY. Las Vegas as we know it today might never have been born if it weren't for gangster Ben "Bugsy" Siegal. Wanted for murder in New York, Siegal was sent out West to set up a booking service for the mob and became obsessed with the idea of creating a "glittering gambling mecca in the desert." He borrowed $6 million in mob money and constructed the Flamingo Hotel, a lavish olive-green castle surrounded by a 40-acre garden that was planted literally overnight in imported soil brought in by truck.

Unfortunately for Bugsy, the Flamingo was initially a bust. To top it off, the mob found out he'd been skimming profits. They had him killed in 1947. But business at the Flamingo picked up, and over the next few years Mafia-owned resort casinos sprang up all along Highway 91, the Las Vegas "strip."

According to *The Encyclopedia of American Crime*, for example:

√ Meyer Lansky put up much of the money for the Thunderbird.

√ The Desert Inn was owned by the head of the Cleveland mob.

√ The Dunes "was a goldmine" for the New England mob.

√ The Sahara "was launched by the Chicago mob."

"Despite the huge profits," the *Encyclopedia* adds, "by the mid-'50s the mob had started selling off its properties to individuals and corporations. In the 1960s billionaire Howard Hughes started buying one casino after another. In the early 1970s the mob's interest in Vegas was reportedly at a low point, but by the close of the decade, many observers concluded, mobsters were returning to the scene."

MEET YOUR COMMIE MASTERS

In 1984, at the height of Ronald Reagan's "evil empire" rhetoric, Robert Conquest and Jon Manchip White wrote a handy book called What to Do When the Russians Come. *You may laugh now, but when the mighty Russian Army marches into your hometown, this could SAVE YOUR LIFE. Here are samples of the authors' penetrating analyses of what Americans from all walks of life can expect in those dark days.*

Y ou will be anxious to know how someone of your particular professional and ethnic and political and temperamental background is likely to fare [under Soviet rule]. In the pages that follow, we look into the special conditions facing a wide variety of these, of a reasonable representative nature, From Academic to Farmer, from Realtor to Industrial Worker, from Homosexual to Feminist...

ACADEMIC. When universities reopen after the crisis, student numbers will have gone down. Some will be dead, some in prison, some in the partisan movement. Private, religious and racially or ethnically oriented institutions will have been taken over by the state. All departments...will be purged of "incorrect" teachers with great thoroughness. Colleges will be run by Communist-appointed functionaries, including representatives of the secret police, and there will be no "academic freedom." If you are at the moment an academic with Communist or Marxist leanings, you can expect to become at least a dean or the head of your department....Sneaking and denunciation will be the order of the day, and since the arrest rate will be one of the highest in any field, you will be hard put to trust your colleagues, for you will not be able to tell which of them have become police informers, either of their own volition or through blackmail....Be generous with your grades, otherwise disgruntled students will denounce you.

BARBER / BEAUTICIAN. Any but the most orthodox haircuts will be heavily discouraged. You...will become standardized and

Most varieties of nuts can remain fresh in their shells for as long as a year.

paid as a public servant, under a new Department of Internal Trade. Most beauty salons will close for lack of patrons with enough money to be able to afford such luxuries. A few will remain open to serve the new Communist elite and the wives of Soviet generals.

DENTIST. The level of dental care in the population will fall. Dental stocks will dwindle and dental equipment will deteriorate for lack of spare parts. Dental techniques will become basic, with extraction taking precedent over filling. Dentures will be poorly made and ill-fitting when available. Extractions will be performed without anesthesia because of the absence of supply. Many dentists will give up in despair.

ENVIRONMENTALIST. No public organization, demonstration, or other activity will, of course, be permitted. As for nuclear power stations, they will be developed to the limit. No sort of objection to them will be permitted under any circumstances. However, there will be one area in which improvement will have been made: the shortage of private cars will mean less pollution from gasoline.

FUNERAL DIRECTOR. Services will be speedy, drab, and uniform. Atheist forms of committal will be encouraged, religious forms banned or perfunctorily performed. Only in rare cases will services be carried out in churches or other religious buildings, the majority of which will be closed. However, Communist burials, while lacking frills, will at least be inexpensive.

GARAGE EMPLOYEE. There will be very few cars on the roads and consequently no need for a large number of gas stations.... Although there are fewer cars, production and servicing standards will be such that motor mechanics' skills will be saleable on the black market. And you may also try your hand at, and profit by, the repairing and refurbishing of bicycles.

JOHN BIRCH SOCIETY MEMBER. Your life will, of course, be automatically forfeit.

If you're average, your feet hit the floor 7,000 times a day.

LAWYER. Lawyers, will, in general, be regarded as a hostile class element. This will be more so in their case because so many of them are...concerned with rights, balances, constitutionality, and common law—all totally opposed to the Communist principle. Casualties, therefore, will be high.

LIBRARIAN. Your old reference books, such as encyclopedias, will be withdrawn and pulped. You should keep handy a pair of sharp scissors and a supply of paste, as you will have to cut out or replace those entries that become politically inconvenient—a normal Soviet practice. As the years go by, even the more harmless books on your shelves will be gradually replaced as works commissioned and printed by the State begin to appear in adequate numbers. If you can safely save and secrete some of the books that are being discarded, well and good; although your superiors will be on the lookout for this, and it may be hazardous for you or your friends to be caught reading them.

PET SHOP OWNER. It is unlikely that families will be able to spare any scraps of food for feeding pets, let alone extra money for grooming them or purchasing accessories. Most cats and dogs will have to be put to sleep or allowed to run free and take their chances. After the fighting stops, there will be a serious infestation of ownerless dogs running in wild packs with which authorities will have to deal. Owners of pet shops should lose no time in making plans for alternative employment.

PSYCHOPATH. If you are able and prepared to control yourself in all matters where you might offend authorities, a wide field of activity of a type you will find rewarding will remain open to you. Those not afflicted with consciences will be in demand not only to occupations offering opportunities of violence, but also in all other institutions, where it will always be possible to denounce anyone who stands in the way of your desires or to blackmail them into submitting. Indeed, the Soviet system...has been described as a psychopathocracy. If your condition is of the right type, you may rise very high indeed in the new hierarchy.

Since 1912, Cracker Jack has given away more than 16 billion toys.

SADIST. Although the secret police will have some use for torturers, such positions are unlikely to be open except to men with political acumen and training, but low-grade thugs, known as "boxers," are often employed for routine beatings....If you apply for the post of an executioner, you might be enrolled in one of the municipal firing squads. Your opportunity to carry out individual executions, if that is your taste, will probably be somewhat limited. The traditional Soviet method of executing single offenders is by means of a bullet in the back of the neck and is invariably conducted neatly and expeditiously by a specialist of officer rank. Mass executions are bound, of course, to occur, and you may well be given a chance to participate in some of them.

YOUTH. You will find yourself under very heavy pressures of a type which your present life has not accustomed you....The special Communist effort to indoctrinate you will mean that you will be under considerably higher pressures than your elders....You will lose several hours a week at compulsory sessions in Marxist-Leninism, in addition to endless harangues about loyalty and the glorious future, which you will be expected to applaud. Still...you have one great point in your favor: unlike your parents, you may find that the overthrow of Soviet power will come when you are still in the full vigor of, perhaps, your forties, when you will provide the leaders to build a new America and a new world.

Just as the airlines hope that their passengers will never have to follow the instructions they give you on what to do in case of a disaster, so we, for our part, hope you may never have to follow the advice we have given you in the preceding pages. But time is running short. We would be deceiving you if we pretended that the nightmare we have described is not a real and deadly possibility. If it does come about, we have one last piece of advice:

BURN THIS BOOK.

MORE EPITAPHS

*More unusual epitaphs and tombstone rhymes from our
wandering B.R.I. tombstoneologists*

Seen in Oxfordshire, England:
Here lies the body of John
Eldred,
At least he will be here when
he is dead.
But now at this time, he is
alive,
The 14th of August, 1765.

Seen in Plymouth, Mass.:
Richard Lawton
Here lie the bones of Richard
Lawton,
Whose death, alas! was
strangely brought on.
Trying his corns one day to
mow off,
His razor slipped and cut
his toe off.
His toe, or rather, what it
grew to,
An inflammation quickly
flew to.
Which took, Alas! to mortify-
ing,
And was the cause of Richard's
dying.

Seen in Luton, England:
Thomas Proctor
Here lies the body of Thomas
Proctor,
Who lived and died without a
doctor.

Seen in Shrewsbury, England:
Here lies the body of Martha
Dias,
Who was always uneasy, and
not over-pious;
She lived to the age of three
score and ten,
And gave to the worms what
she refused to the men.

Seen in Marshfield, Vt.:
Here lies the body of William
Jay,
Who died maintaining his
right of way;
He was right, dead right, as he
sped along,
But he's just as dead as if he'd
been wrong.

Seen in Lee, Mass.:
In Memory of Mrs. Alpha
White, Weight 309 lbs.
Open wide ye heavenly gates
That lead to the heavenly
shore;
Our father suffered in passing
through
And Mother weighs much
more.

Seen in Putman, Conn.:
Phineas G. Wright
Going, But Know Not Where

FAMILIAR MELODIES

These songs are so familiar that it's a little surprising to realize people wrote them. But they did, and these stories are part of their legacy.

DIXIE
Written in 1859 by Daniel Decatur Emmett for a "black-face" minstrel show. Ironically, though his song became the anthem of the South, Emmett was a northerner who detested the Confederacy. When he found out the song was going to be sung at Confederate President Jefferson Davis's inauguration, he told friends "If I had known to what use they were going to put my song, I'll be damned if I'd have written it."

HERE COMES THE BRIDE
Composer Richard Wagner wrote the "Bridal Chorus" in 1848 for his opera *Lohengrin*. He used it to score a scene in which the hero and his new bride undress on their wedding night and prepare to consummate their marriage. It was first used as a bridal march in 1858, when Princess Victoria (daughter of England's Queen Victoria) married Prince Frederick William of Prussia. Interestingly, because of the sexual nature of the original opera scene, some religions object to using the song in wedding ceremonies.

CHOPSTICKS
In 1877, 16-year-old Euphemia Allen, a British girl, published "Chopsticks" under the pseudonym Arthur de Lulli. Included with the sheet music were instructions telling the pianist to play the song "with both hands turned sideways, the little fingers lowest, so that the movement of the hands imitates the chopping from which this waltz gets its name." Allen never wrote another song.

TAPS
As late as 1862, the U.S. military used a song called "Extinguish Lights" to officially end the day. General Daniel Butterfield disliked the song...so he decided to compose a new one to replace it. He couldn't play the bugle, so he composed by whistling notes to his butler, who'd play them back for Butterfield to evaluate. They went through dozens of tunes before he got one he liked.

MEET DR. SEUSS

Say hello to Dr. Seuss. A master of nonsense, he's the creator of
The Cat in the Hat *and* Green Eggs and Ham *and is one of
the most popular kids' authors ever.*

VITAL STATS
Born: March 2, 1904
Died: Sept 25, 1991, age 87

• Although married twice, he never had any children. His slogan:
"You have 'em, I'll amuse 'em."

Real Name: Theodore Seuss Geisel

• He adopted "Seuss" as his writing name during Prohibition, while
attending Dartmouth College. The reason: He was caught with a
half-pint of gin in his room and was told to resign as editor of the
college humor magazine as punishment. Instead, he just stopped
using Geisel as a byline.

• Years later, he added "Dr." to his name "to sound more
scientific." He didn't officially become a doctor until 1956, when
Dartmouth gave him an honorary doctorate.

CAREER STATS

Accomplishments: He wrote 48 books, selling more than 100
million copies in 20 languages. (Including four of the top 10
bestselling hardcover childrens' books of all time: *The Cat in the
Hat, Green Eggs and Ham, Hop on Pop*, and *One Fish, Two Fish, Red
Fish, Blue Fish*)

• As a filmmaker, he won three Oscars—two for documentaries
made in the 1940s ("Hitler Lives," about Americans troops, and
"Design for Death," about Japanese warlords), and one in 1951 for
animation ("Gerald McBoing-Boing"). By that time he had written
four kids' books and turned down Hollywood screenplay offers in
order to keep writing them.

• In 1984 he won the Pulitzer Prize for his contribution to
children's literature.

Flops: Only one—a novel called *The Seven Lady Godivas*, an
"utterly ridiculous retelling of the story of Lady Godiva" first

published in 1937 and republished 40 years later. He always wanted to write The Great American Novel…but the book bombed in 1977, too.

How He Got Started: He was working as a cartoonist in the late '20s for *Judge* magazine. One of his cartoons "showed a knight using Flit insecticide to kill dragons." Someone associated with Flit's ad agency (McCann-Erikson) saw the cartoon and hired Geisel. For the next 10 years he created ads for Flit and other Standard Oil products. His greatest claim to fame at the time: the well-known ad phrase: "Quick Henry, the Flit!"

His contract with McCann-Erikson allowed him to write and publish books for kids, so he wrote *To Think That I Saw It on Mulberry Street.* It was turned down by 27 publishers. Said Seuss: "The excuse I got for all those rejections was that there was nothing on the market quite like it, so they didn't know whether it would sell." Vanguard Press finally picked it up in 1937, and it was an immediate success. So he quit the ad agency and began writing kids' books full-time.

HOW HE GOT HIS IDEAS

"The most asked question of any successful author," Seuss said in 1989, "is 'How do you get your ideas for books?'" Over the years he did reveal a number of his inspirations. For example:

Horton Hatches the Egg

• "Sometimes you have luck when you are doodling. I did one day when I was drawing some trees. Then I began drawing elephants. I had a window that was open, and the wind blew the elephant on top of the tree; I looked at it and said, 'What do you suppose that elephant is doing there?' The answer was: 'He is hatching an egg.' Then all I had to do was write a book about it. I've left that window open ever since, but it's never happened again."

Green Eggs and Ham

• Bennett Cerf, the founder and publisher of Random House, bet Geisel $50 that he couldn't write a book using just 50 words.

• Geisel won the bet. "It's the only book I ever wrote that still makes me laugh," he said 25 years later. He added: "Bennett never paid!"

Food fact: 41% of Americans eat breakfast cereal every morning.

Marvin K. Mooney, Will You Please Go Now?
• "The puppylike creature constantly asked to 'go' is ex-President Richard M. Nixon."

The Lorax
• Dr. Seuss's favorite book, he said, "is about people who raise hell in the environment and leave nothing behind." He wrote the story on a laundry list as he sat at a hotel pool in Kenya, watching a herd of elephants with his wife. "I wrote it as a piece of propaganda and disguised the fact," he told a reporter. "I was on the soapbox. I wasn't afraid of preaching—but I was afraid of being dull."

Yertle the Turtle
"Yertle the turtle is Adolf Hitler."

The 500 Hats of Bartholomew Cubbins
• In 1937 Geisel was on a commuter train in Connecticut. "There was a very stiff broker sitting in front of me. I wondered what his reaction would be if I took his hat off and threw it out the window. I decided that he was so stuffy he would grow a new one."

The Cat in the Hat
• In the early 1950s novelist John Hersey was on a panel that analyzed how reading was taught in a Connecticut school system. In May 1954, *Life* magazine published excerpts of the panel's report (called "Why Do Students Bog Down on the First R?"). In it, Hersey wrote that one of the major impediments to learning was the dull "Dick and Jane" material students were given—especially the illustrations. Kids, he said, should be inspired with "drawings like those wonderfully imaginative geniuses among children's illustrators, Tenniel, Howard Pyle, Dr. Seuss."
• A textbook publisher read the article and agreed. He contacted Dr. Seuss and asked him to create a reading book. The publisher sent Seuss a list of 400 words and told him to pick 220 to use in the book. The reason: People felt this was the maximum that "kids could absorb at one time."
• "Geisel went through the list once, twice and got nowhere," reports *Parents* magazine. "He decided to give it one more shot; if he could find two words that rhymed, they'd form the title and theme of the book. Within moments, *cat* and *hat* leaped off the page. But then it took him 9 months to write the entire book."

CONDOM SENSE

Condoms used to be an embarrassing subject. Now they're advertised in the magazines that B.R.I. members often stash in the bathroom. Here's some condom trivia.

ORIGIN
Condoms were invented in the mid-1500s by Gabriel Fallopius, an Italian doctor. (He was also the first person to describe fallopian tubes in medical literature.) His creation was made of linen (and soon earned the nickname "overcoat"). Fallopius believed that they prevented syphilis. They didn't.

NAME
Legend has it that condoms were named after the Earl of Condom, personal physician to King Charles II of England in the mid-1600s. The King feared catching syphilis from his dozens of mistresses and ordered the Earl to devise a solution.

• Condom's invention, a sheath made of oiled sheep intestine, became popular among the king's noblemen (who were also looking for protection against venereal disease). It was the noblemen, not Condom, who called the prophylactics "condoms." Condom hated having his name associated with them.

• Condoms became known as "rubbers" in the 1850s, when they actually *were* made of vulcanized rubber. These were thick, expensive, and uncomfortable. Owners were supposed to wash them out and reuse them until they cracked or tore. Disposable, thin latex condoms did not become widely available until the 1930s.

MISCELLANY
• Four billion condoms are sold worldwide every year—enough to circle the globe 16 times.

• How does the U.S. Food and Drug Administration test the strength of condoms? By filling them with air until they pop. The average condom swells to the size of a watermelon before it bursts. Government regulators also cut condoms into rubberband-like pieces and stretch them until they snap.

• Most Muslim countries forbid the sale of green condoms, because green is a sacred color in Islam.

If you bury a traffic ticket, it will decompose in about 4 weeks.

CONTROVERSIAL CHARACTERS

Honestly—what kind of political trouble could Mighty Mouse or Barbie get into? Well, as weird as it sounds, times are so volatile that even a cartoon mouse can be accused of being a bad influence.

The Character: Mighty Mouse
   Controversy: Did Mighty Mouse snort cocaine on April 23, 1988, in the TV cartoon show, *Mighty Mouse: the New Adventures* ?

The Fight: In 1988 a Tupelo, Mississippi, watchdog group called the American Family Association (AFA) complained to CBS about a scene in a *Mighty Mouse: The New Adventure* cartoon. Reverend Donald Wildmon, head of the AFA, described the scene as follows: "Mighty Mouse is down in the dumps, and he reaches in his cape, pulls out a substance and sniffs it through his nostrils, and from that point on in the cartoon he is his normal self." Wildmon charged that the substance Mighty Mouse "snorted" was cocaine.

Reaction: CBS producer Ralph Bakshi, who was responsible for the cartoon, angrily rejected the accusation: "This is Nazism and McCarthyism all over again. I don't advocate drugs—that's death. I'm a cartoonist, an artist, not a pornographer. Who are these people anyway? Why does anybody listen to them?" According to Bakshi, Mighty Mouse was actually sniffing crushed flowers he had placed in his pocket during an earlier scene. According to the CBS version of the story, Mighty Mouse was sad because the female character he was attracted to did not love him. So he took out the flowers she'd given him in the earlier scene and sniffed them.

The Characters: Popeye the Sailor and Olive Oyl
Controversy: Should Popeye and Olive take a pro-choice stand on abortion?
The Fight: In July 1992 Bobby London, the artist who wrote and drew the syndicated *Popeye* comic strip for King Features,

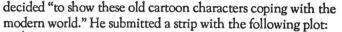

decided "to show these old cartoon characters coping with the modern world." He submitted a strip with the following plot:

√ Olive Oyl receives a baby Bluto doll in the mail and doesn't want to keep it.

√ She and Popeye get into an argument about what to do with it. Olive Oyl tells Popeye that she wants to "send the baby back to its maker."

√ Two priests happen to be walking by and hear the argument. They mistakenly assume that Olive Oyl is talking about having an abortion and try to persuade her not to do it. When that fails, the priests try to get passers-by to help. Olive Oyl tells them that "she can do what she wants to do, because it's her life."

Reaction: King Features fired London and withdrew the strip before it was published.

The Character: Mattel's Barbie doll

The Controversy: Does Barbie promote the "radical agenda" of environmentalism?

The Fight: In the wake of Earth Day 1990, Mattel decided to promote its new line of Barbie dolls with the "Barbie Summit," an all-expenses-paid gathering of children who had submitted winning suggestions on how to improve the world. In the commercial announcing the contest, Barbie asked viewers how they would help make the world a better place—and offered a seemingly innocuous suggestion: "We could keep the trees from falling, keep the eagles soaring," she said.

But the Oregon Lands Commission, an anti-environmentalist lobbying group, was outraged with the ad. They claimed it was exposing children to "the preservationist's radical agenda." "We want to wake up corporate American to the fact that powerful, monied groups are at work shutting down the engines of this country and they are doing it in the name of environmentalism," the commission's spokesperson claimed. The commission organized a boycott, telling its 61,000 members that buying Barbie dolls "would help stop timber harvesting."

Reaction: Mattel went ahead with the promotion, which was a success. "We kind of thought," explained a Mattel spokesperson, "how can anybody criticize a program that is designed to give children a voice in a world they are going to inherit?"

43,000 Americans were injured in accidents involving jewelry in 1991.

INSIDE CITIZEN KANE

Many critics call Citizen Kane *the best American movie ever made. Here's some interesting background material supplied by film buff Ross Owens.*

BACKGROUND

On October 30, 1938, the Mercury Theater of the Air broadcast a radio dramatization of H. G. Wells's *War of the Worlds*, in which Martians invade the Earth (*Ed. note:* See "Mars Invasion," *Bathroom Reader #3*). The plot was implausible, but the performance was so realistic that thousands of Americans believed it—and actually fled their homes or prepared for a full-scale Martian war.

The man behind the radio play was 23-year-old Orson Welles (who produced and directed the broadcast). The publicity he received made him a national celebrity, and two years later RKO studios hired him to direct *Citizen Kane*, a film about a newspaper mogul who destroys his life in an endless pursuit of power.

WILLIAM RANDOLPH HEARST

• In many ways it's amazing that *Citizen Kane* was ever made. Though its characters were supposedly fictional, the film was actually a scathing biography of real-life press baron William Randolph Hearst—head of the Hearst Newspaper chain and one of the most powerful people in America. Naturally, he wanted the movie stopped.

• When he learned that RKO was making the movie, Hearst tried to have the film destroyed. Working through the head of MGM studios, he tried to bribe RKO president George Schaefer with $800,000 (the amount *Citizen Kane* cost to make) to destroy the film's negative. Schaefer refused.

• When that attempt failed, Hearst threatened to sue the studio for libel. RKO took the threat seriously; it delayed the film's release for two months until its lawyers were convinced that the suit wouldn't stand up in court.

• Hearst kept the heat on. Before the film hit the theaters, rumors began spreading that Hearst was planning to attack the entire film industry—not just RKO—in newspaper editorials. This frightened the major Hollywood studios (who also owned or controlled most U.S. moviehouses), so they refused to play *Citizen Kane* in their theaters. *Kane* had to premiere in smaller, independent theaters.

THE OUTCOME

• The film premiered in 1939. It was a commercial flop, due in large part to Hearst's attacks...plus the fact that his papers wouldn't accept advertising for it.

• Hearst's influence was felt even at the Academy Awards—where Hearst supporters in the audience booed loudly every time the picture was mentioned. Nominated in 8 different categories (including Best Picture), *Kane* won only one award—for Best Original Screenplay. It lost Best Picture to a film called *How Green Was My Valley*.

• Orson Welles never recovered from the disaster. RKO refused to give him the level of artistic freedom he had making *Kane*, and most of his later film projects either failed or were never finished.

ROSEBUD BY ANY OTHER NAME

The Idea. The first scene of the movie shows Charles Foster Kane crying out the mysterious name "Rosebud" on his deathbed. The name Rosebud remains a secret until the last scene, when it's revealed that "Rosebud" was the name of Kane's childhood sled. The idea of giving Charles Foster Kane a sled was first suggested by Herman J. Mankiewicz, the film's screenwriter. As a boy Mankiewicz had had his favorite bicycle stolen, an experience he never forgot. He thought a similar story would be useful in the film.

The Name. No one knows exactly how the sled got the name "Rosebud." Some suggestions:

• Orson Welles sometimes told interviewers that "Rosebud" was the pet name Hearst had given mistress Marion Davies's nose...but in other interviews, he claimed it was the nickname Hearst had given to Davies's private parts.

• Welles's biographer, Charles Higham, points out that the 1914 Kentucky Derby winner was Old Rosebud—and that a reporter in the movie suggests that Rosebud may have been a racehorse.

• "Rosebud" may actually have been the nickname of one of the staff's ex-girlfriends. In 1942, a woman threatened to sue Herman Mankiewicz, claiming she'd been the writer's mistress in the 1920s and that Rosebud was a nickname he'd given *her*.

ORDER IN THE COURT!

Disorderly Conduct and Disorder in the Court are two books featuring amusing selections from court transcripts. They make great bathroom reading material—especially for lawyers. These quotes are taken directly from court records. People really said this stuff.

BORED IN COURT

Defendant: "Judge, I want you to appoint me another lawyer."

Judge: "And why is that?"

Defendant: "Because the Public Defender isn't interested in my case."

Judge (to Public defender): "Do you have any comments on your defendant's motion?"

Public defender: "I'm sorry, Your Honor, I wasn't listening."

JUDGE & JURY

Judge: "Is there any reason you could not serve as a juror in this case?"

Potential juror: "I don't want to be away from my job for that long."

Judge: "Can't they do without you at work?"

Potential juror: "Yes, but I don't want them to know it."

Judge to defendant: "You have a right to a trial by jury, but you may waive that right. What do you wish to do?"

Defendant: (Hesitates.)

Lawyer to defendant: "Waive."

Defendant: (Waves at the judge.)

UNTIL PROVEN GUILTY

Lawyer: "Have you ever been convicted of a felony?"

Defendant: "Yes."

Lawyer: "How many?"

Every year, about 12% of the U.S. population is arrested.

Defendant: "One, so far."

Judge: "The charge here is theft of frozen chickens. Are you the defendant, sir?"

Defendant: "No, sir, I'm the guy who stole the chickens."

Defense Attorney: "Are you sure you did not enter the Seven-Eleven on 40th and N.E. Broadway and hold up the cashier on June 17 of this year?"

Defendant: "I'm pretty sure."

ALICE IN LAWYERLAND

Lawyer: "Could you briefly describe the type of construction equipment used in your business?"

Witness: "Four tractors."

Lawyer: "What kind of tractors are they?"

Witness: "Fords."

Lawyer: "Did you say 'four?' "

Witness: "Ford. Ford. Like the Ford. It is a Ford tractor."

Lawyer: "You didn't say 'four,' you just said 'Ford?' "

Witness: "Yes, Ford. That is what you asked me, what kind of tractors."

Lawyer: "Are there four Ford tractors? Is that what there is?"

Witness: "No, no. You asked me what kind of a tractor it was and I said Ford tractors."

Lawyer: "How many tractors are there?"

Witness: "Four."

GOOD CALL

Judge: "It is the judgment of this court that you be sentenced to the state prison...for a term of ten years, the maximum penalty."

District Attorney: "Will that be dangerous or non-dangerous offender, Your Honor?"

Judge: "Well, considering the flagrant nature of his offense, the court finds that he's a dangerous offender."

Defendant: "How in the hell can you find me a dangerous offend-

---

When arrested, the average shoplifter has $196 of stolen goods in their possession.

er? There's nothing in there showing any violent crime. What's wrong with anybody anyway? You take that son-of-a-bitch and—

Judge: "That's will be it; you're remanded to the custody of the sheriff."

Defendant: "You son-of-a-bitch. You bald-headed son-of-a-bitch, when I get out of there, I'll blow your f——g head away. You no-good bald-headed son-of-a-bitch."

Judge: "Get that down in the record, he's threatened to blow the judge's head off."

MISTAKEN IDENTITY?

Prosecutor: "Could you point to someone in this courtroom, or maybe yourself, to indicate exactly how close to a hair color you are referring to?"

Witness: "Well, something like hers (points at the defense attorney) except for more—the woman right here in front (points at defense attorney again). Except for more cheap bleached-blond hair."

Prosecutor: "May the record reflect, Your Honor, the witness has identified Defense Counsel as the cheap blonde."

HOT WITNESS

Prosecutor: "Did you observe anything?"

Witness: "Yes, we did. When we found the vehicle, we saw several unusual items in the car in the right front floorboard of the vehicle. There was what appeared to be a Molotov cocktail, a green bottle—"

Defense lawyer: "Objection. I'm going to object to that word, Molotov cocktail."

Judge: "What is your legal objection, Counsel?"

Defense lawyer: "It's inflammatory, Your Honor."

Judge: "Mr. E., you're charged here with driving a motor vehicle under the influence of alcohol. How do you plead, guilty or not guilty?"

Defendant: "I'm guilty as hell."

Judge: "Let the record reflect the defendant is guilty as hell."

PRESIDENTIAL TRIVIA

More unusual tidbits from the occupants of 1600 Pennsylvania Ave.

George Washington wanted Americans to address him as "His Mightiness the President."

Andrew Jackson, known for his colorful language, apparently taught his parrot to curse. When Jackson died in 1845, the parrot was brought to his funeral. It swore at him through the entire service.

Millard Fillmore was the first president to sign a treaty about bird droppings. It was a U.S.-Peru agreement dealing with bird guano, which has a high nitrate content and is useful in making explosives.

While he was president, Franklin Pierce was arrested for running down an elderly woman in his carriage. He was later found not guilty.

Dwight D. Eisenhower loved to paint but couldn't draw—so he had other artists outline on his canvas the things he wanted to paint. This led directly to the paint-by-numbers fad of the 1950s.

Grover Cleveland, 22nd president, was the first one to leave the country while in office. But he didn't really go anywhere: while on a fishing trip he sailed into international waters 3 miles off the U.S. coast and came right back.

Herbert Hoover was the first president to have a telephone in his office. Earlier, presidents who wanted to use a phone had to use the one in the hall.

After Thomas Jefferson took the oath of office in 1801, he left the Capitol building and walked back to his boarding-house. Several people followed him, giving rise to the traditional inaugural parade every president has had since then.

Bad omen: It was so cold at Ulysses S. Grant's inauguration that the canaries that were supposed to sing during the inaugural ball froze to death.

President Warren G. Harding exercised regularly...by playing ping-pong.

There are 635,013,559,600 different possible hands in bridge.

AND NOW FOR SOMETHING COMPLETELY DIFFERENT

People either love or hate "Monty Python's Flying Circus." Our guess is that most B.R.I. members are pro-Python.

HOW "MONTY PYTHON" STARTED
In the mid-'60s, David Frost—one of England's most popular TV stars—began work on a new series called "The Frost Reports." The staff of young writers he hired included Michael Palin and Terry Jones (who'd performed together since college), John Cleese and Graham Chapman (who'd toured together in Cambridge University's comedy revue), and Eric Idle, a Cambridge student. It was the first time the five of them had worked together.

When Frost's show folded in 1966, they went their separate ways, but they sometimes met and discussed the possibility of doing a program together. When Terry Gilliam (an American friend of John Cleese's) moved to England, he became part of the group. Cleese helped get him a job in the BBC.

In 1969 BBC comedy producer Barry Took tried to team Palin and Cleese in their own show. But they refused to do it unless all six of the group were hired. Took decided they'd complement each other as performers and went along with it. The BBC didn't trust them…but Took insisted.

The BBC had been running a religious program late on Sunday nights, and no one was watching it…so the network decided to replace it with entertainment. That was how "Monty Python's Flying Circus" got on the air.

On October 5, 1969, anyone who tuned in for religion would have seen John Cleese instead, announcing, "And now for something completely different." At first, Monty Python was on so late that almost no one saw it. But eventually it attracted a cult following, which meant, according to the Pythons, "it was seen by insomniacs, intellectuals, and burglars."

American audiences didn't see the "Flying Circus" until years after its British debut. The first U.S. appearance was a group visit to the "Tonight Show," hosted that night by Joey Bishop. The audience had no idea what was going on and didn't find them amusing. But in 1974 Public Broadcasting Station KERA in Dallas picked up the British series, and it became one of PBS's most popular imports.

THE NAME
The group came up with a number of names before deciding on "Monty Python's Flying Circus" They almost used:
1. "A Horse, a Spoon, and a Basin"
2. "The Toad Elevating Moment"
3. "Bunn, Wackett, Buzzard, Stubble and Boot" (an imaginary soccer team's forward line)
4. "Owl Stretching Time"
5. "Gwen Dibley's Flying Circus" (Gwen was Michael Palin's music teacher when he was eleven). Soon Monty Python—a name they made up—replaced Gwen Dibley. At first the BBC rejected the troupe's crazy name, but when the Pythons threatened to change their name every week, the network relented.

THE DIALOGUE
A few samples of Python humor.

Graham Chapman: "I think TV's killed real entertainment. In the old days we used to make our own fun. At Christmas parties I used to strike myself on the head repeatedly with blunt instruments while crooning. (sings) *'Only make believe, I love you,* (hits himself on head with bricks). *Only make believe that you love me,* (hits himself). *Others find peace of mind . . .'* "

Railroad Passenger (who thinks he's been let off at the wrong stop): "I wish to make a complaint."
Porter: "I don't have to do this, you know."
Passenger "I beg your pardon?"
Porter: "I'm a qualified brain surgeon. I only do this because I like being my own boss."
Passenger: "Er, excuse me, this is irrelevant, isn't it?"
Porter: "Oh yeah, it's not easy to pad these out to thirty minutes."

Narrator: "It was a day like any other and Mr. and Mrs. Samuel Brainsample were a perfectly ordinary couple, leading perfectly ordinary lives—the sort of people to whom nothing extraordinary ever happened, and not the kind of people to be the centre of one

The U.S. had 8,915 handgun killings in 1989. Great Britain had 7.

of the most astounding incidents in the history of mankind . . . So
let's forget about them and follow instead the destiny of this man
(camera pans to businessman in bowler hat and pinstripe suit)...
Harold Potter, gardener, and tax official, first victim of Creatures
from another Planet."

Candy maker: "We use only the finest baby frogs, dew picked and
flown from Iraq, cleansed in finest quality spring water, lightly
killed, and then sealed in succulent Swiss quintuple smooth treble
cream milk chocolate envelope and lovingly frosted with glucose."

Government Hygiene Inspector: "That's as may be, but it's still a
frog."

Narrator: "Dinsdale was a gentleman. And what's more, he knew
how to treat a female impersonator."

• • •

BATHROOM ETIQUETTE

In the Middle Ages, it was considered sufficient to step "an arrow's
flight" distance into the gardens before doing what had to be done.
Royalty apparently even thought this unnecessary—one English
noble was appalled to find that the visiting king and retinue defe-
cated wherever they chose throughout his castle—and during a
conversation with a young noblewoman, he was surprised to hear
tinkling water and watch a puddle spreading across his floor beneath her long dress.

Though officially banned as early as 1395 in Paris, it was a cen-
turies-long practice throughout Europe to empty bedpans from high
windows into the street. Oft-ignored etiquette demanded that they
first shout the classic warning "Gardez l'eau!" In Edinburgh you
could hire a guide to walk ahead of you and shout "Haud your
hand!" to people in the windows above.

One of history's earliest etiquette books, penned by Erasmus of
Rotterdam (1465-1536), laid down several laws about behavior
concerning bodily functions. "It is impolite," he wrote, "to greet
someone who is urinating or defecating." He then advises the person in need of "breaking wind" to "let a cough hide the explosive
sound...Follow the law: replace farts with coughs."

ELVIS LIVES

Who really believes Elvis is still alive? Plenty of people do. As RCA Records used to ask: Can millions of Elvis fans be wrong? B.R.I. member John Dollison wrote this piece so you can judge for yourself.

Early in the morning on August 16, 1977, Elvis Presley and his girlfriend, Ginger Alden, returned to Graceland from a late-night dentist appointment. The two stayed up until about 7:00 a.m. Then Alden went to bed. But, according to one source, "because he had taken some 'uppers,' Elvis was still not sleepy."

So the King retired to his bathroom to read a book. That was the last time anyone ever saw him alive.

THE OFFICIAL STORY

• When Alden woke up at 2:00 in the afternoon, she noticed that Elvis was still in his bathroom. So she decided to check up on him.

• When she opened the door, she saw Elvis sprawled face forward on the floor. "I thought at first he might have hit his head because he had fallen," she recalls, "and his face was buried in the carpet. I slapped him a few times and it was like he breathed once when I turned his head. I lifted one eyelid and it was just blood red. But I couldn't move him." The King was dead.

• Elvis was rushed to Baptist Memorial Hospital in Memphis, but doctors could not revive him. He was pronounced dead at 3:00 p.m. The official cause of death: cardiac arrhythmia brought on by "straining at stool." (The actual cause of death: most likely a massive overdose of prescription drugs.)

That is what is supposed to have happened. Nevertheless, Elvis aficionados across the country see a host of mysterious circumstances that suggest that the King may still be alive.

SUSPICIOUS FACTS

• The medical examiner's report stated that Elvis's body was found in the bathroom in a rigor-mortised state. But the homicide report said that Elvis was found unconscious in the bedroom. In *The Elvis*

Files, Gail Brewer-Giorgio notes: "Unconsciousness and rigor mortis are at opposite ends of the physical spectrum: rigor mortis is a stiffening condition that occurs after death; unconsciousness, a state in which a living body loses awareness. Bedroom and bathroom are two different places."

• The medical examiner's report lists Elvis's weight at the time of death as 170 pounds; he actually weighed about 250 pounds.

• Elvis's relatives can't agree on how Elvis died. His stepbrother Rick claims Elvis suffocated on the shag carpet; his stepbrother David thinks Elvis committed suicide. Larry Geller, Elvis's hairdresser and spiritual adviser, claims that Elvis's doctors told Vernon Presley (Elvis's father) that the King had leukemia, which may have contributed to his death. Some theorists charge that the confusion surrounding Elvis's death proves that the star faked his death—if the King is really dead, why can't his loved ones get their stories straight?

UNANSWERED QUESTIONS
Elvis's fans want the answers to the following mysteries:

Did Elvis Foresee—or Fake—His Death?
• Elvis didn't order any new jumpsuits—his trademark outfit—in all of 1977. Why not? Did he know he wasn't going to need any?

• On his last concert tour, Elvis was overheard saying, "I may not look good tonight, but I'll look good in my coffin."

• Was Elvis imitating his manager, Colonel Tom Parker? As a young man, Parker also faked his death. An illegal immigrant from Holland whose real name was Andreas Van Kujik, Parker left Holland without telling his relatives; they thought he was dead.

Was the Corpse in Elvis's Coffin Really Elvis's?
• Country singer Tanya Tucker's sister LaCosta was at the King's funeral, and she was shocked at the body's appearance: "We went right up to his casket and stood there, and God, I couldn't believe it. He looked just like a piece of plastic laying there. He didn't look like him at all…he looked more like a dummy than a real person. You know a lot of people think it was a dummy. They don't think he was dead."

Thomas Edison was afraid of the dark.

• Some observers said they thought the corpse's nose looked too "pugged" to be the King's. They speculated that even if the King had fallen forward and smashed his nose at the time of his death, it would have naturally returned to its original shape, or would at least have been fixed by the undertaker—if the body was really Elvis's. (*The Elvis Files*)

Was the Corpse in Elvis's Coffin a Wax Dummy?

• Some theorists believe that Elvis's coffin weighed more than it was supposed to. Brewer-Giorgio reports receiving a letter from an Elvis fan who claimed to have "personally" known the man who made the King's coffin. The coffin maker revealed that the casket was a "rush" order—and that "there was no way" the coffin could have weighed 900 pounds, as the press reported—even with the King in it. So what was in the coffin with Elvis that made it so heavy?

• According to Brewer-Giorgio, the discrepancy between the coffin's actual weight with Elvis in it and its weight at the funeral is about 250 to 275 pounds, "the weight of a small air-conditioner." "Was there an air-conditioner in the coffin?" Brewer-Giorgio asks, "Wax dummy? Something cool to keep the wax from beading up?"

• To many witnesses, Elvis's corpse appeared to be "sweating" at the funeral. Brewer-Giorgio says she asked Joe Esposito, Elvis's road manager, about TV reports that there were "beads of sweat" on Elvis's body. "He said that was true, that everyone was sweating because the air-conditioner had broken down. Except that dead bodies do not sweat." *But wax melts.*

Why Were the Mourners Acting So Strange at the Funeral?

• Parker wore a loud Hawaiian shirt and a baseball cap to Elvis's funeral and never once approached the casket to say farewell to the King. Elvis's fans argue that if Elvis were *really* dead, Parker would probably have shown a little more respect.

• Elvis's hairdresser claims that he saw Esposito remove Elvis's TCB (Takin' Care of Business) ring from the corpse's finger during the funeral services. Why would he remove one of Elvis's favorite pieces of jewelry—Elvis would surely have wanted to have been buried with it—unless the corpse being buried wasn't the King's?

Is Elvis in the Federal Witness Protection Program?

• In 1970, Presley—a law enforcement buff—was made an honorary Agent-at-Large of the Drug Enforcement Administration by President Nixon after a visit to the White House. According to some theorists, Presley became more than just an honorary agent—he actually got involved in undercover narcotics work.

• In addition to his DEA work, Elvis may have been an FBI agent. During the same trip to Washington D.C., Elvis also wrote a letter to J. Edgar Hoover volunteering his confidential services to the FBI. Hoover wrote back thanking Elvis for his offer, but there is no record of him ever taking it up. Still, Brewer-Giorgio and other theorists argue, the government may have been keeping the King's government service a secret.

• According to Brewer-Giorgio, Elvis was also "a bonded deputy with the Memphis Police and was known to don disguises and go out on narc busts."

• Elvis took his law enforcement role seriously. More than one biography details the time that the King ran out onto the runway of the Las Vegas airport, flagged down a taxiing commercial airliner, and searched it for a man whom he believed had stolen something from him. Elvis looked around, realized his quarry wasn't aboard, and gave the pilot permission to take off.

• Some theorists believe that Elvis's extensive work in law enforcement made him a target for drug dealers and the Mob—and that he entered the Federal Witness Protection Program out of fear for his life. According to Brewer-Giorgio, when Elvis supplied the information that sent a major drug dealer to prison, the King and his family received death threats.

Could Elvis Be in Hiding?

Hundreds of Elvis's loyal fans think they have spotted the King since his "death." He's been sighted at a Rolling Stones concert, working at a Burger King in Kalamazoo, buying gas in Tennessee, and shopping for old Monkees records in Michigan. One woman even claims that Elvis gave her a bologna sandwich and a bag of Cheetos during a 1987 visit to the Air Force Museum in Dayton, Ohio. Could so many people be lying or mistaken?

According to zoologists, elephants love to eat licorice.

OTHER MYSTERIES COLLECTED BY ELVIS FANS

• Vernon Presley never went to the hospital the night Elvis "died."
If Elvis were really dead, some theorists speculate, he probably
would have.

• According to some reports, within hours of Presley's death,
souvenir shops near Graceland began selling commemorative
T-shirts of his death. How could they have made so many T-shirts
in so little time—unless Graceland had let them know about the
"death" in advance?

• Elvis's middle name, Aron, is misspelled "Aaron" on his tombstone. If Elvis is really dead, why don't his relatives correct the mistake?

• Elvis is not buried next to his mother as he requested. Says Brewer-Giorgio: " 'Elvis loved his mother very much and always said he
would be buried beside her,' many fans have noted. 'So why is he
buried between his father and grandmother?' they ask."

• On a number of occasions after the King's death, Priscilla Presley
referred to Elvis as a *living* legend—strange words for a woman who
supposedly believes that Elvis is dead.

• Before he died, Elvis took out a multimillion-dollar life insurance
policy. To date, no one in his family has tried to claim it. If Elvis's
family really believes he is dead, why haven't they cashed in the
policy?

PASSING ON

• The people who were in Elvis's home when he died insist that he
really *did* die. Joe Esposito, Elvis's road manager for 17 years, was
one of the first people to see the body. "Believe me, the man that I
tried to revive was Elvis."

• Elvis may even have committed suicide. According to his stepbrother David Stanley, "Elvis was too intelligent to overdose [acci-
dentally]. He knew the *Physician's Desk Reference* inside and out."
Why would Elvis take his own life? He was getting old, and the
strain of his stagnating career may have become too much to bear.
The pressure showed: in the last years of his life, Elvis's weight bal-
looned to more than 250 pounds, and his addiction to prescription

drugs had gotten out of control.

• The impending publication of a book chronicling the King's erratic behavior and his drug problem may have been the final straw. In August 1977, the month of his death, two of his former aides were about to publish a book revealing much of his bizarre personal life to the public for the first time. He was already depressed, and the imminent public exposure of his drug habit may have pushed him over the edge.

RECOMMENDED READING
The Elvis Files, by Gail Brewer-Giorgio (Shapolsky Publishers, 1990). *A fountain of Elvis conspiracies*.

• • • •

BEAUTY SECRETS OF THE MISS AMERICA PAGEANT
Who says beauty is only skin deep? In September 1992, TV's Entertainment Tonight interviewed makeup artists affiliated with the Miss America Pageant to learn how they keep America's beauties beautiful. Here are some of the tricks of the trade:

Dirty Hair. As Billy Holt, one of the pageant's hairstylists, admitted: "Dirty hair is more manageable. I can make a style fuller and stay better."

Face Putty. Creates "porcelain" complexions by filling in lines, scars, pock marks, and other facial irregularities. One makeup artist, Jane White, admitted "I've even gone so far as to use mortician's wax mixed with the makeup."

Vaseline. Smeared on the teeth so that contestants can smile easily—even if their mouths dry up from nervousness.

Preparation H. The hemorrhoid ointment is smeared on eyelids and under the eyes. According to one makeup artist, "It smells pretty bad, but it removes puffiness."

Sculpted Body Sponges. Stuffed into bathing suits and evening gowns, sponges will "increase contestant's bust size by one cup."

A BREED APART

Ever wonder why a Dachsund is so long and skinny—or why Great Danes are so tall? The answer: They were bred with a specific purpose in mind. Here are the stories behind the names and appearances of some of the world's most popular dog breeds.

BASSET HOUNDS. The name comes from the French adjective *bas*, which means "low thing." Originally bred to hunt rabbits, raccoons, and other small mammals. Their short legs make them relatively slow runners, but they're especially adept at chasing prey through thickets.

BULLDOGS. According to legend, in 1209 A.D. Lord William Earl Warren of Stamford, England, was looking out onto his meadow and saw two dogs fighting a bull. He so admired their courage that he gave the meadow to the townspeople—on the condition that they begin holding annual dog-bull fights. Over the next 600 years, bullbaiting became a popular sport, and the bulldog breed evolved along with it. Like pit-bulls, bulldogs were originally bred to be fearless and vicious. But in 1835, bullbaiting was banned in England. Bulldog lovers used breeding techniques to eliminate their viciousness, making them acceptable house pets.

COCKER SPANIELS. A member of the *Spanyell* family of dogs that dates back to the 14th century. Their small size made them ideal for hunting woodcocks, earning them the name *cockers*, which eventually became *cocking spaniels*, then *cocker spaniels*.

FRENCH POODLES. Actually bred in 15th-century Germany as hunting dogs. The name "poodle" comes from the German word *pudel*, which means puddle or splash. The reason: They're good swimmers and were often used to retrieve game from ponds, etc.

GREAT DANES. Got their name from the French, who thought they were Danish. They weren't: they were actually from Germany, where they were bred large enough to tackle and kill wild boars.

It takes 12 bees their entire lifetime to make a tablespoon of honey.

ROTTWEILERS. When soldiers of ancient Rome went into battle, they had no way of bringing enough fresh meat with them to last the entire campaign. So they brought cattle—and Rottweiler dogs to herd them. In 700 A.D., the local duke in an area of Germany the Romans had once occupied commissioned a Catholic church to be built near the ruins of some Roman baths. Because the baths had red tile roofs, the Duke issued instructions to build at "das Rote Wil,"—the red tiles. Later the area became known as the town of Rottweil, and the breed of dogs the Romans had left behind were called Rottweilers.

GREYHOUNDS. One of the oldest breeds of dogs; dating back as far as ancient Egypt (where they were a favorite pet of the pharoahs). Tomb paintings nearly 5,000 years old depict them hunting wild goats, deer, and other animals. According to one theory they're actually named after the Greeks, taking their name from the word *Graius*, which means Grecian or Greek.

DACHSHUNDS. Although the name is derived from the German words *dachs* (badger) and *hund* (dog), dachshunds have been used to hunt animals as large as wild boars. Their long bodies make them ideal for chasing badgers and rabbits through their tunnels.

BLOODHOUNDS. The bloodhound's unrivaled sense of smell has made it one of the most popular hunting dogs in history. Dog experts believe it dates back several hundred years B.C. and was first used as a hunting dog in and around Constantinople. Its skills were so valuable that it became known as a royal, or "blooded" hound, and was a favorite pet of aristocrats.

PEKINGESE. Came from imperial China, where the purest breeds were reserved for members of the royal family. The dogs were so precious that when British troops sacked the Imperial Palace in 1860, most of the pets were destroyed by their owners...who preferred killing them to surrendering them to the enemy. However one woman—the Emperor's aunt—committed suicide before she killed her dogs, and the British found 5 of them hiding behind a curtain in her quarters. The dogs were brought back to England, and one was presented to Queen Victoria. She fell in love with it, and the breed immediately became popular.

The busiest pay phone in the U.S.—used over 270 times a day—is in the Chicago bus terminal.

ON THE LINE

Here's a great practical joke that can be played from any telephone with two extensions. Reprinted with permission from The Complete Book of Outrageous and Atrocious Practical Jokes *by Justin Geste.*

"Of all telephone pranks conceived, this perhaps is the most ingenious, crafty, perplexing, bizarre, and often hilarious. To execute this practical joke, a telephone with two extensions is required. The most easily adapted for this prank is that model with buttons that are depressed to get a different line. (There is often a "Hold" button on these models as well.) By taking the telephone apart, the two lines can be connected so that two different outgoing calls can be placed at the same time. (Sorry, the details of how exactly to do this are going to be kept a secret. Our intention is to amuse, not dismantle the nation's communications system.)" [B.R.I. note: *You can also perform this prank with any phone that has a "conference call" feature.*]

MAKING A CALL

"Once the two lines are connected, you are ready to go. If you are working alone, you need only dial the first six numbers of one target's phone number, place it on hold, quickly dial the other target's number on the other line, then switch back and dial the seventh number of the first target's phone number. Then press down the buttons for both lines and listen to both phones ring. (Mechanical ingenuity can show you how this is possible.)

"If you are working with an accomplice, you can each dial on separate extensions a different person at the same time, provided one of you has connected the two lines on his phone. Thus, you both dial your different numbers on different phones at the same time, and, voila, both phones at the other end begin to ring at the same time. Both persons who receive the call think the other has phoned him or her. So, if one of you calls your mother and the other calls your father, both your parents will pick up a ringing phone and ask why the other called. If a person has an answering machine at home, you can call him at work, while your accomplice calls

---

Giraffes and mice have the same number of neck bones: seven.

your target's answering machine. The result is the bizarre experience of your target receiving a call from his own answering machine. You can connect old lovers, new lovers, students who cut class with their teachers, criminals with the police, and any unlikely couple you deem fit. Remember, though, the persons you call can hear your voice on the line. You are essentially creating a conference call with your fiddling. See how practical this book is?"

THE CONVERSATION
To show how far this prank can be taken we offer the following true-life example, committed by two pranksters against an antagonist of theirs, here called Wanda.

Wanda had just submitted her undergraduate thesis on barbecue (yes, a thesis on barbecue) to her professor, so John and Alan began by connecting Wanda to her teacher.

"Hello," said the professor.

"Hello," said Wanda.

"Who are you calling?" asked the professor after a pause.

"Who are you calling?" asked Wanda.

"Lady, you called me," said the professor.

"No, I didn't. You called me," said Wanda.

"I certainly didn't. My phone just rang."

"So did mine."

"There must be some problem. Where are you calling from?"

"Hunter County," said Wanda.

"That's where I am," said the professor.

"I'm in Hattersville," said Wanda.

"So am I."

"I'm calling from Monroe College," said Wanda.

"I'm at the faculty building in my office."

There was a pause.

"Professor Burns!" said Wanda.

"Who's this?" asked Professor Burns.

"Wanda Adams."

"Why did you call me?"

"I didn't. My phone rang. I thought you called me," said Wanda.

"I didn't."

Another pause.

"You have my thesis, don't you?" asked Wanda.

"Yes, but I haven't read it. I only got it yesterday."

"Right. I didn't expect you would have. All right, good-bye."

"Good-bye," said the professor.

John and Alan called Wanda back, connecting her this time with a pizza parlor.

"Hello," said Wanda.

"Hello," said an employee at the pizza parlor.

"Yes?"

"Do you want to order?" asked the voice.

"Order what?" asked Wanda. "Who do you want to speak to?"

"Nobody. You called here. We're a pizza parlor."

"You called me," said Wanda.

"No, I didn't. You called me. The phone rang."

"So did mine," said Wanda.

"Lady, we're a pizza parlor. We don't call people to see if they want to make an order."

"Forget it. Good-bye." Wanda hung up.

This time John and Alan connected Wanda to the college switchboard.

"Who is this?" asked Wanda in perplexed tones.

"Monroe College switchboard. Can I help you?" said a woman.

"Why did you call me?" asked Wanda.

"Madam, you called me. Can I help you?"

"But my phone just rang. Why did you call?"

"Madam, the college switchboard does not make outgoing calls."

Survey results: 31% of American women say they wear only comfortable shoes.

After connecting Wanda to Alcoholics Anonymous, John and Alan called her directly.

"This is the telephone company calling," said Alan. "We understand that you're having some problems with your line."

"Thank God. Yes," said Wanda, relieved.

"We're also told that you're playing some sort of prank on persons in your calling area. Would you please stop this immediately?"

"I'm not playing any prank. I keep getting calls from people who say they're not calling me."

"All right, whatever. We're going to do some work on the line in your area. For a few minutes the wires will be exposed to the lineman on the job. So, if your phone rings, please don't pick it up, since that could cause the lineman to be electrocuted."

"All right," said Wanda reluctantly.

Then, as you no doubt have guessed, John and Alan called her back. After failing to respond on several occasions, Wanda finally gave in and picked up the phone.

"Aaaaiieeeeeee!" screeched Alan, in a highly realistic impersonation of a lineman being electrocuted. Wanda screamed and dropped the phone.

After a few minutes, they called Wanda back.

"This is the telephone company," said Alan. "Did you answer the phone?"

"Yes," said Wanda weakly, "I thought—"

"The lineman we told you about has been severely electrocuted."

"Oh, no."

"Oh, yes. We and lawyers will be in touch with you soon, you can be sure." Alan hung up.

Next they connected Wanda with the real phone company.

"Hello," said Wanda, tiring rapidly.

"Hello," said a man at the phone company.

"Who is this?" asked Wanda.

"It's the phone company."

"I'm so glad you called back. What's going on?"

"Ma'am, we didn't call you. You called us."

"No, I didn't. My phone just rang. Aren't you calling about my broken phone?"

"I'm sorry, ma'am, but we have no way of knowing a phone is broken unless a customer calls us."

"But you just called me about the fellow being electrocuted."

"I'm afraid we didn't," said the man, convinced he had some loony on the phone—which was not far from the truth.

When that conversation ended, John and Alan connected Wanda back to the pizza parlor, a crisis hotline, and finally back to Professor Burns.

"Hello," said the professor.

"Hello," said Wanda.

"Adams, what is it now?"

"Professor Burns—"

"Wanda, I have not had time to grade your thesis, so you needn't call me."

"But I didn't call you. My phone rang. Something crazy is going on."

"Get some sleep, Adams."

"Professor, I didn't call you."

"Okay. Good-bye."

Finally, Wanda was connected back to the phone company. In the midst of that conversation, though, Alan let go a burst of laughter which in an instant identified him to his target.

THE BIRTH OF WASHINGTON, D.C.

This fascinating story is from one of our favorite bathroom books—
Extraordinary Origins of Everyday Things *by Charles Panati.*

T he idea for a national capital city in a remote, inconvenient
area originated at a June 1783 meeting of the Congress in
the Old City Hall in Philadelphia.

WHY A NEW CITY?

"While several factors contributed to the decision, one in particular galvanized Congress to action. The War of Independence had
recently been concluded. The treasury was flat broke. The new nation had no credit, still lacked a president, and was heavily in debt
to its soldiers for back pay. On June 20, a large and angry mob of
unpaid soldiers invaded Philadelphia to present their grievances to
Congress. It was not the first such violent confrontation. That day,
though, a number of agitated congressmen—some angry, others
frightened—expressed their weariness with such direct public intru-
sions. They launched a movement to establish a federal city where
lawmakers could transact the business of state without civilian
intimidation."

PICKING A SITE

"Several locations were considered. New Englanders, led by Alexander Hamilton of New York, sought a capital in the north. South-
erners, represented by Thomas Jefferson of Virginia, argued for a location in the south. In 1790, in an attempt to placate both sides,
the recently elected president, George Washington, chose a site
eighteen miles up the Potomac River from his home in Mount Vernon—a location then midway between north and south. In addition, the area was between the thriving seaports of Alexandria, Virginia, and Georgetown, Maryland. No one denied, however, that
the ten-mile-square site was a bog.

"After several years of planning, in September 1793 President
Washington himself laid the cornerstone for the first U.S. Capitol.
Office buildings were quickly erected. By 1800, the U.S. govern-

---

Most experts believe Jack the Ripper was left-handed.

ment had officially moved headquarters from Philadelphia to Washington."

THE UNPOPULAR CITY

"No one was pleased with the new city. Congressmen complained that it was too isolated. A wilderness. They and their families resisted constructing homes there, as did government employees. Groups of citizens petitioned that the capital city be relocated to a more desirable, prestigious, and accessible location. What had been conceived by Washington as a 'city of magnificent distances' was now disparagingly attacked by congressmen as a 'capital of miserable huts,' 'a mudhole.' Abigail Adams, wife of the first president to occupy the presidential mansion, expressed a desire to move out, lamenting, 'We have not the least convenience.'

"By the close of Thomas Jefferson's term of office, in 1809, the population of the nation's new city was scarcely five thousand. To foreign heads of state, America's capital was a nightmare. With a dearth of cultural institutions and personal conveniences, and with the Potomac continually muddying the dirt streets, foreign ambassadors stationed in the capital actually collected 'hardship pay' from their governments."

THE NATIONAL TREASURE

"The advent of the steam engine and the telegraph quelled some of the complaints. These inventions put the city in touch with the outside world. But the real change of attitude toward the new capital, in the minds of both ordinary citizens and government officials, resulted from a national tragedy.

"In August 1814, the British invaded the city. They burned the President's mansion, the Capitol, and the Navy Arsenal. Americans were incensed. And they were united, too, against an enemy that had attempted to destroy the nation's capital—even if that capital was inaccessible, inhospitable, and undesirable to live in. All clamor to relocate the city ceased. An immense and patriotic rebuilding effort began. Jefferson donated his own extensive collection of books to replace the destroyed contents of the Library of Congress. And the badly charred wooden planks of the President's mansion were painted a shimmering white, conferring upon it for all time the title the White House."

WHO KILLED MALCOLM X?

The film version of Malcolm X's autobiography put this controversial leader in the spotlight again, 27 years after his assassination. But it also raised some interesting questions about how and why he was killed. Was it a government plot? Read this excerpt from It's a Conspiracy!, *by the National Insecurity Council, and judge for yourself.*

On February 21, 1965, Malcolm X rose to address a largely black crowd in the Audubon Ballroom in New York City. But before he could begin speaking, a scuffle broke out in the audience.

In *Seven Days,* Alan Berger described what happened next: "All heads turned to see what was happening...Malcolm's bodyguards moved down from the stage toward the disturbance. Malcolm himself stepped out from behind the podium and toward the front of the stage.

"There was a muffled explosion at the rear of the hall and smoke... a woman screamed. A man in one of the front rows held up a sawed-off shotgun and fired into Malcolm's chest. As Malcolm keeled over, two or three men were seen standing in the front row, 'like a firing squad,' pumping bullets into him. After he had fallen, the gunmen emptied their revolvers into the inert body."

According to a 1967 article in *The Realist,* "All eyewitness reports of the assassination indicated a total of five gunmen had been involved, but only one, Thomas Hagan, was caught after he was slowed by a thrown chair and shot in the leg." Hagan was a member of a militant religious sect—the Black Muslims—from which Malcolm had recently broken off. The following week, two more suspects (both Black Muslim "enforcers") were arrested. All three were convicted and sentenced to life in prison.

BACKGROUND
• Malcolm X's pilgrimage from street tough to international figure began in prison when he discovered the writings of Elijah Mohammed. This Black Muslim philosophy of racial separation and black self-reliance appealed to Malcolm, and when he was released from jail in 1952, he joined the group. He quickly became their most effective

evangelist…and their most prominent spokesman. He was often quoted in the national press.

• In 1963, while the country was still grieving the death of President Kennedy, he remarked that the murder was just a case of "the chickens coming home to roost." His remark so incensed the public that the Black Muslims suspended him.

• Unrepentant, he quit the church in March 1964, and started his own group, taking so many Black Muslims with him that Elijah Mohammed's followers vowed revenge. Malcolm repeatedly told aides that he had been "marked for death."

• From the beginning of the investigation, the police and FBI assumed the killing had been ordered by the Black Muslims. The media echoed that official story. The *New York Herald Tribune*'s report was typical: "Now the hatred and violence that he preached has overwhelmed him, and he has fallen at the hand of Negroes."

WAS IT A CONSPIRACY?

Many prominent blacks saw a different reason why Malcolm X had been killed. Some suspected the U.S. government. Said CORE National Director James Foreman in The New York Times: *"The killing of Malcolm X was a political act, with international implications and not necessarily connected with black nationalism."*

A THORN IN THE GOVERNMENT'S SIDE

• In 1964 Malcolm X visited Mecca and Africa. He was greeted as the roving ambassador of an American black nation; he met with presidents, prime ministers, and kings. In Ghana, for example, he addressed a joint session of the Ghanian parliament—the first American to do so. Wherever he went, he encouraged African governments to speak out against American racism. He also reported that wherever he went in Africa, he was followed by CIA agents.

• In July 1964 he traveled to Cairo to address the Summit Conference of African prime minsters. There he introduced a program to "bring the American racial problem before the U.N. under the Human Rights provision of its charter, as South Africa had been." (*The Realist*)

• A few weeks later, the State and Justice departments acknowledged that they considered Malcolm a threat. A spokesman told

The New York Times: "If [Malcolm X] succeeds in convincing just one African government to bring up the charge at the United Nations, the United States government would be faced with a touchy problem."

• After returning to the U.S., Malcolm X continued to push for his U.N. program. In the fall of 1964, he spent most of his time at the U.N., lobbying African delegates to support his efforts. In November 1964 the U.S. intervened in the Congo Civil War. Malcolm X warned African leaders that if they didn't speak out, "the same thing can happen to you."

• They took his advice. During a U.N. General Assembly debate on the Congo, African delegates condemned the U.S. as being indifferent to the fate of blacks everywhere, citing as evidence the U.S. government's attitude toward the civil rights struggle in Mississippi. The State Department reportedly blamed Malcolm X for its embarrassment.

• Friends and family were concerned that Malcolm X was taking a great risk by interfering in American foreign policy. He was under constant surveillance. His half sister, Ella Collins, said she had heard from reliable sources that there were even CIA agents in the group Malcolm X had founded, the Organization of Afro-American Unity. "Malcolm knew the dangers, but he said he had to go ahead." (*Seven Days*)

• Just before he was killed, Malcolm X told his biographer, Alex Haley, that he no longer believed that the biggest threat to his life was the Black Muslim organization. "I know what they can do, and what they can't, and they can't do some of the stuff recently going on." (ibid.)

SUSPICIOUS FACTS
In Cairo
• The U.S. State Department didn't want Malcolm X to attend the summit in Cairo. The U.S. embassy in Cairo tried, and failed, to get the Egyptian government to bar his appearance. (*The New York Times*)

• The day before Malcolm X was scheduled to speak at the summit, he ate dinner at the Hilton Hotel in Cairo. Shortly after the meal, he collapsed with severe stomach pains. He was rushed to a hospital.

• "His stomach was pumped out, cleaned thoroughly, and that saved him," said an associate. "Malcolm said afterwards he would have died if he had not got immediate treatment." Reportedly, a "toxic substance" was found, and natural food poisoning was ruled out. Malcolm suspected the CIA. (*The Realist*)

In France

• Two weeks before he was killed, Malcolm X was scheduled to address a conference in France, as he had on other occasions. But when his plane landed, he was told he could not disembark—the French Government had branded him "an undesirable person." He was ordered to leave the country immediately.

• Three months earlier Malcolm X had visited France without incident, so he was baffled by the expulsion order: "I was surprised when I arrived in Paris and was prohibited from landing. I thought that if there were any country in Europe that was liberal in its approach to the problem it was France."

• After the assassination, a prominent North African diplomat approached an American journalist with information about the incident. "This official, who insists on anonymity, said that the French Department of Alien Documentation and Counter Espionage had been quietly informed that the CIA planned to murder Malcolm, and France feared he might be liquidated on its soil." (*Seven Days*)

Firebombing

• Ten hours after Malcolm X's return from France, four firebombs were hurled into his home in Queens, New York. It looked like a professional hit job, with bombs positioned to block all possible escapes. Fortunately the fourth bomb glanced off a windowpane and exploded harmlessly on the front lawn, allowing Malcolm, his wife, and their four children to narrowly escape. The house was destroyed.

• To Malcolm X, the timing of the attack could not be chalked up to coincidence: "It was no accident that I was barred from

France, and ten hours after I arrived home my home was bombed," he declared at a February 17, 1965, press conference.

• Malcolm X announced, "We are demanding an immediate investigation by the FBI of the bombing. We feel a conspiracy has been entered into at the local level, with some local police, firemen and press. Neither I, nor my wife and child have insurance, and we stand in no way to gain from the bombing....My attorney has instructed me and my wife to submit to a lie detector test and will ask that the same test be given to police and firemen at the scene." But Malcolm X's hopes of pursuing this investigation were cut short eight days later.

THE ASSASSINATION

Police Protection

• Malcolm X had held meetings in the Audubon Ballroom many times before. Usually, there was a large contingent of uniformed police to prevent violence from followers of Elijah Mohammad. But on the day he was murdered, there were only two uniformed police officers—posted at the exit. (*Seven Days*)

• After the murder, New York Deputy Police Commissioner Walter Arm claimed that protection had been offered to Malcolm X, but that he had refused it. According to Alex Haley, however, Malcolm X had made repeated requests for increased protection, but the police had ignored him. (*Seven Days*)

Gene Roberts

• The police certainly knew about the threats against Malcolm X. His chief bodyguard, Gene Roberts—who was with him when he was assassinated—was an undercover New York City policeman.

• Roberts actually did his best to save Malcolm X. He attacked one of the armed assailants with a chair and chased him into a crowd. When the assailant was captured by the crowd, Roberts returned to give Malcolm mouth-to-mouth resuscitation.

• According to *Newsday*, later in the evening, Roberts was called by his supervisors and questioned extensively. Why had he, for example, given Malcolm mouth-to-mouth resuscitation and tried to stop the gunman? "Isn't that what I'm supposed to do?" Roberts responded. "I'm a cop. It's my job to save people's lives. What was I supposed to do...let him bleed to death?"

• Years after the assassination Roberts voiced his doubts about the integrity of the police and raised questions about a larger conspiracy. Certain events at that meeting seemed particularly suspicious to Roberts:

√ After the shooting, "people were trying to get medical help from Columbia-Presbyterian Hospital," which was across the street from the hall. "It damn near took them a half an hour."

√ No other policemen came to Gene's assistance. "The cops were outside. None of them came inside."

The Patsies

• Although eyewitness accounts suggest there were as many as five gunmen, only three were captured, and only one of those was actually apprehended in the ballroom.

• Gunman Thomas Hagan was shot in the leg as he fled the ballroom and was quickly trapped by the crowd and arrested by police. But it was only after an "intensive investigation" that two others, Norman Butler and Thomas Johnson, were arrested weeks later. Both were "enforcers" for the Black Muslims who were awaiting trial for the shooting of a Muslim defector.

• When Hagan stood trial he confessed to the murder, but he told the court that the other two suspects were innocent: "I just want the truth to be known—that Butler and Johnson didn't have anything to do with this crime. Because I was there. I know what happened and I know the people who were there." (*Seven Days*)

• On March 1, 1966, *The New York Times* reported that Hagan "said that he had three accomplices, but he declined to name them. He said he had been approached early in the month of the murder and offered money for the job, but he declined to say by whom....One thing he did know, he said, was that no one involved in the murder was a Black Muslim."

• Regardless, on April 16, 1966, Hagan, Johnson, and Butler were each sentenced to life imprisonment for Malcolm X's murder.

The One That Got Away

• There may have been another suspect caught at the scene who mysteriously disappeared. The first edition of *The New York Times* the next day reported that one of the two police officers at the exit "said he 'grabbed a suspect' whom people were chasing. 'As I brought him to the front of the ballroom, the crowd began beating me and the suspect,' Patrolman Hoy said. He said he put this man—not otherwise identified later for newsmen—into a police car to be taken to the Wadsworth Avenue station." (*The Realist*)

• That second suspect was never heard from again, and the press did not pursue the issue. In later editions of the *Times*, the story had been changed and the earlier subhead, "Police Hold Two For Question," had been changed to "One Is Held In Killing." (ibid.)

• What makes the case of this mystery suspect even more intriguing is that his appearance—"a thin-lipped, olive-skinned Latin-looking man"—matches the description of a man whom Malcolm X had noticed trailing him through London and on the plane to New York one week before his death. (ibid.)

BURYING THE TRUTH

The Films

• According to a February 25, 1965, article in *The New York Times*: "the police were in possession of motion pictures that had been taken at the Audubon Ballroom...where the killing took place." These films would have been invaluable evidence—but there was no further mention of them by press or police. (*The Realist*)

The Mysterious Death of Leon Ameer

• Leon Ameer was the New England representative of Malcolm X's group, the Organization of Afro-American Unity—and many believed him to be Malcolm X's hand-picked successor. On March 13, 1965, he announced, "I have facts in my possession as to who *really* killed Malcolm X. The killers aren't from Chicago [Muslim headquarters]. They're from Washington." (*The Realist*)

• Ameer promised to hold a press conference to reveal evidence proving the "power structure's" involvement in the killing, including documents and a tape recording Malcolm X had given him.

• The next morning, Ameer's body was discovered by a maid in Boston's Sherry Biltmore Hotel. The police announced that he had died of an epileptic fit, but Ameer's wife contended that her husband had had a complete medical checkup just one month before—"and there was no hint of epilepsy." (ibid.)

RECOMMENDED READING

• "The Murder of Malcolm X" by Eric Norden (*The Realist*, Feb. 1967)

• "Who Killed Malcolm X?" by Alan Berger (*Seven Days*, March 24 and April 7, 1978)

• • • •

TALES OF THE CIA

• As the Cold War ended, the CIA decided it needed to project "a greater openness and sense of public responsibility." So it commissioned a task force. On December 20, 1991, the committee submitted a 15-page "Task Force Report on Greater Openness." It is stamped SECRET, and agency officials refuse to disclose any of the contents.

• In its war against Fidel Castro during the 1960s, the CIA literally tried to play hardball politics. "The CIA tried to cut off the supply of baseballs to Cuba. Agents persuaded suppliers in other countries not to ship them. (U.S. baseballs were already banned by the trade embargo the U.S. had declared.)" The bizarre embargo was effective. Some balls got through, "but the supply was so limited that the government had to ask fans to throw foul balls and home runs back onto the field for continued play."

—Jonathan Kwitny, *Endless Enemies*

• Quiz: What motto is inscribed on the wall of the CIA headquarters in Langley, Virginia?

A) "Keep the Faith" B) "And Ye Shall Know Truth and the Truth Shall Make You Free" C) "A Secret Kept Is a Secret Saved"

Answer: B

4% of California automobiles have personalized license plates.

THE TV SPEECH THAT MADE A PRESIDENT

Richard Nixon's "Checkers Speech" was a trademark mixture of self-pity, pathos, paranoia, sentimentality and attack. It was the most important speech of his life, because it saved his career and made him a national figure. But it was also one of the most important speeches ever made on TV because it established the power of the medium to influence the political process.

BACKGROUND

In the summer of 1952, the Republican party nominated General Dwight D. Eisenhower for president and Senator Richard M. Nixon of California for vice president.

Nixon, who'd only been in politics for six years, was clearly the rising star of the Republican party. But in the middle of September, his political career suddenly became endangered. Investigative reporters revealed that for two years, a group of wealthy Californians had contributed $18,000 to a secret Nixon slush fund. Nixon insisted he'd done nothing wrong—the money was simply "to help defray political expenses." But polls showed that most Americans thought he was a crook, and should give up the VP nomination.

Right or Wrong?

Eisenhower wasn't sure. He declared in a formal statement he believed "Dick Nixon to be an honest man." But behind the scenes, his advisors were hotly debating the issue. Was it worse strategy to dump Nixon...or to keep him on and let him drag the whole ticket down?

Eventually, even Republicans began to clamor for Nixon's resignation. At that point, Ike made it clear that unless Nixon could prove he was "clean as a hound's tooth," the veep-to-be would be off the ticket.

After a private meeting with Eisenhower, Nixon announced he would make a nationwide radio and TV address. People wondered whether he would defend himself or resign from the campaign. Nixon wouldn't even tell his own aides what he planned.

Suzuki is the most common last name in Japan.

THE CHECKERS SPEECH

Immediately following the "Milton Berle Show" on September 23, 1952, Senator Richard Nixon took to the airwaves to defend himself.

The program began with a shot of Nixon's calling card. Then the camera focused on the senator, who was sitting behind a desk. Here are some excerpts of what Nixon said:

"My Fellow Americans: I come before you tonight as a candidate for the vice presidency and as a man whose honesty and integrity have been questioned....I am sure that you have read the charge and you've heard that I, Senator Nixon, took $18,000 from a group of my supporters. Now, was that wrong? Because it isn't a question of whether it was legal or illegal, that isn't enough. The question is, was it morally wrong?...

"Let me say this: Not one cent of the $18,000 ever went to me for my personal use. Every penny of it was used to pay for political expenses that I did not think should be charged to the taxpayers of the United States"

Paying Political Expenses

"The question arises, you say, 'Well, how do you pay for these and how can you do it legally?' There are several ways that it can be done. The first way is to be a rich man. I don't happen to be a rich man so I couldn't use that. Another way that is used is to put your wife on the payroll. Let me say, incidentally, my opponent, my opposite number for the vice presidency on the Democratic ticket, does have his wife on the payroll. And has had her on his payroll for the past ten years....

"Now just let me say this. That's his business and I'm not critical of him for doing that. You will have to pass judgment on that particular point. But I have never done that for this reason. I have found that there are so many deserving stenographers and secretaries in Washington that needed the work that I just didn't feel it was right to put my wife on the payroll.

"My wife's sitting over here. She's a wonderful stenographer. She used to teach stenography and she used to teach shorthand in high school. That was when I met her. And I'm proud to say tonight that in the six years I've been in the House and the Senate of the

United States, Pat Nixon has never been on the government payroll."

Here's What I'll Do

"Now what I am going to do—and incidentally this is unprecedented in the history of American politics—I am going at this time to give to this television and radio audience a complete financial history; everything I've earned; everything I've spent; everything I owe. I want you to know the facts. I'll have to start early.

"I was born in 1913. Our family was one of modest circumstances and most of my early life was spent in a store out in East Whittier. It was a grocery store—one of those family enterprises....I worked my way through college and to a great extent through law school. And then, in 1940, probably the best thing that ever happened to me happened, I married Pat—sitting over here. We had a rather difficult time after we were married, like so many of the young couples who may be listening to us. I practiced law; she continued to teach school. I went into the service."

The Respectable Cloth Coat

"Now what have I earned since I went into politics? Well, here it is—I jotted it down, let me read the notes. First of all I've had my salary as a Congressman and as a Senator....I have made an average of approximately $1,500 a year from nonpolitical speaking engagements and lectures. And then, fortunately, we've inherited a little money....

"What did we do with this money? What do we have today to show for it? This will surprise you, because it is so little, I suppose, as standards generally go, of people in public life. First of all, we've got a house in Washington, which cost $41,000 and on which we owe $20,000.

"We have a house in Whittier, California, which cost $13,000 and on which we owe $10,000....I have just $4,000 in life insurance, plus my G. I. policy which I've never been able to convert...I have no life insurance whatever on Pat. I have no life insurance on our two youngsters, Patricia and Julie. I own a 1950 Oldsmobile car. We have our furniture. We have no stocks and bonds of any type. We have no interest of any kind, direct or indirect, in any business."

Financial Whiz: Rock star Mick Jagger went to the London School of Economics for 2 years.

"It isn't very much but Pat and I have the satisfaction that every dime that we've got is honestly ours. Pat doesn't have a mink coat. But she does have a respectable Republican cloth coat. And I always tell her that she'd look good in anything."

I'm Keeping Checkers
"One other thing I probably should tell you because if I don't they'll probably be saying this about me, too, we did get something—a gift—after the election. A man down in Texas heard Pat on the radio mention the fact that our two youngsters would like to have a dog. And, believe it or not, the day before we left on this campaign trip we got a message from Union Station in Baltimore saying they had a package for us. We went down to get it. You know what it was?

"It was a little cocker spaniel dog in a crate that he sent all the way from Texas. Black and white spotted. And our little girl—Trisha, the 6-year-old—named it Checkers. And you know, the kids love the dog and I just want say this right now, that regardless of what they say about it, we're gonna keep it."

Just a Common Fellow
"It's fine that a man like Governor Stevenson who inherited a fortune from his father can run for president. But I also feel that it's essential in this country of ours that a man of modest means can also run for president. Because, you know, remember Abraham Lincoln, you remember what he said: "God must have loved the common people—he made so many of them.""

I'm a Fighter, Not a Quitter
"Now, let me say this: I know that this is not the last of the smears. In spite of my explanation tonight other smears will be made; others have been made in the past. And the purpose of the smears, I know, is this—to silence me, to make me let up.

"Well, they just don't know who they're dealing with....And as far as this is concerned, I intend to continue the fight....because, you see, I love my country. And I think my country is in danger."

Help Me Decide
"And, now, finally, I know that you wonder whether or not I am going to stay on the Republican ticket or resign. Let me say this: I don't believe that I ought to quit because I'm not a quitter. And,

incidentally, Pat's not a quitter. After all, her name was Patricia Ryan and she was born on St. Patrick's Day, and you know the Irish never quit.

"But the decision, my friends, is not mine....I am submitting to the Republican National Committee tonight through this television broadcast, the decision which it is theirs to make.

"Let them decide whether my position on the ticket will help or hurt. And I am going to ask you to help them decide. Wire and write the Republican National Committee whether you think I should stay on or whether I should get off. And whatever their decision is, I will abide by it.

"But just let me say this last word. Regardless of what happens I'm going to continue this fight. I'm going to campaign up and down America until we drive the crooks and the Communists and those that defend them out of Washington. And remember, folks, Eisenhower is a great man. Believe me. He's a great man. And a vote for Eisenhower is a vote for what's good for America."

THE REACTION

When the speech was over, Nixon was depressed—he was sure his political career was over. "I loused it up and I'm sorry," he told his aides. "It was a flop."

But when he arrived at his hotel, the phones were going crazy with pro-Nixon calls. Telegrams supporting him poured into Republican headquarters all over the country. Ike wired Nixon: "Your presentation was magnificent." Even movie mogul Darryl F. Zannuck (who knew good acting when he saw it) called to tell Nixon, "It was the most tremendous performance I've ever seen." Hundreds of thousands of cards and telegrams were received; Nixon flew to Wheeling, West Virginia, to meet Ike and officially rejoin the ticket. Eisenhower rushed to Nixon's plane, and the VP candidate burst into tears, "the most poignant photo of the campaign."

The success of the speech, says one historian, "sent the Republican campaign soaring, establishing Nixon as a national figure and the best-known, largest-crowd-drawing vice presidential candidate in history." Nixon's career was saved, making his election to the presidency—and Watergate—possible two decades later.

According to French tradition, Santa Claus has a brother named Bells Nichols.

SPACED OUT

Some people who claim to have seen UFOs seem completely off their rockers. Others seem more credible. Here are five real-life "sightings." Did they really see UFOs…or are they just making it up? You decide.

T he Place: Gulf Breeze, Florida, November 1987
The Sighting: "Four-foot-tall gray aliens who sometimes speak Spanish."
Background: Ed Walters (a Gulf Breeze developer) and his wife, Frances (president of the local PTA), claim to have had repeated encounters with the Spanish-speaking space aliens over several months in 1987. In March 1990 the couple wrote a book, *The Gulf Breeze Sightings*, that chronicles their experiences.

The Place: Greece, 1979
The Sighting: Space aliens that "looked like fetuses wearing wrap-around sunglasses."
Background: Joseph Ostrom, an advertising executive, was honeymooning with his wife in Greece. One evening, he says, their hotel room "filled with an orangish-red light," and a large alien (wearing a silver suit) led him to the roof of the hotel. His wife stayed behind. Suddenly, a turquoise ray-beam pulled him into the space ship that was hovering overhead. The aliens on the ship examined him, but he didn't mind. "When they did their exam, I felt love and support. It was as if we knew each other." The aliens hypnotized Ostrom to forget the experience, and he did. But several years later he visited an Earthling hypnotist, and the memories came flooding back, changing his life forever.
After a second hypnosis, Ostrom quit his job and moved to Colorado. Today he makes his living conducting New Age workshops and writing. He is the author of the book *You and Your Aura*.

The Place: Mundrabilla, Australia, 1988
The Sighting: A "huge bright glowing object."
Background: Fay Knowles and her three sons were driving along Eyre Highway when their car was sucked into the air. One of the sons told reporters, "we were doing about 68 miles per hour when it

came over us and suddenly lifted the car off the road. We felt the thump on the roof and then it started lifting us. We were frightened and began to yell, but our voices had changed." Then the car was violently dropped back to earth. The shock of the landing blew out one of the rear tires; police officers who later inspected the car said the roof had been damaged and that the car was covered inside and out with "a thick layer of black ash."

Several other UFO sightings were reported the same night—some more than 100 miles away. An airplane flying overhead saw a bright light hovering nearby; a truck driver on the same highway also reported being followed; and a fishing trawler spotted a UFO from offshore. Police officials told reporters they were taking the multiple sightings "seriously."

The Place: Somewhere near the Martian moon Phobos, 1989

The Sighting: A "mysterious...long, faintly aerodynamic shaped pencil-like object with round ends."

Background: On March 25, 1989, the unmanned Soviet space probe Phobos transmitted a photograph to Earth of a strange object that appeared to have darted into the range of the probe's camera. According to news reports, immediately after transmitting the photograph, the Soviet probe stopped transmitting signals back to Earth and "inexplicably disappeared." It has been missing ever since. Marina Popovich, a top Soviet test pilot, displayed the photograph at a UFO convention and explained that the probe's "encounter" and last photograph could be explained either as a legitimate UFO sighting, or the last, faulty transmission of a malfunctioning camera system.

The Place: Mount Vernon, Missouri, 1984

The Sighting: Aliens kidnapping cows.

Background: One morning Paula Watson, a Mount Vernon resident, witnessed space aliens kidnapping cows near her house. Later in the day while canning vegetables in her basement, she noticed a "silvery alien with large eyes" peeking at her through the basement window. She tried to speak to the alien, but it backed away and she fell asleep. The next thing Watson knew she was inside the alien's spaceship being examined. "I was standing up on a white table and the...alien was running his hands down my body, scanning my body." Watson was later returned to Earth unharmed.

For Lone Ranger fans: "Kemo Sabe" means "soggy shrub" in Navajo.

THE SEARCH FOR AMELIA EARHART

Was she the victim of a fuel shortage, a bad navigator, or the Japanese military? America's most famous aviatrix vanished on July 2, 1937. Now, 55 years later, we may be close to finding out what really happened to her.

BACKGROUND

She was the best-known—and perhaps the greatest—female aviator in American history...which is all the more remarkable because of the age in which she lived. Born in 1897, Amelia Mary Earhart began her flying career in 1921, at a time when few women had careers of any kind and had only won the right to vote a few years earlier.

She took her first flying lessons at the age of 24, and, after 2 1/2 hours of instruction, told her teacher, "Life will be complete unless I own my own plane." By her 25th birthday she'd saved enough money working at her father's law firm, as a telephone company clerk, and hauling gravel, to buy one. Within another year she set her first world record, becoming the first pilot to fly at 14,000 feet.

In 1928, Earhart became the first woman to fly across the Atlantic Ocean when she flew with pilot Wilmer Stultz. Ironically, she was asked to make the flight merely because she was a woman, not because of her flying talent. Charles Lindbergh had already made the first solo transatlantic flight in 1927, and Stultz was looking for a way of attracting attention to his flight. So he brought Earhart along...as a passenger.

That was the first—and last—frivolous flying record she would ever set. In 1930 she set the speed record for women (181 miles per hour); in 1932 she became the first woman to fly solo across the Atlantic; on another flight became the first woman to fly solo across the continental United States; and in 1935 became the first pilot of either gender to fly from Hawaii to the U.S. mainland. (She also set several speed and distance records during her career.) By the mid-1930s "Lady Lindy" was as famous as Charles Lindbergh. But her greatest flying attempt lay ahead of her. In 1937 she tried to circumnavigate the globe along the equator.

She never made it.

THE FINAL FLIGHT

Earhart described her round-the-world flight as "the one last big trip in her." Taking off from Oakland, California, on May 21, 1937, she and her navigator, Frederick Noonan, flew more than 3/4 of the way around the world, making stops in South America, Africa, the Middle East, Asia, and the South Pacific. But when they landed in New Guinea on June 28, the most difficult part of the journey lay ahead: the 2,556-mile flight from New Guinea to Howland Island, a "tiny speck" of an island in the middle of the Pacific. It would be difficult to find even in the best conditions.

Monitoring the flight from Howland Island was the Coast Guard cutter *Itasca*. The Lady Lindy, Amelia's airplane, rolled off the runway at 10:22 a.m. on July 2. She remained in contact with the radio operator in New Guinea for seven hours, then was out of contact until well after midnight.

• Finally, at 2:45 a.m., the *Itasca* picked up her first radio transmission. Another short message was picked up at 3:45 a.m.: "Earhart. Overcast."

• At 4:00 a.m., the *Itasca* radioed back: "What is your position? Please acknowledge." There was no response.

• At 4:43 a.m., she radioed in again, but her voice was too faint to pick up anything other than "partly cloudy."

• The next signal was heard at 6:14 a.m., 15 minutes before the plane's scheduled landing at Howland. She asked the *Itasca* to take a bearing on the signal, so that Noonan could plot their position. The signal was too short and faint to take a bearing. At 6:45 a.m. Earhart radioed a second time to ask for a bearing, but the signal again was too short.

• A more ominous message was received at 7:42 a.m.: "We must be on you but cannot see you but gas is running low. Been unable to reach you by radio. We are flying at altitude one thousand feet. Only one half hour gas left." One radio operator described Earhart's voice as "a quick drawl like from a rain barrel." She was lost, panicking, and nearly out of fuel. She would radio two more times before 8:00 a.m. asking the *Itasca* to take a bearing, but each time her signals were too weak.

• Her next message was received at 8:44 a.m.—a half hour past the time she predicted her fuel would run out: "We are on the line of position 156-157. Will repeat message....We are running north and south." Operators described her voice as "shrill and breathless, her words tumbling over one another." That was the last confirmed message she would broadcast.

Then Amelia Earhart vanished.

UNANSWERED QUESTION: WHAT WENT WRONG?

Theory #1: Noonan's erratic behavior and faulty navigation sent the plane off course, dooming it.

Suspicious Facts

• Noonan was an alcoholic. A former Pan Am pilot, he'd been fired from the airline because of his drinking problem. He claimed to have gotten his drinking under control, but during a stopover in Hawaii he'd gotten drunk in his hotel room. According to one reporter in Hawaii, Earhart didn't want him to continue with the flight.

• The episode in Hawaii may not have been the only one. During a stopover in Calcutta, Earhart reported to her husband that she was "starting to have personnel trouble," but that she could "handle the situation." Paul Collins, a friend of Earhart's, overheard the conversation. He took this to mean that Noonan had gotten drunk again. Whatever it meant, Earhart was still having "personnel trouble" when she phoned from New Guinea, the last stopover before she disappeared.

• Why would Earhart have used Noonan as her navigator in the first place? According to one theory, the reason was financial: unlike other navigators, "the reputed alcoholic would work for very little money."

Theory #2: Earhart herself was to blame. Despite her fame as America's premier aviatrix, according to many pilots who knew her, she was actually a poor pilot—and an even worse navigator—who was unfamiliar with the plane she was flying.

Suspicious Facts

• Earhart had very little experience flying the Lockheed Electra she used on the trip. It was her first twin-engine plane, "a powerful, complicated aircraft loaded with special equipment" that was different from any other plane she had owned. Even so, in the eyes of the pilots who trained her to fly it, she didn't spend enough time getting to know it.

• In fact, her round-the-world flight was delayed after she crashed the plane during takeoff on March 20. Paul Mantz, her mentor and trainer, blamed the accident on her, claiming she had "jockeyed" the throttle. Paul Capp, another pilot who knew her, described her as "an inept pilot who would not take the advice of experts."

• Earhart's skills as a Morse code operator were atrocious—even though Morse code, which could be transmitted in the worst of conditions, was the most reliable form of communication. Earhart preferred to transmit by voice, which required a much more powerful signal and was harder to intercept. (In fact, she preferred voice communication so much that partway through the flight she abandoned some of her Morse code radios and flew the rest of the trip without them. She also dumped a 250-foot-long trailing antenna, which made the remaining radios far less powerful.)

• Earhart was also a poor navigator. During the flight to the African coast her miscalculations set her 163 miles off course—a mistake that would have been deadly if the plane had been low on fuel. Some theorists speculate that if her navigation and Morse code skills had been better, she might have survived.

UNANSWERED QUESTION: WHAT HAPPENED?

Theory #1: Earhart ran out of fuel before sighting land, ditched her plane in the sea, and drowned.

Suspicious Facts

• This is the most popular theory...and it's supported by the fact that no conclusive proof has ever been found indicating what really happened. According to one newspaper report, "nothing has been found that can be traced irrefutably to the plane or its crew: nothing bearing a serial number, for example, such as the plane's engines or propellers, nor any numbered equipment known to belong to the aviators."

• However, the islands in many areas of the South Pacific are scattered with the wreckage of 1930s-era planes. A lot of the major sea battles of World War II were fought in the Pacific; many fighter pilots ditched on nearby islands. This makes it next to impossible to confirm that any given piece of wreckage belonged to Earhart's plane, unless it contains a serial number or includes a personal effect of some kind.

Theory #2: Earhart was captured by the Japanese.

• According to this theory, Earhart and Noonan were using their flight as a cover for a number of reconnaissance flights over Japanese-held islands in the South Pacific. The Roosevelt administration believed that war with Japan was inevitable and may have asked Earhart to help gather intelligence information. Some theorists suggest that after one such flight over the Truck Islands, they got lost in a storm, ran out of fuel, and were forced to land on an atoll in the Marshall Islands (which at the time were controlled by Japan). Earhart and Noonan were captured, imprisoned, and eventually died in captivity.

Suspicious Facts

• In 1967 CBS reporter Fred Goerner met a California woman who claimed to have seen two captured Americans—one man and one woman, matching the descriptions of Noonan and Earhart—on the Japanese island of Saipan in 1937. Acting on the tip, Groener went to Saipan, where he found more than a dozen island natives who told similar stories about "American fliers who had been captured as spies," including one man who claimed to have been imprisoned in a cell next to an "American woman flyer."

• Fleet Admiral Chester W. Nimitz, commander of U.S. naval forces in the Pacific during the war, reportedly also believed that Earhart and Noonan had been captured and killed by the Japanese; in one statement in 1966 he said, "I want to tell you Earhart and her navigator did go down in the Marshalls and were picked up by the Japanese." The Japanese government denies the charge.

• Goerner believes that when the Marines recaptured Saipan in 1944, they unearthed Earhart and Noonan's bones and returned them to the United States. He thinks the bones were secretly turned over to the National Archives, which has kept them hidden away ever since. Why? The reason is as mysterious as the disappearance.

• Alternate theory: Joe Klass, author of *Amelia Earhart Lives*, also believes that Earhart was captured by the Japanese. But he argues that Earhart survived the war and may have even returned to the United States to live under an assumed name. According to his theory, the Japanese cut a deal with the United States to return Earhart safely after the war if the U.S. promised not to try Emperor Hirohito as a war criminal. The U.S. kept its promise, and Earhart was allowed to return home. She may have lived as long as the 1970s, protecting her privacy by living under an assumed name.

Theory #3: Earhart and Noonan crash-landed on a deserted island in the South Pacific, hundreds of miles off course from their original destination, where they died from exposure and thirst a few days later.

Suspicious Facts

• For three days after Earhart and Noonan disappeared, mysterious radio signals were picked up by ships looking for Earhart's plane. The signals were transmitted in English in a female voice; some radio operators familiar with Earhart's voice recognized it as hers. They were misunderstood at the time, but if they were indeed broadcast by Earhart, they gave several clues to her whereabouts.

• One signal said, "We are on the line of position 156-157"; another said, "Don't hold—with us—much longer—above water—shut off." Others had similar messages. At the end of the three days, the signals abruptly stopped.

• If those signals were indeed sent by Earhart, she must have landed *somewhere* to have been able to broadcast them. Nikumaroro Island, 350 miles north of Howland Island, is a likely candidate for the crash site. The mysterious broadcasts offer several clues:

√ Nikumaroro is one of the few islands within range of Earhart's plane—and it was in their "line of position 156-157."

√ One of the last transmissions described a "ship on a reef south of equator." For years afterward researchers assumed that the "ship" being described in the transmission was Earhart's plane. But perhaps it wasn't: one of Nikumaroro's most prominent landmarks is a large shipwreck off the south shore of the island—four degrees south of the equator.

√ Why were those final broadcasts separated by hours of silence? For more than 40 years it was assumed that they were broadcast at random intervals. But in the late 1980s Thomas Gannon and Thomas Willi, two retired military navigators, proposed a theory: nearly out of fuel, Earhart and Noonan landed on a part of the island's coral reef that was above sea level only during low tide. This meant that they could only broadcast during low tide, when the radio's batteries weren't flooded and the plane's engine could be used to recharge them.

√ To test their theory, Gannon and Willi compared the times the signals were broadcast to a chart listing high and low tides on Nikumaroro Island the week of the disappearance. All but one of the signals were broadcast during Nikumaroro's low tide.

Other Evidence

• In 1960 Floyd Kilts, a retired Coast Guard carpenter, told the *San Diego Tribune* that while assigned to the island in 1946, one of the island's natives told him about a female skeleton that had been found on the island in the late 1930s. According to the story, the skeleton was found alongside a pair of American shoes and a bottle of cognac—at a time when no Americans lived on the island.

When the island's magistrate learned of the skeleton, he remembered the story about Earhart and decided to turn the bones over to U.S. authorities. So he put the bones in a gunnysack and set sail with a group of native islanders for Fiji. But he died mysteriously en route—and the natives, fearing the bones, threw them overboard.

• Many aspects of this story were later confirmed; in 1938 Gerald Gallagher, the island's magistrate, *did* fall ill while en route to Fiji and died shortly after landing. But it is not known whether or not he had any bones with him when he died.

UPDATE

To date, Nikumaroro Island and nearby McKean Island (thought to be another possible crash site) have been searched extensively. In March 1992 a search team on Nikumaroro found a sheet of aircraft aluminum that they believed was from Earhart's plane...but that theory was later disproved. Other artifacts recovered include a cigarette lighter manufactured in the 1930s (Noonan was a smoker) and pieces from a size-9 shoe (Earhart wore size 9). But no conclusive evidence has been found. The search continues.

THE LAST PAGE

F ELLOW BATHROOM READERS:

The fight for good bathroom reading should never be taken loosely—we must sit firmly for what we believe in, even while the rest of the world is taking pot shots at us.

Once we prove we're not simply a flush-in-the-pan, writers and publishers will find their resistance unrolling.

So we invite you to take the plunge: "Sit Down and Be Counted!" by joining The Bathroom Readers' Institute. Send a self-addressed, stamped envelope to: B.R.I., 1400 Shattuck Avenue #25, Berkeley, CA 94709. You'll receive your attractive free membership card, get a copy of the B.R.I. newsletter (if we ever get around to publishing one), and earn a permanent spot on the B.R.I. honor roll.

ᴄᴓ   ᴄᴓ   ᴄᴓ

UNCLE JOHN'S *SIXTH* BATHROOM READER IS IN THE WORKS

Don't fret—there's more good reading on its way. In fact, there are a few ways you can contribute to the next volume:

1. Is there a subject you'd like to see us cover? Write and let us know. We aim to please.

2. Got a neat idea for a couple of pages in the new *Reader*? If you're the first to suggest it, and we use it, we'll send you a free copy of the book.

3. Have you seen or read an article you'd recommend as quintessential bathroom reading? Or is there a passage in a book that you want to share with other B.R.I. members? Tell us where to find it or send a copy. If you're the first to suggest it and we publish it in the next volume, there's a free book in it for you.

Well, we're out of space, and when you've gotta go, you've gotta go. Hope to hear from you soon. Meanwhile, remember:

Go with the flow.